THE DEMOCRATIC THEORY
AND
PRACTICE IN AFRICA

Prof. W.O. Oyugi
Dr. A. Gitonga

HEINEMANN KENYA

Published by
Heinemann Kenya Ltd.
P.O. Box 45314
NAIROBI.

First published 1987

©Department of Government
University of Nairobi

Printed by
Metro Forms and Systems Ltd.
P.O. Box 52899
NAIROBI.

ABOUT THE AUTHORS

Michael Chege is currently a senior lecturer in Government. He received his doctorate in Political Science from the University of California at Berkeley in 1976. He has published in many scholarly Journals including the *Journal of Modern African Studies, The African Review of African Political Economy*, e.t.c.

Afrifa Gitonga received his doctorate at Toulouse University. He is currently a lecturer in Government at the University of Nairobi.

J. Mugaju is a historian. He received his Ph.D from the University of Bristol. His area of research and teaching is Modern African History — an area in which he has written extensively.

D. Masolo lectures in philosophy   an area in which he is widely published. He received his Ph.D from Gregoria.

Meddy Mugyenyi received his doctoate from North Western University. At the time of submitting the article, he was a senior lecturer in Government, University of Nairobi. Currently he works as a Consultant in Nairobi.

Maria Nzomo is a lecturer in Government. She received her Ph.D in Political Science from Dalhousie University. She has done research and written extensively on Women and Politics among other things.

Walter Ouma Oyugi received his doctorate in Government from the University of Nairobi in 1973. Since 1971 he has been on the staff of the department of Government where he is currently an associate professor and chairman of the department. His publications include: *Rural Development and Administration* (Vikas, 1981), *Bureaucracy and Development in Africa*, University of California I.I.S. He has also published in many scholarly journals and contributed articles to several books.

Vincent Simiyu is a lecturer in History at the University of Nairobi. He received his Ph.D from Toulouse University.

Nick Gatheru Wanjohi is a lecturer in Government. He received his Ph.D in Government from the University of Nairobi in 1980. His area of research and teaching is Political Economy.

Peter Wanyande is a lecturer in Government. He received his M.A. from the University of Nairobi and is currently a doctoral candidate.

Contents

PREFACE

This book is the outcome of a workshop which was held by the Department of Government in June 1985, at Naivasha. The theme — the democratic practice in Africa — from which the title of the book derives, was deliberately chosen by the Department to enable us to reflect on the transformations that have occurred in Africa, especially since independence and to assess, in the process, the effect the said transformations have had on the practice of democracy in Africa. Our aim in putting the book together was to make some contribution, however modest, to the ongoing debate on this illusive concept.

The essays presented here are organized around three sub-themes, namely, the idea of democracy, the democratic practice and democracy and development. Brief introductions to the three parts are presented by Afrifa Gitonga (Part I) and Walter O. Oyugi (parts II & III).

On behalf of the Department, I would like to thank my colleagues in the editorial committee for the diligent work they put in producing the final manuscript. I also use this opportunity to thank the Konrad Adenauer Foundation for the generous financial support that enabled the workshop to be held and the book to be put out in good time. In particular, I would like to thank the Foundation's representative in Kenya, Dr. L. Entrup for his personal involvement and sustained interest in the project throughout the period of its evolution. In addition, I also thank my predecessor Dr. N. Nyangira, under whose chairmanship the project began, for having coordinated the activities that led to the successful holding of the workshop. I wish to thank Miss Elizabeth Mungai for her technical skill and devotion in typing the manuscript.

Last but not least, we wish to thank, in a special way, the contribution made by Professor Atieno Odhiambo during the course of editing the volume.

These sentiments notwithstanding, the views expressed in the book are those of the individual authors and therefore should be associated neither with the sponsoring organisations nor with the Department of Government, University of Nairobi.

Walter O. Oyugi,
Chairman, Department of Government,
University of Nairobi.
22nd April '87

PART I

THE IDEA OF DEMOCRACY

INTRODUCTION
Afrifa K. Gitonga

It is an indisputable fact that democracy, along with a handful of other concerns such as health, development and peace, has become one of the core and foremost preoccupations of the people of the world today. All over the world, millions of men and women are clamouring for it, ready to consent enormous sacrifices of sweat, tears and blood, up to and including death, to secure it. This is the measure of the value of democracy to civilized mankind.

The quest for democracy is the quest for freedom, justice, equality and human dignity. It is the quest for the liberation of mankind from all manner of servitude, injustices, discriminations and humiliations. It is a far-reaching and wide-ranging movement, encompassing the liberation of citizens from local despots and tyrants, women from domestic and social subjugation and nations from foreign domination and exploitation. In one vast fold, it is the story of women's liberation movement (all the way from the suffragettes and their struggle to obtain the simple right to vote and stand for political office); of revolutions and mass uprisings that have changed the landscape and the destiny of nations; of the anti-imperialist struggles of the modern and antique worlds, from that of the Jews of Pharaonic Egypt, through the struggles of the conquered peoples of the Roman, Greek, Persian, Mongolian and other past great and small empires to the collapse of the Nineteenth and Twentieth Century European, Japanese and other empires. From this perspective, the progress towards the realization of the democratic ideal is the great epic of mankind's movement towards civilized political behaviour.

In the long march to the democratic promised land, man has had to constantly sharpen his understanding of the democratic idea, process and experience. He has had to constantly modernize or update his conceptual tools, analytical models and theoretical frameworks for dealing with the democratic problematic. This has been imperative because the practical devices, arrangements and mechanisms for achieving democracy that have so far been tried have required constant refinement and improvement. This, in turn, has been made necessary by the fact that, concretely, freedom, equality and human dignity are goals which are still far from being realized in most parts of the world. More thinking, more action and more sacrifice, therefore, continue to be called for in the move towards the creation of democratic society.

This work is a continuation and an integral part of that universal and timeless tradition of observation, analysis and reflection. Its ambition and objective are to contribute to the development of democractic thought, knowledge, practice and experience. For it remains one of the greatest paradoxes of our time that although there exists a broad consensus that democratic government is the best form of government, it is nevertheless a relatively rare phenomenon in today's world. Even without going into the intricacies of the criteria for judging how democratic a country is, it can be safely advanced as a glaring evidence that only a small minority of world governments qualify to be called democratic.

But the question is: what is democracy? This first part of the book deals with the conceptual and theoretical dimension of democracy. It is devoted to up-dating the concept with the aim of clarifying its meaning in the contemporary context as well as identifying the theoretical bases of democratic practice. The essays in this section address the issues of the objective definition of democracy, the practical ways and means of achieving it and the concrete benefits and/or trade-offs that result from a democratic system. More specifically, the essay by Afrifa Gitonga is an attempt at explaining in general terms (a) what democracy consists of or is all about and (b) the requirements for the establishment of a democratic system of government.

The meaning of democracy that is offered is a synthesis based on the very wide variety of proposed theories and practices. This definition seeks to give the core meaning or essence of the concept. It is argued that the core or quintessential meaning of democracy is "good, fair and just government" according to the three very fundamental meanings of each of these terms (i.e. fair, good and just), corresponding closely to the definition of democracy offered by Abraham Lincholn, viz, "Government of the people, by the people and for the people."

The second part concerns itself with the foundations on which a democratic system is or can be built. It seeks to identify the social, political as well as economic conditions and factors that make it possible and conducive for "democracy to exist, survive and prosper". These conditions, succinctly put, include a healthy and prosperous economy, simple and open electoral rules and procedures and a political culture based on the values of equality, liberty and human dignity.

The essay by Masolo focuses on the relationship between dogma and democratic behaviour. The author decries what he calls ideological dogmatism, which he views as a threat to the openness of mind which characterizes democratic thinking.

CHAPTER I

THE MEANING AND FOUNDATIONS OF DEMOCRACY

Afrifa K. Gitonga

PRELIMINARIES

For millenia, democracy has been the subject of innumerable treatises and discourses from both eminent and not so eminent thinkers, scholars and actors on the social scene. It is however not the purpose of this chapter to make a review of the myriad and diverse theories and practices of democracy that have come up across the ages. Rather it is intended to use these as a broad point of departure and source of inspiration in an attempt to propose a new vision of the concept and the reality it refers to, and some practical and concrete ways and means of establishing a democratic system.

In particular, it is hoped to avoid the principal pitfalls or weaknesses of most traditional approaches to the definition of democracy which are seriously handicapped either by their idealistic and fundamentally metaphysical view of things, or by a narrowly materialistic conceptualization. A prime ambition here therefore is to avoid giving "just another" definition of the concept. We propose, instead, a *synthesis definition* — one that reflects the substance of the diverse, contrasting and sometimes contradictory definitions and usages of the concept of democracy, and one which, at the same time, transcends or surpasses them.

To give the concept a concrete, social and material dimension, the empirical world is then explored in an attempt to discover the raw materials and the implements with which democracy is built. It is these that constitute the foundations of democracy — the prerequisites or the preconditions upon which democracy is predicated or dependent. Put another way, this involves trying to discover what constitutes the building blocks, the energy sources and the "vitamins" of democracy which make it possible for democracy to exist, to survive and to prosper; to be alive, healthy and dynamic.

In the course of the predication exercise, the outline of a distinct theory of democracy should emerge, broaching the answers to such questions as: Why are some societies or social systems democratic and others not? Why are some more democratic or less so than others? What practices or processes, enhance, consolidate, erode or undermine democracy?

DEMOCRACY: USE, ABUSE AND MISUSE

> "In the case of a word like *democracy,* not only is there no agreed definition but the attempt to make one is resisted from all sides. . . . The defenders of any kind of regime claim that it is a democracy . . . ."
>
> George Orwell.[1]

We may add that the adversaries of any regime/system accuse it of being undemocratic or a pseudo-democracy. According to Marxists, for example, liberal democracy is merely formal democracy, democracy in name and appearance only.

Democracy has been described as "a hurrah word" — an umbrella concept used to refer to and to designate a multitude of diverse and varied socio-political systems or realities. This has come about as a result of the progressive sanctification of the democratic ideal. Democracy has become "universally sanctified"[2] and "the name democracy is now so sacred that nobody dares say he is anti-democratic".[3] The term has become more and more "honorific", with an unequivocal "laudatory meaning"[4] attached to it. Supporters or apologists of all kinds of regimes and systems are therefore quick to attach the tag "democratic" onto them. It is not even uncommon to find the term used to signify and thereby to sanctify perfectly antithetical realities and practices.

This quasi-universal acceptance and adoration of democracy as a system has, however, not always existed. Democracy, provisionally and simply defined as "rule of and by the people", has had its enemies. The democratic idea and movement were mercilessly combatted and denounced by the feudal order. They were seen, correctly, as subversive of the rule by God's vicars and representatives who ruled by "divine right" in aristocratic and absolutist monarchies. Elitist ideologies such as those espoused by the Nazi and other fascist regimes have also combatted the idea, denouncing democracy as "massocracy", "mediocracy" and "anarchy". But after the "irruption of the masses into history" in the 19th Century, democracy has progressively gained respectability and acceptance, up to and including the sanctification cited above. Everybody worships the god demoscratos, swears by it.

In view of the great variety and diversity of regimes and systems that pass for democracies, it is not at all an easy matter to establish what the precise and objective meaning of democracy is or can be. Could it be that there are as many *types* of democracy as there are definitions? Or is it probable that each type of system or regime, each definition of democracy incorporates at least an ingredient of what goes for, what it takes to make, a total democratic edifice? This is by no means obvious. But it is plausible.

Many definitions of democracy tend to be taylor-made to fit specific types of regimes/systems. They are often little more than exercises in political marketing destined to sell those particular regimes/systems. The confusion of meanings is primarily due to this propagandistic usage and value of the term as a weapon in the arena of competing and even warring social systems. More often than not it is used and defined in a self-interested, opportunistic and holier-than-thou fashion.

But the confusion and dissension as to the exact meaning, substance or content of the concept are compounded by the tendency to define it in absolute terms. Thus a regime/system is classified either as a democracy or as a non-democracy. All regimes/systems without exception are expected to fit into either of the two mutually exclusive categories. There is no allowance for the *relative* nature of phenomena. There is no recognition of the existence of transition zones between categories, of hybrids, ambiguous cases, unclassifiables, paradoxes. This is the primary weakness of the idealistic and metaphysical approach referred to above.

From a scientific perspective, however, categories and classes in things and phenomena are relative and any established boundaries are a matter of convention and convenience. Unfortunately, in the case of democracy, there is hardly ever any convention or convenience outside the individual political families which use, abuse or misuse the term.

There is no doubt, however, that the substance or content of what is described as democratic is a function of the ideological bent of the user of the term. As the "ideological bents" or "political families" are many and diverse, so too are the meanings attached to the term, across history and across the globe. Obviously the stakes must be high in the struggle for the monopoly of the label. For one, regimes have stood or fallen on their perceived democratic or undemocratic character.

"Democracies" and "democrats" thus come in all colours, shapes and sizes: Social democracy, Christian, Liberal, Popular, National popular democracy, African, Arab, Progressive democrats, (simple) democrats etc. One would imagine that democracy is the antithesis of dictatorship. But no! In Marxist parlance the "dictatorship of the proletariat" is simply another name for "popular democracy". The latter is supposedly a more substantive type of democracy, at least materially or economically, than the purely "formal" one of the liberal/ bourgeois/capitalist variety. One has also heard General Pinochet of Chile speak of his system as being "authoritarian democracy"!

Apart from these more or less partisan, interested, honest or dishonest references to democracy, it is reasonable to assume that the concept must possess a core objective meaning and substance which are at the root of its quasi-universal appeal and which are the reasons for the cult and idolatry reserved for it in the contemporary world. The concept and substance of democracy must possess considerable material, social and sentimental value to warrant such widespread and enduring attachment and devotion: there must be something in it. It is the purpose of this chapter to identify this "something" and indicate how it can be realized.

6

It is no doubt an altruism to state that all human constructions partake of a more or less great degree of imperfection. In the construction of a democratic system, imperfections can and do occur at any of the myriad stages or elements of the project. These imperfections negate *to varying degrees* the validity of the democratic edifice.

There comes a point, however, where the imperfections outweigh the positive characteristics, where they remove the edifice so far from the ideal that it is deemed undemocratic. The debate about democracy hinges on the determination of the exact location of this point. And one of the great tasks of political science is to establish a method, a yardstick for measuring democracy or degrees of it. For it seems evident that in the real world, democratic or undemocratic are a matter of degrees and that between the two extremes, the reality is a continuum along which can be situated all the varieties of social, political and economic regimes/systems.

THE DIMENSIONS OF DEMOCRACY

Democracy can be said to exist in at least three moments or dimensions. In its *abstract* moment or dimension it exists in the imaginations of men and women; in its *practical* moment it exists in the ways and means of men and women; in its *concrete* moment, it exists as the experience of men and women. This multifacetted mode of existence is no doubt one of the principal reasons why there is so much disagreement about what it really is. In the interests of clarity, it is indispensable that those using or defining the term democracy, like the blind men describing an elephant in the fable, should specify at each moment what "face" of democracy they are referring to.

The Abstract Concept

Democracy is first and foremost an idea, an abstract concept, a hypothetical reality or state of affairs conceived of and existing in the minds of men and women. It is an intellectual creation, a mentally visualized reality postulated or proposed as a model of the possible, the desirable in matters of social co-existence, social intercourse and the governance of men and women in society. In this form, it is not situated in time or space: it does not refer to any empirical past or present social system.

In its abstract moment democracy is therefore a vision, a dream. In its pure form it represents an ideal, it visualizes or conjures up a world of perfection, a utopia. For this reason, many people see it as basically impossible to realize: "Democracy is for ever impossible!"[5]

Without belabouring the Greek origins or the linguistic subtleties of the term, we should state that democracy in its etymological sense simply means "rule by the people".

And that is where the problems of definition begin. For as to what is meant by either "the people" or "rule" there hardly exists a consensus. To some authors indeed "Kratia" (-cracy) does not refer to "rule" but to "power".[6] This controversy is not of great consequence for our purposes here, however, because it is possible to define "rule" to include power relations.

To this end, we shall define rule as "the exercise of power, authority and influence in society". Where, succinctly defined, power equals the capacity to enforce obedience or compliance through the use of the means or instruments of exercising positive or negative sanctions; authority equals the right to make binding decisions, to expect or to demand obedience or compliance on the basis of one's position or role in society; and influence equals the capacity to inspire obedience or compliance on the basis of one's personal attributes. The proposition here is that anybody who gets others to obey or comply with one's commands, orders, directives, instructions, requests, advice can only do so through the exercise of power, authority or influence as defined above. And the essence of rulership is in having others obey or comply with commands, orders. As will be readily appreciated, it is the rulers, those who exercise power, authority and influence, who largely determine the character and destiny of human societies.

The democratic ideal or model proposes that the people be the rulers. The people be the rulers of whom? Of the people: of *themselves*. The immediate and critically important implication is that the people should have their destiny, and that of their society, in their own hands. They should rule themselves; order, organize and manage their own affairs. In a word, the people should be free.

But, and this is the other hitch, who exactly are "the people"? Various conceptualizations are possible and have been advanced as to who or what constitutes the people. Giovanni Sartori,[7] gives a list of these possibilities as:

1.   people meaning an approximate plurality, just *a great many,*
2.   people meaning an integral plurality, *everybody,*
3.   people as an entity, or as *an organic whole,*
4.   people as a plurality expressed by an *absolute majority* principle,
5.   people as a plurality expressed by a *limited majority* principle.

The most common conceptualizations across history, ideological camps and individual scholars' idiosyncrasies, however, would seem to be:
(i)   the absolutist or idealistic one in which 'people' refers to each and every(body), all the individuals composing a given community,
(ii)   the mystical conception in which people constitute an *organic* whole, a single entity although made up of a more or less big number of

individuals, groups. People in this sense is seen as some kind of mysterious animal, an almost living entity or organism, a being endowed with a life of its own, with its own rights transcending those of its constituent elements. It is best rendered by the German word *Volk,* the Italian *Popolo* or the French *Peuple.*

(iii) the third essentially distinct conception is the one rendered best by the English word "people". Here "people" is merely the plural of "person". The people therefore merely refers to many individuals and *not* to a quasi-monolithic and transcendental being possessed of its own independent existence. Nor does it refer to some assemblage in which each and all count for the same. Rather, it refers to a relatively big number of people: many relative or compared to another group, assemblage of people. This immediately leads to the idea of *majority* which can be defined as "the many" in contrast to the less many, or, as the expression goes, "the minority" meaning "the few".

It is easy to see that the concept whereby "the people" means each and all, everybody, is objectionable for a variety of reasons. The most important is that it is an *operational non-starter!* It is next to impossible to operationalize it for practical purposes. Before the people can do anything, it would require the concurrence of each and every person/citizen. It would require consensus, total unanimity. And as someone has very aptly put it, "the only place where no dissenting voice is raised is in a graveyard".[8]

The other conceptualization whereby "the people" refers to some kind of supra-individual collective being fails a quite different test — that of *concrete or empirical demonstrability.* Its existence thus becomes a matter of faith! To know its will, needs, nature, and so forth, we have to rely on its self-proclaimed priests, prophets and devotees. For when we look around we can only see individuals or groups of individuals, whose separate activities or lives are certainly often linked or interdependent, but who nevertheless possess unmistakable identities or individualities.

Since the existence, the nature, the will, of this mythical beast can never be empirically and objectively ascertained, it becomes the equivalent of, and often the substitute for the gods of bygone days when kings ruled by "divine" right. More ominously, it becomes the convenient referent for all manner or autocratic, dictatorial and totalitarian regimes. To justify any act, deed, project, they only need to invoke the interests of this sacred entity.

The "Volk" of Hitlerian Nazi Germany and the "Popolo" of Fascist Italy had exactly this significance. The concepts of "people", "society", in communist parlance also partake to a very large extent of this conceptualization. Hence the totalitarian temptations or tendencies of communism and its consequent paradoxical resemblances with fascism.

The only realistic and tenable conceptualization of "the people" would therefore have to be that which is both practically operationalizable and empirically demonstrable or ascertainable. That is, the people as a plurality expressed by the majority principle as defined above.[9]

Most definitions of democracy stop their etymological clarifications at "rule" and "people". It is our contention, however, that the conjunction concepts "by" and "of" are of much more than superficial significance. As many authors define democracy as "rule by the people" as define it as "rule of the people". To those two, Abraham Lincoln in his celebrated definition has added even a third: government (rule) for the people.

Whereas from the beginning the "of" and the "by" the people were clearly and readily understood and accepted, it took the enunciation of the Marxist problematic of historical materialism for the importance of the "for" the people to become evident. We can say in very succinct terms that the "of" raises the question of the "genealogy" of the rule; the "by" raises that of the "mode of existence" of that rule; and the "for" raises the question of the "purpose for existence" of the rule.

In proposing that the rule should be of the people, by the people and for the people, the democratic ideal thereby postulates that this is the only way and means of establishing the ideal, the perfect, the best government of men and women in society. But then, what concrete or substantive meaning can we attach to the concept of ideal/perfect government or rule? What kind of government in real, concrete terms can be said to be ideal or perfect or as close to that as can be?

We propose that the best, the ideal, the perfect government or socio-political system, or the one that comes closest to being such, is the one that can be described as good, fair and just. It is the one which possesses or manifests the characteristics, the properties or the attributes enabling it to be qualified as indicated according to three very precise meanings attached to or associated with each of these three concepts taken as absolute categories.

First of all "good" is a matter of form, a matter of structure and appearance. Is good that which *looks* good, which bears a good image: in terms of proportions, colour, composition, constitution, arrangement of parts? And what is the criterion, the standard of measurement for judging goodness in this regard — ourselves? It is almost a universal constant that each person, each people pose or would like to pose as the model of that which is good among people(s). As a general rule, it can be said that people tend to judge others and their systems, ways, values, attributes and so on, in accordance with how much they resemble or differ from themselves and their own value systems. In this connection we can say that a government or social system stands all the more chances of being qualified as "good" and therefore to that extent democratic, if it is the government of the people judging it or similar to it. By "of" is meant that the rule and the rulers are "born of" the people, "issue of", "begotten of" the people. The rule and the rulers are a creature, a creation of the people. This immediately implies that it is a government/system which is socially legitimate, meaning recognized and accepted by the people who "fathered" it, who "begot" it.

This is the sense in which we say that the "of" of democracy raises the question of the genealogy of the rule/system. A democratic system is one which has its roots in the people. It is therefore not an alien government. It is also not imposed or forced on the people.

Only such can be regarded as satisfying one of the cardinal requirements or criteria for being recognized as a good and, therefore, democratic government or system. It goes without saying that if it is indeed begat by the people, it will resemble that people — it will be in that people's image. That, however, is not the end of the story.

It is not enough that a government has a good appearance or image for it to be certified as entirely good. Apart from being a social category, the faculty of goodness is also a functional attribute. This is goodness as it refers to a good machine, instrument and so on. It means that the machine, is in "good order", i.e. that it not only works but also works according to the established norms.

In the case of a government, it means that the government functions, operates or works according to, in conformity with, the written or unwritten, explicit or implicit rules, procedures and regulations established by the people. In a word it means governing or ruling according to or in conformity with the constitution. To the extent then that there is rule of law as that law is established by the people, it is the people who rule — it is rule *by* the people.

Notwithstanding that it looks good and functions, a system may fail the ultimate test for deciding whether it is indeed a good system. This is in relation to another very critical criterion of goodness — results. A system is good if it "delivers" — if it serves some useful, that is, good practical and concrete purpose. A good and, therefore, democratic government in this perspective is the one which is capable of producing good results — tangible or intangible benefits for the people. It is the one which lives up to *its purpose for existence,* which justifies its existence on the strength of the good it does for the people through the goods and services it provides to them. As a government *for* the people it is one which caters for the material, social and other interests of the people.

The analysis of the meanings of the concepts of "fair" and "just" follow very similar or parallel lines. Is fair first of all that which has a beautiful appearance: as in "fair maiden"? Again the egotistical or narcissistic predilection of people to judge others posing themselves as the standard sees to it that that which is fair is the one which is of the people concerned — "begat" of them, resembling them, "cut in their image". This goes also for the concept of "just". It refers to "just" as a synonym of "exact", as in "just copy" meaning a true copy, a true reflection, representation. A just government then in this context is one which is truly *representative* of the people.

Both the concepts of "fair" and "just" also possess a functional connotation, as in "fair play", — meaning, playing according to the *rules* of the game, adhering to and respecting the procedures, norms, regulations. This functional element in the concept of "just" comes out in its compounded form "justice", as in "Minister for Justice" — meaning, the one who sees to the observance and enforcement of the laws. Again this serves to underline that a fair and just government is the one in which there is rule of law. It is the opposite of a bandit or rogue government which does not respect and enforce the law, which plays foul, which is arbitrary and capricious.

Finally, a fair and just government is the one which is *concretely* so. A government is not there to be looked at and admired as a monument, a work of art or an engineering feat. For it to pass the final test of fairness and justice, it must provide a "fair harvest" and ensure that all those to whom it belongs, or whom it is meant to serve, get their "just" or "fair" share of the produce. In a word, it should be a profitable or beneficial enterprise giving adequate returns in goods and services to the people, as well as ensuring a fair and just distribution of the "cake".

This three-dimensional perspective of viewing democracy immediately incorporates and transcends the various oppositions between "substantive" and "formal" democracy; between "economic" and "legalistic" democracy; between the "material" or "real" democracy and the "mystificatory" or unreal democracy. For whereas the "of" and the "by" of the people are important in that they bring out *l'art et la maniere d'etre* of democracy, that is, its *form* and *mode of existence,* the "for" of democracy is equally important, because it brings out the *substance* of democracy.

The Technical Arrangements

The practical dimension of democracy represents or consists of the how of translating the democratic ideal into a concrete reality. It concerns the technicalities or the ways and means of *implementing* a democratic programme, project or strategy. The question that this poses therefore is, "How should the people organize themselves to exercise their rule?" In other words, what institutional arrangements or mechanisms ensure that in its being (form), in its mode of existence (functioning) and in its concrete effects (results) the government remains or manifests the attributes of a "good, fair and just" government?

Many arrangements, solutions and formulae have been proposed and tried in answer to the above question. Having proposed that "the people", can realistically and objectively only be "the majority", the first practical problem obviously becomes that of knowing how to establish or identify that majority and its will, position or opinion on any given matter. For the tiny city-states of ancient Greece, this was a rather simple affair: all the (male) adult citizens assembled and it was easy to establish where the majority of them stood on any issue. This simple formula of direct rule by the people or direct democracy is, however, impracticable in the gigantic states of modern societies.

For all practical purposes, in the choice of the *modus operandi* of the collective exercise of power, authority and influence in society, the alternatives have been reduced to only one: indirect rule through agents or representatives. And the practical problem then becomes one of devising a mechanism for selecting or designating these "representatives of the people".

Almost universally, the consecrated method for selecting the said representatives is through some form of elections. The basic idea is that sub-groups of the main polity elect an individual, or a small number of individuals, to represent them in a gathering or assembly of representatives, which assembly or gathering is deemed in turn to represent the people as a whole. The logical inference is that the majority among the representatives represents a majority of the people themselves.

The manner of delimiting these sub-groups, the rules and procedures of selecting the representatives, all provide opportunities for myriad variations on the basic electoral theme. And with each variation, different effects, different results ensue in terms of the representativity of the group ultimately designated as "the people's representative".

Ideally, this group should be representative of the people in the fullest sense, that is, according to the three basic meanings of the term:

(i)   First of all, it should constitute a "representative sample". It should represent a cross-section of the population in terms of such things as race, religion, sex, socio-economic classes etc. In this sense, the proxy rulers will pass the test of goodness, fairness and justice because they will be "cut in the people's image".

(ii)   Secondly, the group should be representative in the sense which would be best rendered if we disaggregate the term to read "re-presenter". In this sense the group would merely be a kind of "re-sayer", a spokesman, a mouthpiece, an echo: the repeater, conveyor, transmitter of messages that the people would like to send. In a word, the representatives would merely be "their masters' voice"!

(iii) Finally, the group should be representive in the sense of being an agent, that is, a fully mandated delegate authorized to act *on behalf and in lieu of* some other person — the people. To this extent they would have authority to use their judgement to decide in matters of interest to, and, ideally, in the interests of, the people. They would thus have a margin of discretion enabling them to interpret the messages (the will) of the people, to amplify or tone them down as necessary, to initiate action.

Once the people are constituted in the form of a majority of the people's representative, they must then organize themselves to govern, to rule — they must constitute a *government*.

To organize is to structure. It is, first of all, to institute some kind of division of labour and specialization of tasks among the organs of an entity, which, in this case, is the government. This is a necessary practical step, of course, for no other reason than that the tasks entrusted to or performed by governments, especially modern ones, are of an extreme diversity and multiplicity. This exercise is what is commonly called the "separation of powers" of government. In other words, quite apart from its value as a means of obviating tyranny and despotism, thanks to the wisdom of the adage that "no person should be accuser, judge and executioner all in one", this device is also a matter of practicalities and is based on the need to share out work for greater operational efficiency. This part of structuring or organizing corresponds to the "There shall be . . . . . ." part of constitutions, which establishes the organs of government and specifies their respective tasks and duties.

Organizing also means structuring the relations among the organs or constituent elements of an entity. It means, in this case, deciding what power, authority and influence relations shall exist between and among the specialized organs of the government. Among other things, this specifies what organs shall take orders, commands and instructions, from which; which are accountable or report to which. This is what is specified, for example, by provisions such as:

"In the exercise of the functions vested in him . . . the Attorney-General shall not be subject to the direction or control of any other person or authority."[10] or,

"The office of a Minister shall become vacant if the President so directs."[11]

A kind of departmentation and hierarchy of organs is thus created. Traditionally, the assembly of the respresentatives of the people is the supreme authority and all the other organs (institutions) of government are subordinate to it.

Once the organs of government are in place and their mode of operation specified, it is necessary, as a final practical measure, that there be established a mechanism of control for ensuring that the people's will does (indeed!) get implemented — that it is indeed the people's government which gets instituted or which results from the arrangements.

Like all control mechanisms, this one rests on a system of information generation, storage, transmission and dissemination. It rests on all the means that allow the people to *know* what the various organs of government are doing and thus enabling them to decide what to do about it. This includes information contained in all manner of records, reports, the media, plus the evidence of direct observation.

Once the arrangements outlined above are operationalized, it is then expected that a democratic system will be in place and that fruits or benefits will accrue.

The Concrete Reality

"If there were a people of gods, they would rule themselves democratically. So perfect a government is not suited for men."
Jean-Jacques Rousseau.[12]

Guided by the vision of the democratic ideal and armed with all the practical tools his intelligence and creativity could fashion, man has for centuries been striving to install a democratic order. The concrete dimension of democracy concerns the balance sheet of the past and present experiments and efforts of the peoples of the world.

The question that this raises is: what has come out of the immeasurable sacrifices of blood, sweat and tears that have been shed at the altar of democracy? In other words, in terms of the democratic ideal, where does the world stand today? What reality do the people of the world actually live? What is the hiatus between the real and the ideal? What distance has been covered and what remains to be covered before mankind finally reaches the democratic promised land?

If democracy means good, fair and just government of men and women in society according to the various connotations of the concepts outlined above, it follows that it can only be established, it can only live, survive and thrive in a country of good, fair and just men and women. The question is: where is such a land? And the sad answer is: nowhere on earth! And the equally sad conclusion is that there is no democracy on planet earth! At least not in its ideal or pure form. Democracy in the real world is negated or limited in the fullness of its concrete manifestations by the existence of non-ideal or limited men and women to nurture or to operate it.

Contrary to the many holier-than-thou attitudes, accusations, counter-accusations, controversies and polemics that oppose supporters, apologists, opponents and detractors of all types of regimes on the basis of their being or not being democratic, the sobering conclusion is that none of them is democratic: at least not in the sense of the democratic ideal outlined here.

When it comes to the various structural, organizational or institutional arrangements — the electoral procedures and rules, the division of labour among the organs of government, the mechanisms of popular control over the government — we find that different combinations and systems necessarily produce different effects: each is of a different value in terms of how much they contribute towards the realization of the democratic ideal. Single party systems, multi-party systems, direct elections, indirect elections, simple majority rule, absolute majority rule, majority representation, proportional representation and differing combinations of all these produce governments of varying degrees of goodness, fairness and justice.

Thus, by the very fact that different peoples possess different mechanisms of implementing democracy, they also harvest different crops of its fruits. Many electoral systems for example are institutionalized frauds. They include the so-called "democratic centralism" of communist systems and most one-party systems. In these, the people have hardly any choice in who their representatives shall be. One way or another the choice is made for them!

Again, many rulers/governments/peoples pay only lip-service to the procedural aspects of their electoral system, such as it may be. The rules of the game are not adhered to except in the most perfunctory, formalistic and ritualistic manner. Quite often they are openly, directly or indirectly, violated, through such practices as vote rigging, fraudulent disqualification of candidates, harassment and intimidation of others, illegal arrests, corruption, bribery, violence. It is certainly not through the most scrupulous adherence to the letter and the spirit of the electoral rules and procedures that, for example, some African rulers manage to be regularly reelected with majorities of 99%!

Moreover most electorates are incapacitated by objective socio-economic conditions from playing an effective role in the choice of representatives. The television and other avenues of mass media political marketing, for instance, are used with extraordinary effectiveness in the manipulation of the electorate and public opinion, especially in such countries as the United States and Western Europe. At the other end of the scale, the illiteracy, ignorance and poverty of Third World masses plus such factors as poor communication facilities, militate to a large extent against the full development of the democratic process.

Thus, if it is not failed by defective procedures or mechanisms of implementation, then it is failed by the bad faith of the implementers or, if not that, by objective conditions of the social and material life of the people until, in the final analysis, democracy in its ideal form, in its fullest sense, remains what it has always been — a dream!

To say that democracy does not exist in its ideal form, however, is not to say that it does not exist in any form! To that extent we can advance the proposition that, rather than being either democratic (or undemocratic) systems existing in the world are *more or less* democratic (or undemocratic) depending on the perspective one chooses to look at them from. What exists in the real world, as always when the ideal meets the real, are only *approximations of varying degrees of fidelity* to the ideal, to the proposed model.

The uncontestable fact is that some governments are more representative, more "cut in the people's image" than others; some observe more scrupulously the rules of the game (primarily the letter and spirit of the constitution) than others; and some are more useful, deliver more tangible benefits, (goods and services) to their people, than others. All these are parameters for measuring democracy.

Thus, *for convenience and as a matter of convention* only, it can be advanced that, in terms of those parameters, once the democratic content of any given system reaches a certain point, then, for *all practical purposes,* that system can be said to be democratic. Conversely, all those systems which do not attain the said level, degree or "amount" of democratic content should stand condemned as undemocratic. And once objective, precise methods and standards for measuring democracy along the lines of the said parameters are established, the only point at issue will remain the exact location of that all important threshold.

Concretely, in terms of the balance sheet of mankind's democratic enterprise, the picture remains ambiguous. Although much has been accomplished towards the establishment of a democratic order since the democratic ideology took root in the world, much, nevertheless, remains to be done and it is still a matter of great uncertainty whether the people of the world have crossed the rubicon in the progress towards democracy. The balance sheet is inconclusive.

For if government by "divine right" has virtually disappeared from the face of the earth, there still remain a dozen or so of them, and in democratic terms, those are a dozen too many. If many have "gone down under", we still have too many social political systems where racial, religious, ideological, tribal, sexual minorities and privileged elites, castes and/or socio-economic classes, maintain oppressive and repressive hegemonies over the majority of the people. Although many tyrants, dictators and despots of various hues (the Somozas, Bokassas, Idi Amins, Pol Pots, Pahlavis) have continued to bite the dust, it nevertheless remains true that there are still too many brutes ruling with "iron fists" and sitting heavily on their people.

And finally, if much has been accomplished in terms of liberating man from material misery and exploitation by fellow man, it is nevertheless incontestable that in many parts of the world, extreme poverty and deprivation are the order of the day, while slave and near-slave conditions are the daily lot of millions of men and women in such places as the sugar plantations of Haiti, the haciendas of Latin America, the gold and other mines of South Africa, the labour camps of Siberia, the brothels of the entire world. . . The list is long indeed!!

THE FOUNDATIONS OF DEMOCRACY

Like any other social phenomenon, democracy is the result or the product of definite social and material factors: it is a function of identifiable and quite probably measurable social and material forces. This is what explains the fact that some societies or social systems manifest a high degree of closeness, faithfulness or fidelity to the democratic ideal while others present caricatured, even grotesque images of it. The amount or degree of democracy that any given people enjoy is explainable by, and is predicable upon the existence or otherwise of these factors/forces and their dynamic interactions.

The said factors/forces operate or are to be found at all the three fundamental levels, dimensions or moments of human social existence and life: the material (or infrastructural) level, the institutional (or techno-structural) level and the human relations (or superstructural) level. For democracy to exist, survive and prosper, it must have its roots firmly grounded in *all the three levels*. In other words, the amount or degree of democracy in any given society at any given moment depends upon the nature and state of its material infrastructure, its institutional techno-structure and its human superstructure.

The Infrastructure of Democracy

"A hungry man is an angry man."
— Bob Marley!

Like any other kind, democratic rule, or rule by/of/for the people, requires, as the first and *sine qua non* condition, that the ones to be governed (ruled) be governable! If that sounds like a statement of the obvious, the foundations of a people's governability are far less obvious. And even if they were, they are nevertheless more than commonly overlooked or forgotten. And because of this, it has happened countless times in history and in many lands, that rulers have been rendered incapable of maintaining their rule by a people who have become ungovernable!

The first more or less obvious foundation of a people's governability is that they be of healthy and sound body and mind. They must be both physically and mentally fit, not only so that they may be able to do what the rulers tell them to do (to obey or comply with orders, instructions and commands), but also so that they can be in a position/state to understand those orders, instructions and commands, and the need to obey or comply with them.

It requires no special feat of intelligence or imagination to know what it takes to make a healthy body and mind. It is nothing more, and certainly nothing less than those things that are necessary for man's social and material life — the wherewithal to meet and satisfy the so-called basic human needs: biological or physiological needs i.e. the needs for the sustainers of life: food, shelter, clothing; security needs: freedom from danger, fear, anxiety; affiliation or belonging needs i.e. the need for human acceptance, affection, love, "human warmth,"; recognition needs: respect, esteem, status; and self-actualization: need for accomplishment.

Without going into the controversy as to whether there exists a "propotency" or a "hierarchy" among these needs as advanced by Abraham Maslow[13] and without worrying whether some are "fundamental" and others "secondary", the fact is incontrovertible that failure to meet these needs leads to a state of physical and/or mental unhealth which can go as far as death. Anything therefore that contributes to the betterment of a people's *material and social welfare* contributes towards making them governable and to that extent must be regarded as one of the most sure foundations of any rule — including the democratic one.

Obviously a society satisfies most of its needs through the economic production of goods and services. The infrastructure of democracy therefore lies in the economy — the system of production, distribution and consumption of material goods and services. To this extent, democracy is served by the existence of a healthy and prosperous economy. The reverse is also true: a weak and badly functioning economy is a mortal danger for democracy. Therefore, as a first requirement, the solidly anchored democratic system should enable the people to get in quantity and quality, an adequate supply of goods (food, shelter, clothing) and services (education, security, entertainment), to meet and satisfy their material, social and other needs, wants and desires.

Empirical evidence in this regard is overwhelming. Among a thousand and one other examples of a time-honoured pattern, one needs only recall the direct link between the Great Depression of 1929-33 and the rise of fascism, and nazism and the Gulag Archipelago. Globally, governments become destabilized and are quite often overthrown altogether in times of economic adversity. At such times people tend to "loose their heads"!

We can say, figuratively that democracy is founded on full bellies and peaceful minds! And the "proteins" or the building blocks of democracy are such things as a stable currency, low, or better, no inflation, high, or better, full employment, a growing gross domestic product (without worrying, at this stage, whether or not it is equitably distributed).

The Technostructure of Democracy

"As you make your bed, so shall you lie on it"!
— Proverb.

The other level at which democracy needs to be anchored is the institutional technostructure of society. As indicated earlier, in the case of governments this refers to the structural and functional arrangements of the governmental apparatus and process. It refers to or raises the question of how adapted the mechanisms of government are, in terms of their objective value as promoters of the ambitions of the democratic ideal. Democracy can be defeated on technicalities just as certain technical arrangements can make it more difficult to undermine. For this reason, certain arrangements are more adapted than others to the democratic task. And the technical refinements to the machinery of government, in all its multifarious aspects, can obviously vary almost infinitely.

Whatever the technical minutiae, however, certain principles of organization are fundamental in laying the foundations of practical democracy. Among these are: (i) the openness of the system; (ii) the simplicity of the operational mechanisms and (iii) the clarity of the institutional role structure. The openness of the system refers primarily to the degree of freedom that the participants enjoy in making their contributions to the operation of the system. It therefore refers to how receptive or accommodating the system is to inputs from individuals or groups of citizens. In this connection, for democracy to function optimally, the people should be as free as possible in the choice of their representatives. And this freedom constitute another *sine qua non* of democracy. The people must be free to choose their representatives; otherwise, how can the latter be considered as representing them?

The openness of the system also refers to the latitude the prospective candidates are allowed to organize themselves for the purpose of offering their services to the people. It is in the interest of democracy that the system should accommodate as many parties, groupings and campaign styles as possible. Multi-party systems are therefore, as a general rule, a better foundation of democracy than single-party systems. It is even possible to advance that no-party systems are the best!

The openness of the system extends also to the latitude that the citizens have in exercising their choice of representatives. This is a necessary corollary to the openness of the candidates' nomination process. Thus, not only should the people have the widest possible choice of candidates, they should also have the greatest freedom of choice in selecting from amongst them. And it is in this connection that the secret ballot becomes a technical device of the greatest importance as a foundation of the democratic process. It ensures that at the moment of deciding, the citizen makes his own choice — free from manipulation or undue influence of whatever kind. Corruption and intimidation, for example, are rendered inoperative by the impossibility of verifying compliance.

If the people's rule can only be exercised through a detour, that is, through proxy, it is essential, in the interests of democracy, that the said detours be kept to a minimum. For the more detours there are, the more the people's will risks getting hijacked on the way!

Thus the simplicity of the operational mechanisms becomes another key foundation of democracy. Among other things, this means that elections should be as direct as possible. There should be no intermediaries, go-betweens or middle men between the people and their representatives. The people should choose their own representatives — not choose the choices! This implies, among other things, that the idea of electoral colleges is fundamentally anti-democratic. It merely transforms a system into an oligarchy.

Simplicity in such things as procedures and rules is also important in more ways than one. For one, it makes the system easier to operate or manage, thus helping to avoid even unintentional shortcomings and human failures. For another, it facilitates supervision and control, thus keeping the system less vulnerable or open to fraudulent manipulation. Finally, simple rules and procedures make the system more easily understood and followed by the citizenry — thus enhancing the quality and even the level of their participation in the whole process.

For its part, institutional role clarity touches on the system of division of labour and specialization of tasks within the government. As a foundation for democratic practice, the roles (duties, tasks, responsibilities) of the various organs and the authority, power and influence relationships among them should be as clearly defined as possible. Each organ's functions and area of jurisdiction should be spelt out in unequivocal terms. This, among other things, helps to smoothen operations by minimizing conflicts of jurisdiction and competence. More than this, it fosters institutional autonomy, thus helping to avoid undue hegemony by one organ over the others with the attendant dangers to the separation of powers principle.

The clarification of role and authority relationships among the institutions of government also provides the opportunity for establishing the famous "checks and balances" in their operations. These constitute an extra guarantee for the all-important freedom of the people.

The Superstructure of Democracy

"Umleavyo mtoto, ndivyo akuavyo"![14]
— Swahili saying.

Democratic behaviour is not a genetically conditioned, inborn or inherited faculty — it is learned. The practice of democracy must therefore be taught to its practitioners. It belongs to the cultural patrimony of a people.

Culture generally means what a person learns from, and in relation to, his/her material and social environment. It refers to *acquired* knowledge: about what *is,* what is good, bad, useful, useless, what to do, when, how. This education or culture is what fashions values, attitudes, beliefs and habits, of individuals and social groups. It is thus at the root of behaviour and conduct in society. It is through it that individuals and groups learn to recognize, accept and respect established social institutions and practices.

The superstructural foundations of democracy are therefore to be found in the values, beliefs and attitudes of the people. To this extent, and in this regard, we can advance that, other things being equal, the amount or degree of democracy in any given society is directly proportional to the degree of acculturation of the people in democratic values, attitudes and beliefs. For democracy to exist, survive and prosper, it requires that the people be bathed in and drenched with the democratic ethos!

It is in this manner that education and culture constitute one of the most fundamental foundations of democracy as of any other social system. And, naturally, for the particular culture to be a foundation for democracy and not for any other system, it must be one whose teachings promote the democratic ideal. Among other things, that education must preach the gospel of equality, freedom and human dignity.

Equality is needed because *people* is merely the plural of person: each person should count for the same as any other person. Inequalities of fact (e.g. in education or wealth, for example, or of attribution that is, based on religion, race, colour, or sex of the person), are therefore antithetical to a democratic life and practice.

If freedom of the people is the cornerstone of democracy as previously argued, then for democracy to survive, the people must *value* freedom sufficiently to treasure and nurture it. They should be prepared to defend it with the requisite sacrifices of sweat, tears and blood!

And since the people must govern together, collectively, there is no way they can do so without a minimum of respect for one another, without according each other the right to full human dignity. Their *attitudes* towards each other must be proper, correct, in a word, civilized!

REFERENCES

1. Orwell, G. *Selected Essays,* Baltimore, 1957, p. 149
2. Eliot, T.S. *The Ideal of a Christian Society,* London, 1939, p. 11.
3. Sartori, G. *Democratic Theory,* New York, 1965, p. 9.
4. Lively, J. *Democracy,* London, Oxford Univ. Press, 1975, p. 1.
5. Carlyle, T. *Latter-Day Pamphlets I,* "The Present Times", London, 1850, p. 27 In Sartori, *Op. Cit.* p. 52.
6. Cf. Sartori, *Op. Cit.* pp. 17 and 22.
7. *Ibid.,* p. 18.
8. A commonly held view is that the eternal woes of the Polish nation and state could very well have their origins in the unanimity rule of its ancient Council of State!
9. Obviously we can take the majority concept further and say that it does not refer to "the many" in terms of all the citizens but in terms of all those among them who have "attained the age of majority".

10. Republic of Kenya, The Constitution of Kenya, Government Printer, Nairobi, 1969, Sect. 26 (8).
11. *Ibid.,* Section 16 (3).
12. Rousseau, J.J. *Social Contract,* Vol. III p. 4.
13. Maslow, A. *Motivation and Personality,* Harper and Brothers, New. York, 1954.
14. Approximately: "The way you bring up a child is the way it grows up."

CHAPTER II

IDEOLOGICAL DOGMATISM AND THE VALUES OF DEMOCRACY

D.A. Masolo

INTRODUCTION

Democracy has become the most appealing form of government in the modern age. Plato and Aristotle had refuted it largely as an unworkable form of rule that complied fully with their metaphysical elaborations of man and reality. J.S. Mill and Hegel exalted it as the form of government most compatible with a high stage in the dialectical development of the spirit.

In our own time, to subscribe to democracy as a form of government is a source of respect, a reflection of good and sound reasoning and respect for human dignity and rights. That democracy is so popular is evident from the number of rulers and regimes that claim to belong to "the democratic world", including not only the late Allende's regime in Chile, but also the apartheid regime in South Africa.

All this not only shows how much democracy is often abused when portrayed as a mere ideological slogan, but probably how vast and varied a concept it is. In this varied use, the overriding element is that democracy is a term that describes actions in the art of governing, either as a method or as the acts themselves. In the discourse that follows, it is taken as axiomatic, in the words of the Ghanaian philosopher, Kwasi Wiredu, that action — by an individual or group of individuals —.needs to be guided by ideas and that philosophy attempts to elucidate the most fundamental of such ideas. We shall attempt to show here how many of the problems democracy suffers from today are due to certain intrinsic cognitive issues of ideology as a whole. In the end, it may appear as if a new kind of liberation is necessary before democratic systems can take root in Africa: a mental liberation from arbitrary dogmatism to a state of liberal cartesian *dubitatio*.

Democracy is both an attitude and a value. It is an attitude because it is a way of doing things that is dependent upon how we regard ourselves, our abilities and those of others. As an attitude, no doubt democracy can be taught and people educated about the limitation of men as opposed to the *tout puissant* attitudes that underlie most undemocratic systems. Whether we talk of the rulers' self promotion or of rampant detentions without trial, we are still addressing the fundamental issue of the uncompromising and absolutist attitudes of those who refuse to recognize the value of others' contributions to the socially constructed truths and values. It is paramount in any democratic system that what is to be considered as good rests with those that are governed.

This chapter does not present an expository analysis of the problems of democracy in Africa but it is hoped that the analysis of the idea, which is our primary concern, may throw as much light as possible on the obscurization of the concept and method of democracy on the continent. The chapter is divided into two parts. The first part is basically an attempt to bring out some fundamental characteristics of dogmatism in ideological assumptions. Part two approaches the issue of democracy as a body of values vital to social life whose knowledge, use and achievement in socio-political experience call categorically for the demolition of ideological dogmatism and for an openness to a certain kind of liberalism as an attitude of mind essential to a democratic exercise of government.

IDEOLOGICAL DOGMATISM

Dogmatism in Social Sciences

Dogmatism is essentially a problem of the humanities, or of the Social Sciences and we want to begin by proposing that the origins of dogmatism must therefore be sought within the poverty of the humanities and social sciences themselves — that is, of those sciences that do not have any specific claim to any body of principles or criteria other than logical consistency and moral appeal, to make their propositions demonstrable.

David W. McKinney Jr. writes that "Since there exists no body of demonstrable knowledge in the social scineces, it must be presumed that the various *approaches* to social science data are inadequate for the task for which they are employed".[1] This is due to the fact that the area or range of human activity is unlimited and that man's behaviour patterns are exceedingly difficult to fix and make constant under a limited number of laws. Correspondingly, therefore, the inadequacy of any given single approach is due to the failure of theory, methodology, specific research techniques and procedures to comply with the requirements induced by the initial and corollary assumptions which underlie the broad body of data for which the specific unit of study represents only a particular and limited instance.

This inadequacy must not therefore be seen as a question of the legitimacy or validity of any specific approach taken separately, but rather as lying in the inability of each approach to cover the broad area of the data. Each approach thus forms its own world, remotely open to other approaches' assessment, but at the same time holding on to some form of absolutism, ultimacy, (although open to development from within), and authoritarianism. Thus each social science discipline is dogmatic in relation to others. But are all these dogmatic qualities for mere self preservation and identity?

Of course, these questions would be more relevant where one talked of personality and/or areas of activity that are controlled by and dependent on human character. Ideology is such an area. But what do we mean by dogmatism? Just what is dogmatic statement? And how is this related to ideology? These are the questions we wish to attempt to clarify rather than answer.

Dogmatism: Irrationality, Idolatry or Faith?

By dogmatism we commonly refer to an attitude of mind of whoever makes affirmations in an absolute manner without giving intrinsic proofs thereof, and often with a claim to authority. Dogmatism thus inhibits rational discussion, with the indication that if the claim were to be dispassionately examined, it would turn out to be unwarranted. The strength of dogmatism thus lies in its invocation of authority as its basis rather than in the demonstrability of the claims made therein. A historical survey of the use of the term, so closely connected with religion, reveals this authoritative character of dogma as "authentic, authorized and infallible declarations, judgements or decisions," on the part of the *magisterium* (authority).

In the history of the use of dogmatism within the Catholic Church, the authority of dogma shifted from the *magisterium* (teacherhood) of the doctrines themselves to the personality of the leadership of that institution. Thus Vatican Council II ratified the infallibility of the Pope. "He who is in power must be above the institution he so leads", as Bishop Gasser of Brixon commented on complaints that the draft on the infallibility of the Pope (made doctrinal by Vatican Council I) was separating the Pope from the rest of the Church. Said he: "We are not separating the Pope, we are not in the least separating the Pope from the consent of the Church, provided that such consent is not understood to be a condition, whether antecedent or consequent — This consent (of the Church) can never be lacking (to papal definitions)"[2]. Thus dogmatism plays a vital role in developing the authoritarian personality in whoever holds power. And once achieved, power engenders the attitudes of dogmatism.

The attitude of the authoritarian character towards life, his whole philosophy, is determined by emotional strivings. The authoritarian character loves those conditions that limit human freedom. He loves being submitted to fate. And "fate may be rationalized philosophically as 'natural law' or as 'destiny of man'; religiously as the 'Will of the Lord', and ethically as 'duty'. For the authoritarian character, it is always a higher power outside of the individual, towards which the individual can do nothing but submit."[3] Such people have a logic of their own which integrates all life for them in such a way as to make their actions not only understandable but, from their own point of view, quite justifiable and correct.

Behaviour is essentially an expression of motivational intent. Thus because philosophy, as a discipline, seeks truth in general, it is characterized by a "behaviour" of openness, critical attitude and ability to spread over a variety of issues and comparative approaches. But because ideology, as defined by Professor Wiredu, is "a political weapon in the relentless pursuit of power or when attained, the determined retention of it at all costs"[4], it is dogmatic, closed and exclusive in character or "behaviour". Behaviour is an expression of interests. Thus dogmatism, as a *pattern* or set of behaviour, is a particular type of prejudice based more largely upon factors in the subject and his total situation as far as his conception of a given reality is concerned. Hence to understand why this particular conception of reality occurs rather than some other possible conception, it is necessary to focus attention on the needs and wishes of the holder of this conception.

Ideologies, whether "specific" or "total", according to the Manheimian distinction, are a set of dogmas, social formulae or even belief systems normally held by specific groups or classes as justifications for some specific set of interests. In any given society, therefore, there is to be found multiple ideologies — some dominant, others dominated; still some manifest while others suppressed — but all openly or silently colliding in a constant struggle for power.

Each ideological framework contains not only interpretative schemes ("*weapon*" in Wiredu's definition), but also normative propositions regarding specific truths about the intelligible reality. Ideologies are always a function of interests, or its uses. We may, however, distinguish the use of ideas for descriptive and explanatory purpose from other uses of them — such as making requests and giving orders, making value judgements, expressing moods and feelings, and so on.

An ideology is overtly descriptive and explanatory. Sets of beliefs or theories that are ideological purport to tell us how things are or were, and how they come or came to be. Ideology is also prescriptive in that it often takes a moral position or makes a value judgement in relation to a certain interpretation of reality, be it a state of affairs or a set of actions. But the ideology that we have in mind here is the type analyzed by John Plamenatz as one which "would contain also an idea of man, an interpretation of his activities, compatible with but not presupposed by the findings of the psychologist and the sociologist. . . . a product of reflection, a fruit of experience. It would be a belief or set of beliefs about man and not just a feeling or attitude or disposition expressed in words".[5]

As Plamenatz himself suggests, this is the kind of ideology we often get in philosophical hypotheses and accounts or in dogmatic religions with elaborate theological doctrines.

Social and Political Ideology

But there is still another type of ideology which despite the fact that it lacks the clear and overt philosophical exposition of the one we have described above, still remains different from the kind of "false-consciousness" with which Marx painted religion as class ideology. In other words, this kind of ideology is not mere fantasy. It is theory about society and about the social world. Of course, to Marx this would only apply to the bourgeois class. The lower classes have religion as their *ideology* (fantasy) in the manner of false consciousness. However, at one time or another, even the lowest class in a class society also acquires an ideology in the theoretical sense, and this may include even religion since ideology is a body of truth propositions.

In each society, every social group has its own perception of reality to which it resorts, and which guides its aspirations and expectations regardless of its truth. But who would have to judge it true? The truth value of each ideological framework is judgeable by the other ideologies only in terms of whether or not the activities and ideas of its adherents are conformant with those of the opposing or judging point of view. The ruling class will hold the workers' ideology as true only in so far as it does not embody any ideas that threaten their own. Social truth thus becomes synonymous with social consciousness, and the latter, to use the words of R.J. Njoroge, "can be viewed as a normative stance towards social phenomena." Njoroge calls this interest conflict between the rulers and the masses a sign of the second phase of social consciousness, marred by hostile diversity and dogmatism in regard to concepts and values which are, in themselves, not truths of fact, but of the moral and metaphysical kind. The situation is even more complicated than this.

There are situations where this conflict in ideologies either does not exist or does so only in a mild way, but their maintenance in their respective places is one of mutual interaction and influence. Houseboys may help their employers in maintaining their status of houseboys by acting towards the employers in a manner suggesting that they recognize and accept their role in that specific interaction. In such a situation, conflict would only arise when and where the hoseboys began to desire to become the employers. But in the latter case, we observe a change both in the interests and in the ideology of the houseboy group. And what brings this change is probably more of a psychological factor than one of understanding or "false-consciousness". The former is often deemed "reactionary" ideology and the latter revolutionary.

However, in conflict or in conformity, each group endeavours to achieve and then maintain its interests. Ideology and the field of social goals can therefore be characterized as primarily constituting an area of idealizations, concept formations or projections to be converted into action, and cuts deeply into the concept and problem of truth. We have used the term "interest(s)" here in a manner comparable to "point of view" (Wiredu) or "context" (Odera Oruka). Ideologies are not mere sets of beliefs, but rather theories that attempt to explain how some part of life fits into a larger context; and this fitting is patterned according to the general picture an individual or class has of the larger context — that is, from their own painting of the ideal social reality.

Hence, in claims or policies, we often use ideas and advance demands which fit into our general ideological positions and attitudes, whether we make them in the name of a class or category to which we may belong. We use such ideas both to make claims and advance demands and to resist claims and demands that conflict with them. Hence dogmatism in ideology is not to be seen as an attitude bent towards the retention of the *status quo* of any social group, but as an uncompromising attitude bent towards the achievement of defined aims. Those aims and the conditions for their achievement may be denied to one group by another, and the former's struggles to grab them from the latter may be as dogmatic and uncompromising as the struggle by the latter to maintain the *status quo*. Thus scientific socialism is just as dogmatic as staunch capitalism.

The Elites and Society in Africa

What we have said above about ideology in general implies that every social group in a society is conscious or aware of its unity, role and interests in relation to other social groups, and that, therefore, there is always implied a social conflict in society. Sometimes, however, as Plamenatz says, members of two or more social groups may be passive as groups in terms of their interaction while remaining highly active in their respective internal group roles.[6]

Generally, this has been, and largely is, the situation in modern Africa. The ruling elite, deeply engaged in carrying out their duties of running the state machinery set and left behind by the former colonial elite, has done little, if anything, to establish a meaningful relationship with the large number of peasants dwelling and working in the remote countryside. Given the diverse interests of these two groups (due to the differences in their ways of life), each lives "beside" the other without any meaningful contact or awareness of the other, though they are of common origin. The peasants form a passive social group. They are unaware of their being a distinctive class in the society. Nor are they aware that those others who portray elements of difference from them — like possession of cars, big

houses, better (different types of) clothing, difference in eating habits, etc.
- have anything to do with them. One could even dare to say they lack an ideology except for the traditional *weltanschauung* and some other scattered detail.

The elites, on the other hand, are an active class or social group, for they are aware of their common belonging, ingrained further by the constant competitive conflicts between them. Whether in terms of power or wealth, they are, in every sense, an active group. The passivity of the peasantry is even a further contribution towards the sustenance of their position. Their conceptions of reality and of social goals and values are more comprehensive and clearly defined. This comprehension and definition may not be clearly exposed in any theoretical form, but all their activities ranging from political slogans to the choice of the administrative structure are consciously made to fit into these well-conceived aims. Even educational systems are designed and structured to promote the sustenance and continuation of these ideological interests of idolatry rather than rationalism.

In education the humanities and social sciences are deliberately given a lower grading because they lead to political awareness while religious education is promoted so as to instill obedience and pious servility and subservience as a high god-given virtue. Thus the educated class, though trained primarily to assist the ruling elite in the management of the infrastructure, poses itself as essentially the only possible threat to the masters. This suspicion on the part of the rulers triggers off measures to close most of those gaps that may lead to the top of the ladder. And as a counter effect, these measures themselves have prompted criticisms from the intellectuals who are therefore seen as the real threat to the positions and privileges of the ruling class and their administrative aides.

But to what extent are the intellectuals a real or mythical threat to the ruling class?

More often than not, the intellectuals themselves have been responsible for their fate in this struggle. And this is mainly due to the language in which they express their idealization of the better society. They make it look a society ruled by the peasants, — and this term, in many parts of Africa, has come to mean the poor and illiterate masses, dwelling and working in the countrysides — people who by the standards of their experience and understanding are unable to handle the matters of a modern state. And because they are educated and bound to know these simple facts, the intellectuals are deemed by the rulers not only as a threat to their positions and privileges, but also as liars who want to achieve their own goals by riding on the back of the peasants. And because the rulers themselves have control over the machinery of contact with the public, they have all the chance to hang the intellectuals on the necks of the peasants: all detentions without trial, closures of higher educational institutions and other acts of repression become "legitimate" for the "protection" of the majority. The intellectuals then become the "real" enemies of peace, justice and order in the definition of the rulers.

On the other hand, the intellectuals are a committed class without distinctive aims or interests of their own. They are a class of liberals acting as mercenaries for the proletariats and peasants. Between them and the rulers, the problem is not so much "about the range of allowable personal aims and about the opportunities and rights people must have to be able to pursue these aims effectively" as "about the conditions, social and economic, for providing these opportunities."[7]

In condemning the intellectuals, the ruling elite intentionally wishes to kill two birds with one stone. By portraying the intellectuals as liars and seditious characters it wishes to diminish their potential of enlightening the masses. By so doing it serves to "disarm the oppressed classes of the more revolutionary theory" which is increasingly being exposed by intellectuals. By condemning the intellectuals the ruling elite also wishes to perpetuate the *status quo* by indicating to the masses that any change is only equitable with chaos and lawlessness. Any opponents are thus portrayed as disgruntled elements — to mean a disjointed group of individuals apparently misled by ignorance and inapplicable, unworkable "foreign ideologies".

Ironically, therefore, it is the intellectual who is termed ignorant. Cries for equality, justice and a halt to corruption are termed effects of unworkable "foreign ideologies". It is obvious that in such a situation there can be no dialogue between different interpretations of reality. The ruling ideology thus becomes highly exclusive and dogmatic as the intellectual, the sole possible interlocutor, is termed a "false revolutionary" and is left out not only without a platform on which to present his contributions on matters of common good, but also without listeners.

However, "if the development of an ideal of society had convinced one that one's own society contained radical faults, then one would surely wish to see it changed. If, on the other hand, one's own society seemed to measure up well against one's ideal, then one would surely want to maintain it against ill-conceived changes. However, in either case, the question of the nature and justification of social change becomes important."[8]

Ideology and Science

In all these ideological conflicts and unwavering faithfulness to one's class or group position, there is one fundamental assumption or claim being made and this is that each group's assertions reflect the *truth* or state of provable facts in the way we talk of scientific assertions.

The assumptions of ideology, like those of philosophy, are sometimes said to be "self-evident"; but, as they differ from one class or group to another, or from one school to the next, it is clear that this can only mean that there is no unquestionable outside evidence for them. "There cannot be: their truth or falsehood is intrinsic. They cannot be proved or disproved; they can only be taken or left."[9]

The assumptions of ideology cannot be fully substantiated by an empirical observation, for they are assertions not of material fact, but of reality and meaning. For example, a wealthy ruler's conception of the *true* needs of the poor peasants may range from tractors to efficient highways for the transportation of the peasant's produce for sale in the urban areas

unaware that such *truth* reflects or is so only in terms of the magnanimous way of looking at and expecting things from the point of view of a wealthy ruler.

The peasant, on the other hand, knows his needs to be a cheap hoe to enable him to cultivate subsistence crops. Hence truth in this aspect is relative, not absolute. It is often not realized by people deeply involved in ideological framings and in activities based on specific ideological positions that their axioms are primarily dogmatic assumptions based on unprovable claims. They are also integral and absolute, and their strength or weakness lies just in this.

It is no less a necessary condition of ideology that its objective reference should be taken as scientifically valid. The conditions of a peasant can be described in no better terms by a social scientist than by a politician. The facts in his life   the physical environment, the tools he uses, the quantity and quality of his produce, his health conditions and so on, are observable and indisputable facts. Ideology, like philosophy, goes further than this domain of facts in trying to fit these facts into a larger context of reality. The factual data are thus trimmed or stretched to fit into this magical box of ideology. They are interpreted, and thus enter the domain of dogma as "an affirmation of a certain integral character resident both in events, things, persons and peoples, and in reality as a whole."[10]

Thus while different ideological aims and prerequisites may vary widely from one class to another, they all claim that the unity and coherence reflected in the structure of their patterns are *manifested* in the different areas of life, that is, politics, economics, religion, family, group relations, education and so on. The same facts may be cited to support end-theories or aims diametrically opposed to each other.

It is sometimes contended in social science that in certain respects there are bodies of verified interrelated explanatory proportions or theories that make comprehensible a body of verified empirical findings, and that to this extent such propositions consist of an end product   a body of demonstrable knowledge.[11] But unless we are talking of numerical calculations like we get in economics, in ideology such logic is intrinsic to broader assumptions of valuational elements and can often contain "biased" and "false" assertions.

This scientific view of ideology is as old as Destutt de Tracy who "assigned to ideology the tasks of defining the sources of human knowledge, its limitations, and the degree of its certainty" and investigating the origin and law governing the formation of ideas in a scientific manner that could provide an adequate foundation for the political, moral and educational sciences.[12] Since, to him, right thinking was the basis of right political action, ideology as the science of ideas, could not be short of certainty and truth in the manner of physics. In ways reminiscent of Plato, de Tracy held that "only such indubitable knowledge would enable the legislator and ruler of the state to establish and maintain a just and rational order.[13]

Destutt de Tracy's philosophy is a firm claim to realism. And all rulers, including our own rulers in Africa, however mediocre they may be, have a similar claim. Yet only a few of them perhaps understand that even the details of such realism are "meaningful" only because they fit within a more general and broader context of their application which no longer has the image of an indubitable reality of mathematical precision, but one of valuational and metaphysical images specific only to the perceiver(s). "Interests" may not be immediately evident in such a broad metaphysical reality, but the point is that as a conception of reality from a given context, it always carries with it feelings of satisfaction to the perceiver in the corollary desire and wish that such a world be ever realizable. This alone has both emotional and physical or material interests in that it implies a "model" of life or man's place in a so-conceived world.

Being the work of the intellect, however, this world is many times illusory, and a dogmatic and exclusive attachment to it for action-orientation always hides the danger of perpetuating falsehood and deception. Our point here is that it is the power interest elements of ideology that often erode its significance, both in the field of knowledge and in matters of social construction, by hindering its openness and constant re-evaluation in order to achieve a more adequate and truer assessment of facts than those that are available or in use rather than the doctrine that forfeits its claim to objectivity because it contains judgements of value.

Many times too, the wheel of ideology rolls endlessly on the very dogmatism that keeps it up, especially in our young countries where such concepts as responsibility for other people's lives and national interests either have no meaning or have not taken root at all.

Either upon realizing this, or in fear of their own self-deception or deception by others, or deception about the nature of the world (because it is falsified by events), the leaders undertake to further and aggravate their mistakes by forcefully remaining in indisputable power positions by declaring themselves life presidents and amending constitutions to safeguard such interests and aims. Falsehood is thus intentionally made to run people's affairs. In the platonic sense, the *doxa* is made the *episteme* and vice-versa. Man becomes chained forever in the cave of slavery and appearances. The irony is, however, that even the philosopher who has raised some doubt regarding the permanence (objectivity) of this world is not allowed to enlighten those entrusted to him, so that the question about the difference between *doxa* and *episteme* should never arise except in reminiscences after death. In a manner similar to this, Francis Bacon asserted that unless great care was taken, *idols* can be obstacles in the path to true knowledge.[14]

Karl Mannheim puts it even more to the point. He observes that the modern meaning of the term "ideology" originated with Napoleon from a contrast between thought (theory) and political action or practice, and was used by him to ridicule and discredit his critics. He says that "the new world gives sanction to the specific experience of the politician with reality, and it lends support to that practical irrationality which has so little appreciation for thought as an instrument for grasping reality."[15]

In such circumstances, such rulers, especially in Africa, have come out strongly against the intellectuals who belong to differing camps or who hold different views by challenging them to demonstrate the "realism" or their "talks" by action. In turn, however, the rulers are often themselves at pains to answer to the challenges their own assailance has put them in by demonstrating a pragmatism based on a realistic or "true" consciousness. Thus "the necessarily supplementary relationship between action and perception speaks immediately against the entirely arbitrary handling of tested and testable evidence in ideologies and in any kind of action-oriented belief system."[16]

Perception is an essentially subjective phenomenon and activity, and the truths about its "total" structure are possible only within an intersubjective dialogue, by relating the various facts to one another, so that we are able to judge our own perceptions and the perceptions of others, since "the account we give of our experiences and more especially of our motivations may be faulty."[17]

Recapitulation

The validity of a theory essentially lies in its testability, body of proofs or accountability. Proof or experiment, however, does not only aim at verification, or justification of the contents of a proposition. Justification is also reached, however negatively, from lack of contrary evidence. So Sir Karl Popper added to the positivist principle of verification that of falsification. A simple way of saying this is that, we do not, for example, prove the durability of our plates in the houe by storing them away and letting the children use woven baskets. In order to have a ground for claiming their durability we must expose them to constant and proper use.

The number of tests or length of time required will both depend on our natures and habits. In the domain of socio-political truths and tests, the situation is even more complex as both the subject and object is man himself.

Man interprets and transforms according to a general context into which specific beliefs and belief-derived actions fit. This is the area of his ideological fumbling. Whether clearly outlined or not, every human individual capable of using his reason normally is not only capable, but always has this often-called "philosophy" of life. But man is a complex being; he is a cultural, social as well as ecological or natural creature. His life "philosophy" often reflects a complex of the specific impact of all these "modes" of his existence. Hence diversity in these philosophies varies from individuals, through groups and classes to categories. Each has its own ideology or life-philosophy.

In primitive and recent traditional times, each ideology was exclusive of the other, co-existence was unthinkable. Elimination of the other (and this meant physical elimination of people belonging to a different and rival ideology) was the best guarantee for survival. This resulted in frequent jihads and other types of war aimed at subjugating or eliminating ideological adversaries. As ideological co-existence was out of the question, dogmatism thrived in the absence of reason with its powers of investigation and assessment. It thus became a powerful instrument for securing obedience, and upholding unity. In this respect it has held religious systems and political parties together by closing doors to heresy, schisms and revolutions. The rewards for violation of such dogmatic attitudes in religion or racial ideologies are often executions or ex-communications. From Hitler's Germany to Khomeini's Iran and Botha's South Africa, the trend has been this absolutist approach to matters of socio-political values and ideals, based on an absolutist ideology of race or religion.

Dogmatism, however, thrives only in a situation of inversely proportional decline or suppression of reason. Even in the established Christian churches or religious systems, it was at its peak only before the Renaissance and Enlightenment periods. With reason more fertile soil is quickly gathered where some was eroding below the feet of dogmatism. Theology has grown into a formidably strong and rich science or discipline today, for example, as a result of the decline of dogmatism in Christian Churches, especially in the post Vatican II period.

The qualities of diversity and even opposition that often go along with reason, have not so much shown fragility of systems and power grips as they have demonstrated constructiveness, better understanding and better management of the affairs of men by integrating diversity for a richer and more diversified human life. And this can be reached only through tolerance and participation. Intellectuals and other persons capable of formulating and articulating concepts and ideas should be given the opportunity to contribute to the formulation of national policies and ideological frameworks. We must learn to accept that many times it will be the man who objects to and opposes the *status quo* who has the well-being of his country and people deepest at heart. The developing countries cannot afford the luxury of dogmatism in any form. Given their diverse and complex social, cultural, political and economic problems, diverse thoughts, ideas and opinions from within are urgently required for the planning and construction of a better and true society of men.

THE VALUES OF DEMOCRACY

A number of things are inferable from the above analysis of the cognitive nature of ideology. Firstly, on the purely cognitive level, ideologies tend towards absolutism or totalitarianism, thus defying the role of inter-subjectivity in human knowledge. On the political level, they either ignore or totally reject the value of participation as central to the making of any tolerable society of men.

These characteristics of political ideologies run counter to the values of democracy, which idea not only believes in public opinion as the criterion of truth in socio-political life situations but also transcends pure relativism and replaces it with intersubjectivity which alone offers us the dialectical elements of progress which in turn guarantees the achievement of a certain measure of happiness.

At least two essential characteristics define the ideology of any democratic society or system: its innate and natural cartesianism and the recognition of public opinion by the authorities.

We are talking of natural cartesianism because we do not expect everybody to know or to have an interest in philosophy. So we talk of cartesianism merely as an attitude of openness in thought, an openness that embraces scepticism as a method leading to truth. In social and political life and practice this scepticism may be expressed in the form of consideration for the stands and views of different political camps, and parties, or just the views and opinions of people from different social bases, because the truth in it is some kind of order or value — a social good — meant to affect the whole society and not just a class of it.

In most African countries, however, this is hardly the actual behaviour. People in power rarely recognize their role vis-a-vis the social good whose realization they have been delegated to supervise. Instead, the powers that go with this delegation are often confused with or taken to embrace the absolute cognitive authority of the delegates. As a consequence, and as we said earlier, any opposition or variety of opinion is viewed as misguided. The cartesianism of democratic ideology demands that no truth or claim of a social or ideological nature be considered final or sacrosanct.

This confusion of power and knowledge must therefore be dismantled if we are to build the bases for democracy. First, we must accept a variety of equalities of men and encourage individualism in a specific sense. This equality will encourage all individual members of a society to trust their own reason as the source of ideas and opinions which are necessary for the conduct of life. A healthy society is that which encourages its members to think for themselves and which recognizes the right of each one to form his own opinion. Such a society will be cartesian in its ideology as much as it will be individualistic in its everyday political and social life. Intellectual liberty as well as the principle and practice of individual conscience examination are paramount characteristics of any democratic ideology.

In Africa, these characteristics are painfully lacking. The responsible citizen is seen as the one who totally ascribes to the beliefs and doings of the class in power. Intellectuals have been dragged to questioning rooms to ascertain whether or not their purely professional or academic beliefs conform with the dominant ideologies. Decisions taken unilaterally by politicians in matters affecting the entire republic have been declared undebatable by the very public that the policy is meant to affect. And in such cases where policies are unilaterally upheld by those in power without proper public participation, the affected people, or those who think they are disadvantaged as a result of the policy, often revert to private negotiations and bargains with the relevant authorities. Private bargains never rule a nation. They may for a time, but they do not offer lasting solutions as a method of rule. Public affairs are different from private interests and must be treated as public through all the stages of their realization.

Democracy and Public Opinion

It has been suggested against democracy that "the people" are always inept and unrestrained. But this ineptitude and lack of restraint can only be tamed through the promotion of "the moral, intellectual and active worth of all individuals". This does not mean an indiscriminate popular participation in politics. In *The Logic of Discovery* Karl Popper defined scientific statements as those which deny that something logically conceivable is actually realized. Accordingly, he said, it is not sufficient for a statement to be counted as scientific, that there may be confirmatory observational evidence for it; it is essential for such a statement to be capable of being disproved by some conceivable spatio-temporally located event which, were it to occur, would exemplify the possibility that the statement excludes. This statement may by analogy apply well in the social domain. But it demands the use of general ideas on which to base policies, a fact which hardly exists in African political practice.

These general ideas or statements need to be exposed to criticism, not only in parliaments, but also in informed circles, especially among the intellectuals, so as to assess their validity where this merely means accord with the tastes and desires of the people whether or not such tastes and desires are beneficial. To be democratic does not require that you must of necessity be of material benefit to the people. It means only that you do what people want.

In Africa it appears that the material benefit of policies and leaders is often the yardstick for measuring what and who are democratic. A good leader is defined as he who "understands" the needs of the people, where "understanding" becomes nearly equivalent to "intuiting". It has been argued that it is the general will for national unity and economic development that defines democracy in Africa and the underdeveloped countries at large.[18] The determination of the accuracy of this claim is beyond the scope of this paper. However, this theory of the "general will" seems to be in line with what we said earlier about the prescriptive nature of ideologies on the basis of certain interpretations of reality.

In the pre-independence period it might have been apparently easy to assume the presence of this will as a "general" desire for a different state of affairs (freedom or independence from the colonial powers) and it could be reasonable to "assume" further that whoever went to the front to fight for the achievement of this good had the support of the people and represented their united will. We use the word "assume" and the word "general" in quotes because the presence of this will or its generality is not an observable fact as such, but a matter of conjectures and interpretations of the frontrunners and theorists of the struggle of the time. It appears that this assumption is quite basic even to the present form of African democracy, either by anachronism or merely as a result of a theoretical position about its truth or relevance to the existing socio-political situation in Africa.

Either way, such method of politics or conception of democracy fails to take note of the changes in basic social relations that have taken place in the lives of Africans and the moral implications which such changes entail and which demand from us a constant revision of our social theories. This assumed "general will" is easily manipulated to advance misconceived policies in the name of economic development. In political organization, democracy may or may not bring material benefits to all the people or even to the majority of them. Even if it did, democracy is not, and must not be identified with, beneficial dictatorship. If material benefits were the yardstick for assessing and grading the various possible forms of government, then the one in which the least possible number of men was involved in the actual ruling but delivered the desired goods would be the best. But this would obviously limit the amount of another value which, we think, gives democracy its desirability: freedom.

Democracy is more than just a method of delivering material goods. It is an embodiment of non-material values, moral or ethical as one may wish to call them. It describes a state of affairs whereby man actually enjoys the freedom to develop and realize or utilize his higher potentialities such as the development and effective use of his intellectual abilities. It is true that the majority of people have neither an immediate interest in nor a clear perception of such values. It is on the basis of this fact that Plato and Aristotle discredited democracy and defended elitism against it.

In his *Principe* Nicolo Machiavelli theorizes that if a prince wants to survive in power, he must keep his subjects not only constantly well-fed, but also ignorant, because many people are more interested in the things of the senses, in what they see and eat, than in things of the mind.[19] But values as "ought" conditions do not exist only for the knowledgeable man. They are goods for man as man, whatever they may be at the level of "material" principles or actual experience.

In the empirical political arena in Africa this materialistic yardstick has been applied to its fullness in certain areas. To support all this, there is another "mislogic" used which makes "giving" a necessary logical consequence of "having". The reasoning runs somewhat in this form: since a democratic government is defined by the ability of the leaders to bring about the material benefits that the general will desires, and since it is those who have these benefits that can give them, they are the ones to form the democratic government. The result is that power is placed in the hands of those few who have material wealth whether or not they have the mind and/or time to reflect on matters of the State. The characteristic features of this kind of rule are wealth and a lack of brains.

In a paper entitled "Philosophy and Democracy", Prof. H. Odera says of such elitist conception of democracy:

> "Government is something which is supposed to help secure and deliver the goods for its subjects. Yet not one individual or group is capable of knowing exactly what such goods are. The people themselves must as a collectivity determine what their goods must be. And this can best be done only through democracy."[20]

Democracy as a form of government has had opponents throughout the history of ideas. Plato and Aristotle are classical examples of those whose rationale for the support of elitism was based on the ineptitude and lack of restraint on the part of the majority that made democracy a form of government incapable of great achievements. According to them matters of State are a prerogative of the elite born with or made, through education, to acquire superior moral qualities and political insights. They placed emphasis on the moral and intellectual abilities of those considered for rulership.

In Africa, on the contrary, there appears to be a special hatred on the part of rulers for intellectual elites, due more to ideological polarization than to a distinct social theory. But whether or not intellectual ability is a positive requirement for good ruling, democracy must first of all be an attitude of mind, a new form of knowledge in the fashion of cartesianism. Of course, this does not go without difficulties in human experience. Most of the time, men have neither the time nor the patience to form by themselves and evaluate all those ideas and opinions which they need in their everyday life. They simply make use of a certain number of dogmatic ideas and opinions which they believe in without taking time to reflect sufficiently. Yet it is these very same abilities and inabilities that make up a whole world of difference between good and bad rulers both in matters of public administration and those of private lives.

REFERENCES

1. McKinney, D.W., *The Authoritarian Personality Studies: an inquiry into the failure of Social Science Research to produce demonstrable knowledge*, Mouton, The Hague - Paris, 1973, pp. 14-15.
2. Cfr. Groot, J.C., *Aspects horizontaux de la collegialite*, in Barauna, G. and Congar, Y., (Eds.), *L'Eglise de Vatican II*, Paris, 1966, p. 816.
3. Fromm, E., *Escape from Freedom*, Rinehart Co. Inc., New York, 1941, pp. 170-171.
4. Wiredu, K., *Philosophy and an African Culture*, Cambridge University Press, 1980, p. 86.
5. Plamenatz, J., *Ideology*, Pall Mall Press, London, 1970, p.83.
6. *Ibid.*, pp. 99-100.
7. *Ibid.*, p. 105.
8. King, J.C. and McCilvaray, J.A., *Political and Social Philosophy: Traditional and Contemporary Readings*, McGraw-Hill Book Co., New York, 1973, p. 9.
9. Wilson, G.M., *The Analysis of Social Change*, C.U.P., 1968, p. 65.
10. *Ibid.*, p. 68.
11. Cfr. McKinney, D.W., *Op. Cit.*, p. 16.
12. Cfr. Barth, H., *Truth and Ideology*, University of California Press, London, 1976, pp. 1-3.
13. *Ibid.*, p. 6.
14. Cfr. *Novum Organum*, p. 38.
15. Mannheim, K., *Ideology and Utopia*, Routledge Paul, London, 1968, p. 64.
16. Seliger, M., *Ideology and Politics*, George Allen & Unwin, London, 1976, p. 160.
17. *Ibid.*,
18. MacPherson, C.B., *The Real World of Democracy*, Oxford University

Press, 1966, pp. 30 ff.

19. Machiavelli, N., *The Prince,* London, Hammondsworth Books, 1970, pp. 46-48.

20. Oruka, H.O., *Philosophy and Democracy,* (The ethical basis for democracy), seminar paper (unpublished), Nairobi, 1981, p. 7.

PART II

THE DEMOCRATIC PRACTICE

INTRODUCTION

Walter O. Oyugi

That most African regimes today are undemocratic has found expression in many books and journals. The question usually is why should that be the case? What is unique about the political terrain in Africa that militates against the establishment of democratic behaviour?

It has been asserted by some political anthropologists that the problem of undemocratic behaviour in African politics is a post-colonial phenomenon. According to this view, the pre-colonial African states were, in the majority of cases, open and participatory. Decisions were often made on a consensual basis — the concern always being the welfare of the community. However, exceptions were to be found in those states which had stratified socio-political systems and a rigid structure of authority. Here, it has been suggested, the bureaucratization of the socio-political life acted against democratic behaviour. But the problem was confined to a few areas only.

The intervention by colonialism in many instances changed the existing situation fundamentally. Regardless of the form of government found in existence, the colonial situation at once brought with it a new form of authority to which all had to relate. The unification of the locus of authority in a territorial sense had introduced a new form of governance which the old political order had to contend with. The progressive loss of traditional institutional structures and authority that accompanied the consolidation of colonial authority was to deprive the old order of some of its democratic character and later, when independence was achieved, the situation tended to deteriorate in many respects.

The idea that pre-colonial Africa was by and large democratic, in the sense that the common citizens had a say in their governance, is questioned in this volume by Vincent Simiyu. Drawing his examples mainly from Central Africa, he argues that, to a large extent, there was no democracy in traditional African societies. While observing that the problem was more accentuated in the stratified, centralized polities, he is also quick to point out that even in the so-called democratic decentralized political systems, the gerontocratic principles and practices tended to act against openness and popular participation. Therefore to him, the notion that pre-colonial African states were democractic is but a myth.

The volume provides no further debate on the nature of the state in pre-colonial Africa. Neither is there a discussion that bridges the pre-colonial and the independence periods. Indeed, if anything, Simiyu's contribution is intended to question the popular assumption that the authoritarian character of political behaviour in post-independence Africa has no import from the pre-colonial period. It would have been interesting, however, to find out what would have been said about the contribution of colonialism. But since a lot has already been written in this area, we leave the reader to draw his own inferences.

The question to pose at this point is whether indeed the establishment of a democratic society has been a major concern of African regimes?

Upon the attainment of independence, many African countries were primarily concerned with the consolidation of power at the centre. This was so regardless of the form of constitutions inherited at independence. The popular argument then was, and still is, that the plural character of most states as characterized by both secular and non-secular cleavages potentially militated against national unity. National unity in turn was regarded as a major ingredient of national development. Therefore, if development (broadly defined) were to be achieved, the centre had to assert its complete control over the localities. The manifestation of that control was the centralization of authority and power in the hands of central institutions. It meant, in practice, depriving local institutions of their decision-making powers, where such existed.

The emerging monolithic perception of political life had a direct effect on the nature and character of the political system. Instead of inheriting and fostering, for example, the multi-party systems extant at independence in many African countries, the new regimes at once began to introduce practices that made it difficult for opposition parties to operate freely. Political unity was, according to the then emerging trends, possible only within the context of a single party — the ruling party! The roots of the phenomenon of the one-party system were thus being laid.

The emergence of one-party ideology brought with it a lot of debate about its implication for democratic practice. The critics argued that by its very nature, which does not allow for the existence of opposition parties or political opposition as such, it was undemocratic. But supporters, such as Julius Nyerere, argued that since democracy is an attitude of mind, its practice would not be confined to the multi-party system. It could equally be practised in a one-party system.

The argument aside, what has been the experience? Notwithstanding the military intervention in African politics since the 1960s, the institution of the one-party system has survived in many countries. Two brands have existed: the *de facto* and the *de jure*. In practice, however, the two systems have operated on quite similar lines. There has been a lot of talk of the supremacy of the party in political life without the party being allowed in practice to exercise that authority.

In virtually every country that has experimented with it, the one-party system, has been riddled with factionalism and internal rivalries. These have at times resulted in the emergence of new opposition parties when none existed before (e.g. Kenya in 1966); or in the case of dominant

45

one-party states, the emergence of a third political force (e.g. Zambia in 1971). These developments have tended to lead to even more centralization of power — this time not in the hands of central institutions *per se* but rather in the hands of the chief executive. Over the years, this has given birth to the phenomenon of personal rule ably analyzed by Rosberg and Jackson in their "Personal Rule Theory and Practice in Africa", *(Comparative Politics,* July 1984, pp. 421-442).

Personal rule, they say, is a dynamic world of political will and activity that is shaped less by institutions or impersonal social forces than by personal authorities and power . . . . it is a distinctive type of political system in which the rivalries and struggles of powerful and wilful men, rather than impersonal institutions, ideologies, public policies or class interests, are fundamental in shaping political life. The major indictment of personal rule as behaviourally undemocratic comes where they wrote "personal rule is an elitist political system composed of the privileged and powerful few in which the many are usually unmobilized, unorganized and therefore relatively powerless to command the attention and action of government". In that sense, personal rule is "a form of monopolistic rather than pluralist politics". This has, in some countries led to the emergence of "presidential monarchs".

If the above be the developments that have sprung from the emergence of the one-party practice in Africa, then Peter Wanyande is probably right in concluding that the one-party practice is incompatible with democracy and democratic politics. He presents data to show how undemocratic African one-party regimes have been in the manner in which the major political institutions and processes have been manipulated to suit the interests of the power holders.

But if things have not gone well within the one-party systems, the multi-party systems have not done well either. Mugaju, for example, argues that in spite of the existence of more than one party in Uganda in the 60s, the democratic experiment did not take roots. He attributes this to the fact that at the time, the country lacked democratic traditions and consciousness at all levels of the society. This was to be compounded by the political intrigues and manipulations that were put in motion immediately after independence especially by the various parliamentary factions. He is also critical of the independence constitution which, he argues, was based on questionable democratic legitimacy. The essay ends by lamenting that Uganda as a backward country could not and still cannot be considered as a fertile ground for the germination of the seeds of democracy.

The link between development and democracy raised in Mugaju's paper supports the contention in Mugyenyi's paper that "whereas development can occur in the absence of democracy, the latter cannot operate in the absence of development".

If African governments have been as undemocratic as they have been portrayed in these essays, can their major delivery agency — the bureaucracy, escape the indictment? It was Hegel who once gave bureaucracy a rather neutral position in society by claiming that its major role was to act as a bridge between the civil society and the state. Taking the work of Hegel as his starting point, Marx was later to deny bureaucracy that role by asserting that in a bourgeois society (by which he meant at the time the industrialized West), it was first and foremost merely an instrument of domination by the power holder.

In practice what has been the experience and performance of the bureaucracy in Africa? The question is taken up by Walter Oyugi who argues that bureaucracy is a creature of its environment. Therefore to the extent that the African environment is hostile to democratic behaviour, the bureaucry cannot be expected to behave otherwise. Indeed, he rejects the idea that bureaucracy as such can be an instrument of the democratization of society, observing that in the context of Africa, the symbiotic relationship between it and the "political class" has turned it into an instrument of control and, therefore, an enemy of democracy. However, like Mugyenyi and Mugaju, Oyugi too suggests that at the present stage of development in Africa, it is rather premature to expect key institutions in society such as the bureaucracy to become agencies for the democratization of life.

Away from the polity and her institutions, the next paper in this section addresses the gender issue. Using a Marxist framework, Maria Nzomo submits that democracy in a class society (it is implied most African countries are such societies) is an ideological weapon that serves the interest of the dominant class. Her basic argument is that women in Africa are an exploited lot and she presents data to support her contention. She makes a strong plea for the independence of women which she sees as coming through a socialist revolution; yet at the same time she is quick to recognize that all has not been well for women in countries such as the Soviet Union and Cuba where such a revolution has occurred. Whether one agrees with this framework of analysis or not, the proponents of male chauvinism have been given something in this chapter to ponder.

The last chapter in this section is unique in a way. Written by a non-African, Franz Ansprenger, it tries to focus on the external influences on the African democratic experience. The essay's main concern is to examine the extent to which conditions affecting democratic behaviour and experience in Africa can be traced to Africa's past and present relationships with the external environment. The author observes that the external environment has little or no influence on the democratic practice in Africa since the relationship between African and international systems is influenced more by the economic interest of the latter than by whether the African state is democratic or not. Indeed there is enough evidence to support the above contention. Some of the most repressive regimes in

Africa happen to be at the same time the best friends of the self-appointed guardians of democracy in the world, namely the Western democracies.

In summary, the essays indicate that the way to democracy in Africa is still a long one and that there does not seem to be any indication as to how and when Africa is likely to get to the end.

CHAPTER III

THE DEMOCRATIC MYTH IN THE AFRICAN TRADITIONAL SOCIETIES

V.G. Simiyu

INTRODUCTION

The study of African traditional societies has raised more problems than it has solved. Pertinent issues include such questions as: were there or were there not social classes in the African traditional societies? If there were, are these classes to be conceived of in the classical Marxist-Leninist paradigm of the incompatibility of class interests and the attendant class struggle? Or, were these societies egalitarian in essence and perspective as Mwalimu Julius Nyerere has tried to show? In other words, were these societies without any class interests or class conflicts? What was the nature of political power in the centralized and in the so-called decentralized polities? Were concepts like democracy part and parcel of egalitarianism? Or is the idea of democracy, as C.R. Macpherson says, a new development within the Western liberal state that may be quite foreign to the African traditional societies and cultures?[1]

Many African scholars and politicians have portrayed the African societies before colonialism as harmonious, undifferentiated entities enjoying democratic tranquilities. This Rousseauist view of the Noble Savage at the state of Nature, seems to be the background against which Julius Nyerere propounds his *Ujamaa* philosophy. He says:

> "The equality of all members is fundamental to any social grouping to which an individual freely belongs — the ideal society is based on human equality and on a combination of the freedom and unity of its members."[2]

He points out that the traditional African family was the most satisfactory institution for all its members. He argues:

> "Despite all the variations and some exceptions where the institutions of domestic slavery existed, African family life was everywhere based on certain practices and attitudes which together mean basic equality, freedom and unity."[3]

As we shall see later, these are some of the tenets of a democratic system. Indeed, for Nyerere, the political authority in this traditional set up was based on democracy and free discussion among the elders. "They talk till they agree," he writes.[4] This free discussion, which the Francophone call

'*Palabre*' was the "Very essence of African democracy."[5] to use Mwalimu Nyerere's own words. These were political systems which cherished and practised "government by discussion."

Property ownership was also governed by the same egalitarian principles and no individual hoarded wealth while others starved in poverty. There were no exploiting classes. African traditional life was a socialist one, Nyerere argues.

Here Mwalimu Nyerere seems to have taken democracy to mean or include concepts and practices like equal access to the means of production, which was basically land and probably cattle also.

He further argues that inequality only set in with the advent of the capitalist money economy during colonialism when this delightful harmony of egalitarianism was disrupted. After that the principle of belonging to a community of equals was replaced by sordid individualism which hence forth expressed itself in terms of personal enterprise, ambition, search of profit and more seriously, the thirst for the accumulation of wealth to the detriment and, indeed, at the expense of others.

Jomo Kenyatta, writing in 1938, was even more forthright about the existence of democracy among his Kikuyu people and by extension among all African traditional societies before the advent of colonialism. In his words:

"Before the coming of the Europeans, the Gikuyu had a democratic regime."[6]

According to Kenyatta, originally the Gikuyu had a monarchy which was vested in a tyrannical sovereign who was overthrown in a revolution. This people's revolution held a representative council at *Mukurwe wa Gathanga* where a democratic constitution based on the people's general will was drawn up. The new constitution was based on the following principles: freedom of land acquisition; equality among the members of the tribe who had the right after initiation to take part in the government. There were to be regular elections *(itwika)*. This democratic government was vested in the Council of Elders *(Kiama)* who had passed the stage of warriors, that is those who had attained the age of forty years and above. It was this that was supposedly destroyed by European colonialism.

However, Godfrey Muriuki, an authority on Gikuyu pre-colonial history, says that there is no evidence that there was a monarchy of the Gikuyu people which was overthrown in the distant past.[7] Muriuki is also silent on the establishment of a democratic regime. We shall return to this. Other scholars, foreign and African, especially anthropologists and historians, have described African social and political institutions before the advent of colonialism either as detached observers or more importantly with that sympathy that betrayed the same assumption that the nature of African traditional governments and social systems was egalitarian and democratic. As was argued by Fortes and Evans-Pritchard:

"It is possible that groups are more easily welded into a unitary political system without the essence of classes, the closer they are to one another in culture."[8]

C.B. Macpherson, a political theorist, seems to go along with the above scholars, emphasizing the classless nature of the African societies. He writes:

"Colonial countries . . . at the time of the revolution (independence) (had) relatively little internal class division of an exploitative kind."[9]

Leopold Sedar Senghor of Senegal argues along the same lines. Outlining the weakness and limited scope of dialetical materialism in so far as the authors, Marx and Engles, did not take into consideration what he calls "the West African realities", the Senegalese scholar and statesmen writes:

"West African realities are those of underdeveloped countries — peasant countries here, cattle countries there — once feudalistic, but *traditionally classless* and with no wage-earning sector. They are community countries where the group holds priority over the individuals; they are especially religious countries, unselfish countries, where money is not King."[10]

For Senghor, one of the most important realities of the Negro African is his high sense of humanism and emotion which Africa should rekindle since it was destroyed by European colonialism.

Another scholar who has indicated that in the African traditional societies there were some forms of democracy is historian Joseph Ki-Zerbo of Burkina Faso. Writing about societies with community based social and political structures Ki-Zerbo argues that political authority in such societies was vested in the hands of elders who only had the right to deliberate on matters of the "city". But he adds:

"But, by and large, these gerontocracies were moderated by *democratic assemblies* which assisted the head of family, village or district through an advisory role if not a deliberative one." *(my emphasis)*[11]

Our argument in this chapter is that it is quite elusive to try to prove that democracy existed in these societies before the coming of colonialism. Indeed, we argue that what comes out of a careful examination and analysis of the political institutions and mechanisms of the pre-colonial African societies is a mixture of rudiments or democratic tendencies and practices on the one hand and aristocratic, autocratic and/or militaristic practices and tendencies, with varying degrees of despotism on the other.

When colonialism came to Africa, it did not find a pure democratic tradition and base, as others have argued, but, rather, various mixtures of rudimentary democratic institutions and despotism. Some of the institutions ranged from mild ones and hardly noticeable models like in the so-called acephalous societies, to quite brutal ones in the highly centralized states which tended to deny any democratic practices.

However, colonialism unleashed such violence, discrimination and exploitation, that Africans, young and old, educated and uneducated soon forgot the violence and undemocratic practices of their traditional rulers. Therefore, the past was portrayed as a bygone world of bliss, harmony and democracy. The pre-colonial African leaders were now seen as heroes who had championed the cause of democracy and people's sovereignty in the face of foreign invasion. Colonialism and then imperialism had made a *tabula rasa* of the African traditional institutions — political, economic, social and cultural. Africans were lumped together as natives, without much distinction, and Macpherson may have been right in saying that at independence, Africans constituted only one class — the class of the exploited and the dominated.

But, had the situation always been so? It is the contention here that if modern Africa is to build democratic socio-political and economic institutions and mechanisms, we have to understand the nature of power, authority, government and politics in traditional African societies without bias. Although we have to identify the positive aspects that promoted and enhanced democratic principles, this does not imply that we should be complacent about the despotic, militaristic and brutal regimes that prevailed in some of the regions of Africa.

DEMOCRACY: A HISTORY

The idea of rule according to the wishes of the majority of the people is quite ancient in the political history of mankind. The democracy of the ancient Greek city-states consisted not only in the rule according to the wishes of the majority of the people, but also in the actual participation of the people themselves. They actively participated in the running of the affairs of the state and government. Through various modes of recruitment, all free adult males, so defined as citizens, took turns in the running of the affairs of the state and in the dicision-making process of the entire government. Governance was in accordance with the general will of all these citizens. It was also a government by direct representation because the leaders were chosen openly from among the entire crowd of citizens by the citizens themselves through the lot system. This was the democracy that prevailed in Athens during the time of Aristotle and Plato both who denounced it as quack and argued in favour of a politico-military elite rigorously selected and headed by a philosopher king.

But democracy itself as an idea and as a political movement has not done well in the history of mankind. The reason is fairly obvious. Ingrained in the concept is an element of subversion against the established order of things: the right of the people to overthrow a ruler or a government or both, who might go against the perceived general will and restore the old order. One of the first scholars to express this idea was Marsilius of Padua, who postulated a secular relationship between the sovereign and the government on the one hand and the people, the ruled, on the other. He argued that the people must give their explicit and deliberate consent to be ruled according to the mutually acceptable secular law before any obligation can be demanded of them. Should the sovereign break the established principle, then the people are free to remove him. His ideas embodied a fundamental democratic principle, that the people have control over the rulers and the government; and that any of the citizens can be vested with the highest responsibility.

Other scholars who advanced the theory along similar lines were John Locke and Jean-Jacques Rousseau, with their theories of the Covenant and the Social Contract respectively. The essence of their argument is that men should not be ruled arbitrarily. A Covenant or a Social Contract should be made on the basis of the General Will. The people are the sovereign authority but since they cannot all rule at the same time, they have to elect one of them, who must then rule according to the principles and the terms of the Covenant or the Social Contract. As long as the ruler acts in accordance with the terms of the contract, the people have the obligation to obey him and to be ruled. But should he break the spirit and the terms of the contract, they have the equal obligation to do away with him and his government and install another government.

This was the time when the basis for a liberal state was being established. In fact, democracy as such was not yet evident in the character, policies and practices of the state or governments in Europe at that time. Liberalism simply called upon the governments to promote free enterprise among the profit-oriented individuals. The state, instead of interfering in economic matters was only to step in to help individual enterpreneurs, the capitalists, the new class of owners of means of production, to achieve more profits and secure their investments. Society was expected to automatically benefit from the accrued wealth.

Macpherson points out that Western-liberal democracy is a recent development. He states that when the market economy developed to a highly sophisticated level, politics itself became a commodity in the society and there emerged the idea of choice between various brands. The multiplicity of political parties with various programmes became the order of the day. The only rule of the game to be observed was that the social ideology of capitalism, liberal democracy was taken for granted as immutable. Parties and candidates had to operate within the parameters of that general philosophy which promotes private enterprise and individual freedoms.

However, the social and political movements in Europe in the 19th century produced another variant of democracy, at least in theory: the proletarian democracy, or what Lenin called "Democratic Centralism". Marx and Engels argued that liberalism and the type of social justice it contained was a one-sided democracy for the dominant social class, the bourgeoisie. The workers, who were the actual producers of wealth and the numerical majority in society were excluded from the public affairs of the state and the government. The workers should have not just a say in the affairs of the state, but should qualitatively control those affairs because economically they are the real force, and should *ipso facto* also be the real political force. They should carry out a proletarian revolution against the bourgeois state and establish a workers' democracy. And since the workers are numerically the majority in the society, their democracy would be a people's democracy.

But since not all workers can run the affairs of the state, or lead the proletarian revolution, the idea of an elite vanguard was invented to cater for the assumed interests of the proletariat. This vanguard was to be the party. The party would be the basic organization. It would not be a mass party, but a party of the most enlightened echelons of the workers who would spearhead the movement, through propaganda and actual seizure of power. The people, theoretically would still be the supreme authority. But in reality, it is the elite that would hold the reins of state power and governmental machinery.

The present-day African sitution is compounded by various dilemmas. At the out-set, African leaders rejected the Western model of democracy on the grounds that it engendered selfish individualism and set in motion a whole process of differential accumulation of wealth, creating classes to the detriment of the traditional African philosophy of egalitarianism. The Africans too rejected the communist democratic centralism as antagonistic to the African classless harmony. African leaders were particularly unhappy with the atheist conception of the world as propounded by the supporters of scientific socialism. For them, the African is basically a religious man. As Senghor has argued:

> "Finally... we have a choice to make in our final option. Everything in scientific socialism is not to be accepted, especially its atheistic materialism. I do not say its dialectical materialism."[13]

And so the question may be formulated as follows: Is the basis of the rejection of both the Western and Eastern European models valid? Is there anything in the African political tradition that can be called an African form of democracy on which new structures may be built?

As stated earlier in this chapter the answer is likely to be in the negative because the premise of the problem is different. When Sydney Webb eloquently steered the 1917 British Labour Congress to declare that the colonies were destined to an eventual self-government, or when his counterpart on the continent, Albert Sarrault of France declared that colonies were destined to some kind of autonomy, the assumption then and long after was that the African peoples would have assimilated enough principles and practices of the Western liberal democracy to rule themselves. There was nothing in the traditional African institutions worthy of note, so they thought. The scheme has largely failed due to the non-understanding of the nature of the African political tradition, which, to repeat, was not an entirely democratic tradition.

AFRICAN POLITICAL SYSTEMS: AN ANALYSIS

To support the argument we would like to analyze a few African political systems within their traditional set up. We shall examine these systems in relation to four basic areas of the democratic concept and practice, viz: access to property; the decision making process; role recruitment; and rule adjudication, that is dispute settlement. This will be particularly so with regard to the so-called decentralized societies, whose structures and political systems may have fined the "democratic" imagination of those who have found democracy in traditional African political systems. We shall briefly examine the centralized and class structured societies so as to show that by and large, on the whole of the African continent, there were hardly any democratic traditions in the pre-colonial days. But first, a few general remarks.

The first general principle which seemed to lie at the base of nearly all African political systems was the concept of hierarchy. The societies and therefore the political organizations were conceived in a hierarchical structure with little or no horizontal checks and balances. The second was the insular type of structures, in other words, structures without upward mobility or open recruitment outside the laid down rigid rules of procedure. In some instances, there was no chance of any upward mobility at all. Thirdly, the age-set systems which were found in the majority of the African societies tended to thwart or contain the aspirations of the more volatile, active and probably intelligent younger generations. In some cases the age-set system might have combined with the class structure to suppress forever the aspirations and rights of the lower echelons of the society.

Now, let us examine a little closely, the centralized states. In the interlacustrine region of Eastern Africa there were quite a number of centralized states: Buganda, Rwanda, Nkore, Burundi, Buha, Bushubi, Bunyoro, Bushi, Karagwe and Wanga. Generally, their regimes varied from strong absolutism to moderate aristocracy. Buganda, Rwanda and Nkore were quite absolutist, while Burundi, by the end of the 19th century, could be described as a moderate aristocracy. The political power and life in the 19th century Burundi revolved around the personality of the *Mwami*, the King, and his aristocratic entourage.[14] The socio-political hierarchy in the Rundi society could be reduced to four social categories:

1. The *Baganwa* who were said to be the direct descendants of the original founder of the Rundi monarchy. They owned large herds of cattle and large tracts of land. They took most of their wives from the Tutsi, a social category that was predominantly pastoralist. Their claim to political power was on the basis of the tradition that linked them to the very foundation of the Rundi monarchy. They were popularly called "the children of the Belly of the Drum". They were responsible for the formulation and execution of the laws of the land; they constituted the army and were in charge of the control over and the distribution of agricultural as well as pastoral land. They were, therefore, a very powerful group in the political economy of the Burundi kingdom, claiming a direct blood filiation with the king with whom they shared power. And so in the four departments of power, authority, judicial process and wealth, they were at the top.

2. *The Banyamabanga* were the next most important category. They were the keepers of the state secrets, organizers of cults and royal festivities. They organized the popular manifestations among the common masses, and also had access to cattle and land wealth. Their riches and power, like those of the *Baganwa,* were hereditary. They also participated in the legal processes of the society. This category, together with the preceding one, could be lumped together as the ruling class.

3. The third social category that formed a class of its own was that of the *Batwara basanzwe* and the *Bakozi b'abakuru.* They were the administrative and technical workers within the state machinery. They were the king's attendants and assistants to the *Baganwa* chiefs. They served as a link between the upper ruling class and the masses below. The members of this class had some access to land and cattle property which could be given to them by the king or by *Baganwa* chiefs. They also never paid any tributes and never took part in the decision-making process, the latter being reserved for the ruling class.

4. Finally there was the commoner class, the people so to speak. These were collectively known as the *Banyagihugu.* The term itself derives from the word *igihugu,* meaning the country. So, these were the actual countrymen, the subjects of the ruling classes. Indeed, as Emile Mworoha puts it, the structure can be reduced to three social classes: (i) the ruling class composed of the *Baganwa* and the *Banyamabanga,* (ii) the working middle class and (iii) the subjects.

The classes had antagonistic interests because the *Baganwa* chiefs in charge of large provinces had to collect tribute from the rural masses and remit them to *Mwami's* mobile capital. If they did not or if they showed any lenience towards the peasants, they were sacked and punished. Within the structure, there was no chance of upward mobility. And so, the system, unlike a democratic one, did not have open recruitment from the lower classes, precisely because the social, political and economic roles were hereditary and therefore permanent, or ascriptive.

The only restraint to the *Mwami's* power came from two close blood relatives, the paternal uncle of the King and the King's mother — the *Mugabekazi,* who in some cases, through intrigues, could prove quite astute, cunning and powerful against the *Baganwa* chiefs and other co-queens. We can only classify this type of moderation as part of court intrigues and fraternal restraint. It would be dangerous to qualify such practices with any democratic concepts.

The system of education for the royal youth reinforced the royal values according to sex. The young princesses, were taught to use a refined royal language towards the princes. They were taught to show respect and obedience towards the male members of the royal family in all circumstances. Chastity was a prime virtue, to the extent that anybody found making love to a princess was put to death instantly and on the spot. The princes, on the other hand, were taught military, political, administrative and judicial techniques. When grown up, they were posted to head the provinces to avoid the hatching of intrigues at the royal court. They became the *baganwa bakuru,* literally, the "Big Chiefs".

The *Banyagihugu* were the basic producers of wealth while the *Baganwa,* the *Banyamabanga* and the *batwara basazwe* were the owners of the means of production. The only participation of those lower classes in the political system and machinery was as producers and during wars when they were called upon by the chiefs to take up arms and defend the regime. They had no political, social or economic rights. In all, our submission is that the Rundi political system was not democratic at all.

The Nkore Kingdom at the end of the 19th century was organized on the same model. The central power was vested in the *Mugabe.* He also incarnated the state itself. The symbols of power were the royal drum, *Bagyendanwa* which could only be struck by the *Omugabe;* the spear, *Nyamiringa;* the shield, *Kashazyo;* the axe, *Kaitabagone;* the veiled pearl, *Rutare;* the arrows, *Nyarwampi;* and the royal stick.

The royal court was a big center of attraction for members of the royal family, dignitaries of the court and other pretenders. The dignitaries came from special clans which enjoyed special status in the polity and at the royal court. The *Bagache* clan, for example, supplied wives for the *Mugabe* while the *Baruru* clan was the guardian of the royal drums.

The king, *Omugabe,* had three categories of assistants or political advisers. First were the *Abakungu abaruhwekira,* who had direct access to him. They took part in the deliberations of the royal tribunal. They, therefore, enjoyed some share of power. Next were the men of arms, the *emitwe* (literally, heads), who lived at the royal court and in the neighbourhood of the royal domains. The military men were actually real holders of power in the ancient Nkore Kingdom. Lastly there were the *entumwa,* messengers who ensured the liaison between the central authorities and the provinces.

These three categories of state officials had access to economic power as well. They were paid cows, land and appointments to chieftaincies. There were also the ordinary courtiers who fed the *Mugabe* with intelligence reports about the country.

As can be seen, the real political and economic power in the kingdom was exercised by the king and his entourage. One can hardly call such a system democratic, particularly in the light of yet another fact: possession of large herds of cattle was the key to the central and higher echelons of the political system. The *Bahima,* who owned large numbers of cattle were a privileged class compared to the *Bairu,* the cultivators who were prohibited from owning cattle.

However, the Nkore society had internal mechanisms of patronage that tended to reduce the excesses of the system. Through the mutual exchange of gifts of cattle, known as the *Okutoija,* ordinary people could have access to the "corridors" of power and establish friendship with the authorities. For this reason, one can say that the subjects were not totally cut off from the political system. They could rub shoulders with the real holders of power within the political system. Nevertheless, such mechanisms cannot be likened to any democratic practices.

In conclusion, we can say that the two examples cited above, tended towards strongly centralized monarchies that entertained a royal rather than a democratic tradition. The essence of the two political systems was the relative exclusion of the common man from the centers of power — both economic and political.

The above models could be applied with some local variations to the general interlacustrine region of East Africa where centralized polities existed. By further extension, they can apply to the centralized states of central and western Sudanic regions. The most important addition in the societies of those regions was the clear distinction between the social classes. According to Lansine Kaba the society of the ancient kingdom of Songhay was divided into two groups of economic production.[15] "Large estates belonging to the crown and employing an extensive labour force" and those that belonged to the elite in the provinces and near Gao, the capital. The classes that possessed these estates were the crown, the elite and the military, who were very powerful in this militaristic regime. These classes had access to resources, trade, power, knowledge and prestige.[16]

Then there was the class of commoners, to which also belonged the conquered peoples. These were large groups of dependent farmers who owed free services to the upper classes. Islam served as the ideological vehicle for the maintainance of this inegalitarian and undemocratic system. The only important factor for any upward social mobility was through the army, precisely because the very foundation of the Songhay

Kingdom, right from the days of Soni Ali its founder, was militaristic. The soldiers were handsomely rewarded — sometimes with whole domains fully settled with a permanent population to supply free labour.

The moderating factor that could resemble democratic tendencies is contained in the very essence of military service. Able young men, whether from the aristocracy, commoners or even slaves, could use the army to ease their ways into high appointments. If we consider this upward mobility then the ancient Songhay society had some elements that tended towards some democratic principles. However, we have to add that the very military expansion kept alive a permanent source of a slave population that constituted the foundation of the Songhay economy.

Elsewhere in West Africa, we notice a similar class structure. Majhemout Diop,[17] states that in ancient Mali there was a three-tier system of castes composed of (1) *Rimbe Benangatobe*, (2) *Rimbe Nangatobe* and (3) *Matioube*. The *Rimbe Benangatobe* had two categories which were the pastoral *Fulbe* and the *Torobe*. They constituted the upper class from which chiefs and the *Almamy* were recruited. The *Fulbe* and the *Torobe* were actually the ruling class. Indeed in the same social category but at a lower rank were *Sebbe* (warriors, farmers, hunters and the occasional fishermen), the *Soubalbe* (professional fishermen) and finally the *Diawanbe* who were the non-professional individuals. All these others paid tributes to the *Fulbe* and the *Torobe*. In case of disputes it was the *Fulbe* and the *Torobe* who arbitrated.

The second caste *(Rimbe Nangatobe)* was basically composed of handicraft professionals: *Maboube* (spinners), *Sakebe* (cobblers), *Laobe* (wood-hewers, carpenters), *Waylibe* (blacksmiths, jewellers, armourers), *Wambabe* (musicians) and the *Aouloube* (griots, singers). Members of this caste also paid tribute to the *Fulbe* and *Torobe* in terms of what they produced. Finally the third caste, *Matioube*, was the caste of slaves, who were sub-divided into first generation slaves on the one hand and the second and third generation on the other.

The members of these last two castes, *Rimbe Nangatobe* and *Matioube*, never took part in the decision-making process and they had no authority. Disputes involving them were resolved by the ruling class, and in the case of slaves they had no access to property. In other words, the members of the inferior castes were excluded from the political process. Such a system cannot be said to be democratic.

There were some moderating factors in the slave conditions in some societies in West Africa, like the *Lobi* of Gabon, where the slaves were considered as "new children". Among the Massangou people of Chaillou Hills, also in Gabon, war captives were incorporated into the entire community to replace those the community had lost in war. But this practice might have been dictated by the weak demographic situation in Gabon where diseases have sometimes tended to decimate whole villages.

In Dahomey the children of slaves were free people incorporated into the master's family with all the rights except the right to inherit political leadership.

The above descriptions fit what we may call centralized political systems. And as stated earlier, we have analyzed these societies to hammer the point home that they were by no means examples of a democratic tradition.

Let us now turn to what may have fired the imagination of those who hunt for a democratic tradition in the African traditional setting: the clan or decentralized system. We shall once again examine the four areas of access to property, decision-making process, recruitment into the various roles and dispute settlement.

The general characteristics were that the political authority was held either by one leader/chief or by a council of elders. The leader was normally the oldest member of the clan or where such an individual was visibly senile and inept, then a younger elder was chosen by the consensus of the members of the council of elders. Normally the elders were the custodians of the clan's or tribe's secrets and traditions. They jealously kept those secrets as sources of their power over the entire social group and especially over the ambitious younger generations.

The elders also had the absolute control over the tribal/clan property, whether it was land, be it for agricultural or grazing purposes or livestock, in the name of the clan or tribe. The accumulation process, normally minimal, was done by the elders, through various forms of "gifts", free labour, priority in the cultivation and harvesting cycles and so on.

The age-set system worked in favour of these elders because recruitment into higher grades was done on the basis of the age-grades. There was a feeling of fraternity and freedom among the members of the same age-grade and it is probably at that level that one can talk of the rudiments of democracy in the sense that opinions were aired freely between coequals. Among the Malinke of Western Sudanic regions, this type of organization was typical. Other socio-professional groupings also existed. There were the warrior societies, for example, who specialized in raids, either for themselves or for other individuals who hired them.

There also existed secret organizations like the awe-inspiring black panther men. But these groups generally escaped from the political control. However, the majority of other people came under the sway of the political control of the elders.

Succession to authority followed a hierarchical pattern of the initiation grades. From the oldest member of the family and/or clan, authority went to the next dean of the oldest generation, then from the eldest brother to the youngest, from uncle to nephew and so on. Although the chief or the elder might be the custodian of the clan heritage, he could not dispose of it at his will.

Let us take the case of the Bukusu of the Western Province of Kenya. The political authority was highly decentralized to such an extent that every clan or local community had its own council of elders. Where the people lived in forts (walled villages) each fort had its council of elders. For matters involving more than the members of one fort, a wider council composed of elders from other forts was involved. Their leader was called *Omwami we lichabe.* How were the members of these councils recruited? Gunter Wagner has observed that:

> "Although. . . there were no individuals or bodies which wielded clearly defined political authority entailing explicit rights and duties, a number of ways (existed) in which individuals could gain prominence over their tribesmen or clansmen and find recognition as leaders by certain groups within the tribal unit and with regard to certain activities."[18]

There were several ways through which individuals were recruited into certain roles. They included the privileges of primogeniture, whereby the eldest son was automatically recognized as head of the family in the absence of the father. As such, he inherited a larger share of his father's property than that which went to his other brothers, whether it was land or cattle. The father paid for his brideprice earlier than for his other brothers and if the cattle were not enough, the others could wait long before marrying. He also inherited the younger wives of his father in case the latter died. Indeed, when the father died the eldest son assumed full authority over the entire family and became a member of the council of elders of the clan or fort or community. He made his decisions as he saw fit although he consulted one or two of his brothers and sometimes other elders.

In this system therefore, the senior members of the lineage system had more privileges, material, legal and moral, than the junior members in the same lineage structure.

Wealth, accumulated either through raids, heritage or trade, could also enable an individual to gain prominence and thus become *Omukasa,* that is a *rich and influential person* because he could offer lavish feasts to the public who could eat and drink in praise of him. Personal merit also came in, for example when one excelled as a warrior or one was endowed with intelligence and sharp memory useful for remembering the history and the traditions of the Bukusu. In this latter case, he was recognized as *Omuseni we kumuse,* one who presided over the funeral oration of a deceased elder. Finally, age also counted for much when it came to the recruitment into the council of elders. The members of the most senior age-group such as the first two oldest age-groups in a community were generally selected by fellow coequals already on the council to join them. All the members of the council had to be married men with already circumcised children.

Members of younger generations, even if some of them happened to be very brave at war and/or intelligent, were strictly excluded from being members of the council of elders. Women too were excluded. Indeed, women, for all their longevity on this earth never became members of these councils.

It is obvious that such systems could not be democratic. Members of the council normally arrived at their decisions by consensus, and it was this procedure that Nyerere has called "the essence of the traditional African democracy".[19] The elders sought the opinion of the majority of the people in the fort or community or clan, before making a decision.

Disputes were generally settled within the family or the clan. Small offences were generally disposed off quickly by the council of elders. But when somebody became a habitual offender who wronged even members of other clans, he could be ostracized and expelled from the clan and, in such a case, even if he were murdered the clan did not pursue the matter. The elders usually sat at a particular place to solve disputes or talk about the affairs of the clan, fort or village. The place was called *Ekokwa*. They usually took their meals there as well. The basic principle underlying the judicial system was compensation, whatever the crime, theft, adultery or murder.

In case of murder involving two clans, clan solidarity played a very important role. Every member of the murderer's clan contributed towards the payment of the "blood fine" to the wronged family. If the murderer's clas failed or refused to pay the "blood fine" the wronged clan was entitled to kill a member of the opposite sex of the murderer's clan. Then, elders of the two clans sat together and ordered the members of both clans to stop the feud.

Elsewhere in Kenya, W.R. Ochieng' has described the political organization of the Gusii people. According to him,

> ". . . the Gusii society did not constitute one political unit. It was a collection of many political units, based on exogamous, patrilineal clans or clan groupings which often consisted of a large clan with a number of smaller clans or sub-clans or families, who normally occupied a distinct territory over a ridge or a succession of adjacent ridges."[20]

He asserts that among the Gusii the clan was the most effective political unit. They had a system of chiefs, *Abagambi*, who were supposed ". . . to lead and make decisions with the consent and support of the elders".[21] However, the chief had very little coercive powers to enforce his decisions. These chiefs were actually heads of clans. The chieftainship was hereditary.

> ". . . persons . . . automatically assumed their positions of chiefs by virtue of being the most senior survivors of the agnatically leading clan families."[22]

A chief as a symbol of continuity of the clan had several privileges above the common man. He would be the first to cultivate, first to sow, first to taste the new crops and the first to harvest. However, Ochieng' argues that these chiefs were sometimes looked upon as ordinary individuals who were constantly reminded by the people to mind their domestic affairs. He further argues that the Gusii society was egalitarian because "everybody was entitled to equal rights and privileges of their society."[23]

However, the same author gives evidence which contradicts the statement. He says that among the Gusii there was also another type of leadership, *Omotang'ani*.

> "a person who by force of example, talents, or qualities of leadership, played a directing role, wielded commanding influence, or had a following in any sphere of activity or thought."[24]

Here we would be tempted to see a democratic essence of the recognition of personal merit. But the description of the lines of authority rules this out. From the homestead level, the head of the family had enormous powers. All disputes were handled by him. His wives, sons and daughters had to submit to his authority. However, certain wrongs like fratricide or incest could only be referred to clan elders who would decide on the type of punishment to be meted out to the offender.

The clan chief presided over a council of elders who were generally homestead heads. The clan council of elders dealt with more serious offences like cattle thefts, murder, land or boundary disputes, rape or incest. In the Kitutu, a sub-tribe of the Gusii, there was a sub-tribal political organization which was hereditary. The most important personalities were chiefs of big or militarily strong clans.

Access to land, property and cattle was governed by the authority of the homestead chief who distributed it among his sons, starting with the eldest of the first wife and so on down the ladder. This practice, therefore, defeats any argument of egalitarianism or democracy among the Gusii. Indeed, although the young men were the warriors who brought in the cattle, they were excluded from the council of elders and so their rights and ambitions were thwarted. The only moderating factor was that great warriors amassed a lot of cattle, therefore wealth, and so there existed some openness in the society with regard to their merit. But actually, the society had no mechanisms for controlling such strong individuals. The women were also excluded from political activities except as observers.

H.E. Lambert and G. Muriuki have described the political institutions of the Kikuyu. Muriuki writes:

> "By the end of the nineteenth century, Kikuyu society was patriarchal, uncentralised and highly egalitarian."[25]

However, on reading through his text, the egalitarian aspect does not come out. What comes out clearly in the works of the two scholars is the age-set system which embodies the political institution. The age-set system, *Mariika,* cut across the kinship system of *Mbari* which even though weakened by the dispersal of members into various Kikuyu areas, still remained the forum where disputes were settled.

At the nuclear level, the head of the family was the supreme authority. In his absence, normally after death, the eldest son of the first wife took over. The father decided virtually on all matters except really serious ones where he consulted the members of "all the initiated males who had attained elder status".[26] The attainment of elder status was a long process which involved the payment of various forms of fees. These payments were "obligatory associated with status" as Lambert records.

The *Mbari* council chose a head known as *Muramati* who was actually the custodian of the *Mbari's* patrimony and also its spokesman in inter-*mbari* affairs. He also administered the *mbari* land. How was he selected? He was "the eldest son from the senior house line"[27] *githaka.* The age-set system had more or less the same function as in other societies where similar institutions existed. Initiation was considered very important because it was through it that young people became adults. The initiated young men also formed the military force. In Kikuyu, they had their own *njama ya anake a mumo* council and very rarely did they participate in the council of elders. Muriuki states that although they had "enough power and privileges in (their) hands . . . they were strictly governed by their council"[28] like all other age-groups. Their titular head was the *muthamaki* who was their spokesman and who also reprimanded wrong-doers. They had grades in their structure: from junior warrior to senior warrior. The advancement to a higher rank was subject to, among other things, the payment of an entrance fee. Indeed Muriuki notes that the age-set system acted as "a very important agent of social control".[29]

Lambert states that the choice of a *muthamaki* was meticulous and normally only very intelligent and prudent people were chosen. The word *muthamaki* means "adviser, ruler" and is derived from the verb — *thamaka* meaning "to lead intellectually". This is a clear case of the selection of a leader on the basis of personal merit and it could be considered as a case of giving everyone equal opportunity to rise up in the social and political ranks. This could sound democratic.

However, the equal opportunity is only exercised at the level of the age-group. The *muthamaki* could not sit on the council of elders unless he was invited, and even then he would hardly be consulted by the elders when deliberating. Indeed, Lambert has put it quite clearly:

> "He will remain the *muthamaki* of his *riika* in his *mwaki* and when he has paid the *hako* and the *ndong'o* he will, if he has retained his reputation for intelligence and a quiet mind, be invited to sit near the elders of the *Kiama* in their determination of suits."[30]

And so, not every *muthamaki* joined the council of elders.

The *athamaki* (pl.) settled disputes within their age-group and in the local community. It was only when one distinguished himself that one became the judge of a ridge or *rugongo* and as such also represented the ridge on the council of elders. Not all *athamaki* were judicial leaders. They could be *athamaki* in other fields such as religious matters.

A quick survey of dispute settlement may bring out the point a little more clearly. At the nuclear family level the father settled the disputes. In his absence, his eldest son of the first wife assumed authority. When the dispute went beyond the nuclear family but within the *mbari*, the family heads were involved. It was only family heads of appropriate grade of the *Kiama* who were called upon and not every family head.

Beyond that, the *Kiama kia itura*, or *Kiama kia mwaki*, composed of clan heads, took over the settlement of disputes between members of unrelated individuals. The parties had to pay a fee. In serious disputes like homicide involving two *mbaris*, the *athamaki* from outside the two clans were called to settle the case and restore peace and equilibrium. This independent court was not a permanent institution. It was *ad hoc*, and each party was advised by his *muthamaki*, but the members of the public who knew the facts could be called upon to testify. The parties were then instructed to choose about four *athamaki* each, leaving out close blood relatives. The eight would then join the independent *athamaki* to constitute the complete court that deliberated *in camera*. This court was called *ndundu* meaning secret. The judgement was pronounced publicly. If any party was dissatisfied with it, they could resort to a supernatural oath.

In analyzing the above judicial process, there is an element of fairness and rudiments of democratic practices, particularly at the level of constituting an independent court. However, right from the nuclear family level, the rights of the individual are subordinate to the need for peace and equilibrium. Whether the head of the family was the father or, upon his death, his eldest son, the point is that all other family members, even male adults who were already married, had to submit to his authority without much say. Moreover, the involvement of the age-set system such that the *athamaki* had to come from senior grades only tended to thwart the aspirations of the younger generations. And once again women were excluded.

Property was vested in the kinship group but in reality it was governed by the family head who gave priority to the eldest son of the eldest wife. Indeed, the *kiama* of elders could not interfere with the distribution of land even if one clan had a lot of it and the neighbouring one little.

It can, therefore, be argued that although the Kikuyu political and judicial systems had some rudiments of democratic practices, such as the settlement of disputes by deliberation and discussion at the various councils, the rigid age-set system curtailed any such tendencies and reinforced gerontocratic principles and practices. The system taken as a whole was not egalitarian at all unless by egalitarianism is meant equality among members of the same age-group. Finally, the exclusion of women from the political and judicial processes except as observers or victims was undemocratic. What was more, in case of homicide, the compensation varied according to sex. The compensation for a murdered man was one hundred and ten goats, while for a female it was only thirty goats and three rams.

Let us now turn to the case of the Arusha Maasai of Tanzania. They also have quite an elaborate age-set organization. According to P.N. Gulliver, the age-set structure has formal stages and when these are exhausted, the cycle starts again.[31] He enumerated fourteen stages, the fourteenth being a retirement stage after a lapse of about 49 years following an initiation ceremony. The divisions most pertinent to our discussion are those of junior *murranhood,* senior *murranhood,* junior elderhood, senior elderhood and finally retired elderhood.

All the age-groups must pass through these major stages. Recruitment to an age-group is by circumcision according to the Maasai rituals. There is a clear distinction in seniority and in privileges between the age-groups. The *murran,* for example, are not allowed to eat meat. They can only do that on entering the rank of junior elders through a special ceremony. There is even some generation conflict because the junior age-group must assert itself against the immediately preceding senior age-group. Each has a kind of "godfather" *menye laiyok* who comes from the senior age-group and represents his own age-group in their responsibility to the juniors. He advises the young men as to their place in the total maturation cycle. There is cooperation among all the groups in terms of procedure and rituals to ensure that the maturation cycle in the entire Maasai society has some continuity. A ceremonial leader organizes the passage to the next age-group.

This age-group organization is the basis for administration. Each age-group leader exercises his authority within the age-group and within a given locality with fixed boundaries. Gulliver calls it a "parish". But, the age-group as a whole is what gives the individual his identity. The leaders of age-groups are chosen by the members of the same age-group who know their leadership abilities very well because they have grown up together.

Indeed. the most important institution for an individual is his age-group. Within it he enjoys equality, familiarity, sympathy and support. This is particularly so among the *murran* who are the warriors and who are responsible for security in the community. In fact, the age-mates call each other "brother" and cannot marry each other's daughters. But they may marry the duaghters of a "godfather". At funerals it is the age-mates who mourn publicly one of theirs.

The roles are also assigned according to the stages of the maturation cycle. The junior *murran* have almost no responsibility, whether public or private. They do not participate in the ritual or in the politico-juridical affairs. They are actually servants who do some physical chores requiring little skill or judgement. They do not even herd cattle although they may take care of a cattle "boma". However, they help the senior *murran* in house-building.

The senior *murran* are usually experienced warriors and have some responsibilities. They do not take part fully in the rituals or politico-judicial affairs. When they attend the "parish" assemblies, even their spokesman keeps quiet. But they are the actual police in the locality. They also act as messengers for the elders in matters requiring discretion and diplomacy.

Next are the junior elders. They participate fully in the rituals and politico-juridical affairs and their spokesman can even convene and administer parish assemblies. They take part in the decision-making process together with other junior elders who are their age-mates. These are the ones who form the backbone of the political economy of the Arusha Maasai society because they are the household heads of their ever-increasing families. They are the cultivators, cattle owners and general overseers of the development of their farms. They do not do a lot of heavy physical work. They do not even carry spears. They have no food restriction rites and drink beer freely. They spend their leisure time in the company of senior elders learning the laws, rituals, techniques and ceremonial conventions of the Maasai society.

Senior elders, though less active than the above, are experienced, expert custodians of knowledge, diplomacy and the judicial system of the entire society. They consolidate their farms, livestock and families. Their children are marrying in and off and so they oversee the new extended relations and responsibilities. They drink less. They have to distribute land to their maturing sons. Finally the retired elders are like old discarded locomotives despised by younger generations as too old to do anything. Their authority is usurped by their adult sons.

Leaders are chosen by age-mates and not always on the basis of popularity. Intelligence and prudence also count and the "godfathers" with the help of their age-mates help the young age-groups choose their spokesmen, the *olaigwenani,* carefully. Each age-group has two sub-sections, the junior and the senior. There is usually a conflict between the two sections when it comes to the choice of age-group leaders, though they, normally agree.

Generally, the sense of equality among age-mates is very strong. Gulliver describes a case of a senior elder spokesman who, by virtue of his position in the traditional Maasai set-up, qualified to be a voter in the modern system in 1958. He was so reluctant that he said that he had to get the approval of his age-mates first. And even then, he would only vote according to their wishes.[32]

Finally, let us turn to dispute settlement within the parish. Most of the disputes are settled in the parish assembly. The assemblies are composed of age-group spokesmen of the senior and junior elders. Sometimes spokesmen of senior *murran* may take part. Other members of the public of equal rank may or may not attend. The assembly deals with many matters: land disputes, adultery and livestock thefts, to name a few. It is interesting to note that support for parties goes along age-group lines. Often they agree. In 1958 senior elders accused senior *murran* of adultery and other offences and threatened to withhold the up-grading ceremony for them until the senior *murran* had rectified their conduct and paid the relevant fines.

An analysis of the above structures and practices brings out a few outstanding aspects. There is equality, indeed, egalitarianism among the members of the same age-group. Once again, it is at this level that one can say democratic principles and practices prevailed among the Maasai and societies with similar institutions and structures. The other aspect is the balanced composition of the parish assembly. No particular age-group could dominate the scene. The active role of junior elders was moderated by the presence, though non-participative, of the senior *murran* and especially by the cool-minded serenity of the senior elders. The choice of the age-group spokesman was democratic in that it was based largely on personal merit.

However, as we have noted earlier, the very rigid structure of the age-set system tended to thwart the aspirations of the younger generations. The junior *murran*, for example, although initiated, had no voice at all in the affairs of the community. They were left out just like women were. The rigid rules of procedure with threats of ritual curses and/or of withholding the upgrading of an age-group to a higher rank, was definitely despotic and undemocratic. Finally, the opposite of the equality between the age-mates prevailed when it came to inter-age-group relations. Indeed, taken as a whole, the system was very inegalitarian. The retired elders virtually lost their rights.

CONCLUSION

In Black Africa, whether the political system was that of the highly centralized states or of the *amorphous* non-centralized communities, it did not belong to a democratic tradition. There were rudiments of democratic principles and practices, especially in the non-centralized communities, but it would be dangerous to equate those practices with advanced forms of democracy. At best we can only call upon scholars to delve a little into the study of these societies so that they can bring out what we may be able to blend with the present political structures, institutions and practices. In some societies, the class structure prevented the development of democratic tendencies. There may have been checks and balances against the absolute authority and power of the king, but the exercise of those controlling forces was done by the immediate members of the ruling aristocracy without any participation of the commoners. For example, the members of the royal council in the Oyo Empire, the *Oyo-mesi*, could present a deadly gift of a parrot's eggs to the king if they were disatisfied with his style of ruling. He had only two options: commit suicide or run away. But the commoners had no role in these court intrigues.

On the other hand, the non-centralized societies, sometimes due to the unsophisticated nature of the economy, technology and the social system, gave the impression of egalitarian and democratic tendencies. However, a closer examination reveals the same hierarchial structure and actual aristocracies in embryonic form. What is more, African traditional political structures were so geared to gerontocracy that there was no open way of recruitment from below. This gives a somewhat mixed bag of some rudiments of democratic principles and practices on the one hand and tradition and practices on the other, which tend to thwart individual freedom and promote gerontocracies. Such gerontocracies established quite an un-democratic tradition.

REFERENCES

1. Macpherson, C.B., *The Real World of Democracy*, London, O.U.P., 1966.
2. Nyerere Julius, *Nyerere on Socialism*, Dar es Salaam, O.U.P., 1969, p. 10.
3. *Ibid*.
4. *Ibid*., p. 104.
5. *Ibid*.
6. Kenyatta, Jomo, *Facing Mount Kenya*, Martin Secker and Warburg Ltd., London, 1938, p. 131.
7. Muriuki, Godfrey, *A History of the Kikuyu, 1500-1900*, Nairobi, O.U.P., 1974, pp. 110-1.
8. Fortes, M. and Evans-Pritchard, E.E., *African Political Systems*, London, O.U.P., 1970, pp. 9-10.
9. Macpherson, C.B., *op. cit.*, p. 32.
10. Senghor, L.S., *On Socialism*, New York, Fredrick A. Praeger, 1964, p. 77.
11. **Ki-zerbo** Joseph, *Historie de l'Afrique Noire*, Paris, Librairie A. Hatier, 1972, p. 176.

12. Onwuejeogwu, M. Angulu, *The Social Anthropology of Africa,* London, Heinemann, 1975, p. 159.
13. Senghor, L.S., *op. cit.,* p. 83.
14. Mworoha, Emile, *Peuples et rois de l'Afrique des Lacs,* Dakar, Les Nouvelles Editions Africaines, 1977.
15. Kaba, Lansine, "Power, prosperity and social inequality in Songhay, (1464-1591)". Unpublished paper. By courtesy of Dr. E.S. Atieno-Odhiambo of the History Department, University of Nairobi, 1980.
16. *Ibid.*
17. Diop, Majhemout, *Histoire des classes sociales dans l'Afrique de l'Ouest. I. Le Mali,* Paris, Francois Maspero, 1971, pp. 46-47.
18. Wagner, Gunther, "The Political Organisation of the Bantu of Kavirondo", *African Political Systems,* p. 230.
19. *vide supra.*
20. Ochieng' William, R., *A Pre-colonial History of the Gusii of Western Kenya, C. 1500-1914,* Nairobi, E.A.L.B., 1974, p. 193.
21. *Ibid.,* p. 196.
22. *Ibid.*
23. *Ibid.*
24. *Ibid.,* p. 197.
25. Muriuki, G., *op. cit.,* p. 110.
26. Lambert, H.E., *Kikuyu Social and Political Institutions,* London, O.U.P., 1956, p. 85.
27. Muriuki, G., *op. cit.,* p. 116.
28. *Ibid.,* p. 121.
29. *Ibid.*
30. Lambert, H.E., *op. cit.,* 104.
31. Gulliver, P.H., *Social Control in Society. A Study of the Arusha: Agricultural Maasai of Northern Tanganyika,* London, Routledge and Kegan Paul, 1963, Chapter 3.
32. We have used the present tense in this section because most of the principles, structures and institutions are still current and are very different from what they were at the end of the 19th century.
33. Gulliver, P.H., *op. cit.,* p. 49.

CHAPTER IV

DEMOCRACY AND THE ONE-PARTY STATE: THE AFRICAN EXPERIENCE

Peter Wanyande

INTRODUCTION

The attainment of political independence by African countries was followed by two striking political developments. One was the emergence and establishment of one-party systems of government in virtually all the independent states on the continent. To date, out of the forty-nine independent countries, less than five can be described as multi-party states. Even Zimbabwe which only attained independence in 1980 has already indicated its intention to work towards the establishment of a one-party system of government.

While in some countries such as Tanzania and Kenya the establishment of a one-party system was done through acts of parliament which made opposition parties illegal, in other cases it was simply achieved by the voluntary dissolution of the smaller parties with the leaders and supporters of such parties being absorbed into the ruling parties, thus making such countries *de facto* rather than *de jure* one-party states. In theory, the people of such countries are free to form opposition parties if they so wish. In the *de jure* one party states on the other hand, it is illegal to form an opposition party as this has been proscribed by law. Apart from ensuring that no one would organize and form an alternative party to the ruling party, the fact that parliament passes a law proscribing such parties is often cited by governments in such countries as evidence of popular support and, therefore, of the legitimacy of their decision to establish a one-party system of government.

The second striking political development is the incidence and frequency of army take-overs and the subsequent establishment of military governments. *Coups* have been so frequent that by 1986 out of the forty-nine independent countries of Africa two-thirds are under a military government of one type or another with some having experienced several *coups* since they became independent.

These two developments, and in particular the phenomenon of one-party states and systems of government, gave rise to a debate about their implications and the prospects for democracy, not just in Africa and the Third World but elsewhere too. The debate was essentially between those who associate democracy with multi-parties on the one hand and those who argued that one-party systems of government were not incompatible with democracy. Below we briefly summarize some of the major arguments of the supporters of the one-party system of government.

THE CASE FOR A ONE-PARTY SYSTEM

In the debate that ensued, the protagonists of one-party regimes or systems of government dismissed the fears that their systems would undermine democracy. Instead they argued that one-party systems would be just as democratic, if not more so, than the multi-party systems and they have continued to justify their regimes and political behaviour on democratic grounds.

Leading in the defence of the one-party system was Nyerere of Tanzania who contended that "where there is one-party and that party is identified with the nation as a whole, the foundations of democracy are firmer than they can ever be when you have two or more parties each representing only a section of the community".[1] The people of any one country on the continent were, according to this argument, assumed to hold common or identical political views that could easily be accommodated in a single party. The argument could also be interpreted as implying that any social differences in any one nation were without significance or meaning and, therefore, did not require articulation through the medium of different political parties.

The argument appears to have been influenced by the fact that during the mobilization phase of the struggle for independence in many countries of Africa, the people abandoned their political and ideological differences and came together to fight one common enemy, the colonialists. It was therefore assumed that this apparent consensus would be maintained even after independence. Later events were of course to prove this assumption wrong.

A further argument in defence of a one-party system of government was that in cases where there were differences of opinion such differences could be accommodated through what the African leaders called opposition from within the party. To demonstrate that this was possible, leaders like Nyerere practised in the initial stages what has been called the politics of accommodation in which they avoided taking disciplinary action against politicians who openly contradicted official government policy. However, this did not last long.

In fact, many leaders of one-party regimes throughout the continent referred their critics and those who were skeptical about the democratic nature of one-party systems of government to the practice in the traditional African past where many different shades of political opinion were discussed in one meeting, under one and the same leader, until a consensus was arrived at. African leaders consequently argued that a system could not be more democratic than this. Their concept of opposition from within the party approach has been influenced by the assumption they all seem to have made about African traditional systems of government. A one-party system of government and opposition from within was African and democratic, they argued.

Related to the above was the argument by the advocates of the one-party system that a multi-party system of government was foreign to Africa as it was Western in origin. In rejecting multi-party systems of government, therefore, the advocates of one-party regimes strongly challenged the relevance of the multi-party system in contemporary Africa. These countries, being underdeveloped, needed to concentrate on economic development rather than politics. Being characterized by internal divisive forces such as tribalism, they needed to concentrate on nation-building rather than party politics. The fear thus was that multi-party systems would emphasize politics at a time when these countries needed to play down politics and concentrate on achieving political stability and socio-economic development. Nyerere made the point when he said that a genuine and responsible opposition (may) arise in time but that the present was a time of national emergency when unity was necessary.[2] It was considered important to organize politics in these countries around single parties as a means of fostering unity and socio-economic development.

The emphasis placed on (a) the "Africanness" of single-party systems, (b) the need to play down politics and to concentrate on nation-building and economic development and (c) the argument that multi-party systems of government are foreign to Africa, raises the question of whether democracy was truly a major concern of the protagonists of the one-party systems of government or whether their advocacy and defence of it amounted to anything more than just a demonstration of their desire and ability to break away from the shadow of their former colonial masters and to establish their own distinctive political identity. Alternatively, were these leaders not merely looking for political arrangements that would ensure their firm hold of power in the face of the many challenges confronting their countries, some of which threatened the very basis of their power?

Writing about the one-party system in Zambia, for example, Chikulo observes that Zambia's adoption of the one-party constitution in 1972 could be regarded as an attempt to create an institutional structure capable of constraining certain types of conflict and competition, which had affected the stability of the political system. The one-party and electoral systems it entails are thus primarily a device for conflict management.[3] The point is that with the establishment of a one-party system of government, all potentially organized opposition in society is brought under the party which in most one-party states is accorded paramountcy over all such institutions, thus sharply limiting their range of activity. Since those who control the party also control political power, they are clearly able to ensure their dominance in the political system.

In order to determine whether or not one-party systems of government in Africa are democratic, a review of how the various political institutions are used as instruments of operating the one-party political systems will be undertaken. This is done because as one writer puts it, "a country's proximity to democracy is more accurately measured by the working of its (democratic) institutions rather than their forms".[4] An appropriate point to start this discussion would therefore be to ask the question: what is democracy?

Neither the long history of the existence of democracy as a political system, nor the debate just referred to, has helped students of political theory to arrive at a consensus on the precise definition of the term "democracy" and particularly on the arrangements and political institutions and processes and the form in which they must exist and operate in order that the system may qualify as democratic.

The problem of definition has been compounded by the fact that in the twentieth century, almost all countries, irrespective of the differences in their political order and institutional arrangements, have devised ways and means of retaining the word "democracy" to define and describe their political systems. This they have done, for example, by prefacing democracy with qualifying adjectives to explain differing political arrangements. Thus Cuba's Castro describes his political order as "true democracy" — the leadership of the state through a party,[5] while Nasser gave the name "party-less democracy"[6] to his political order. Terms like "participatory democracy" and "guided democracy" are commonly used by leaders, especially in Africa and the Third World, to describe their political systems. Thus all leaders assert that their political authority is derived from popular support and is exercised in the interest of the people. They go to great lengths to show how their regimes derive legitimacy from the people.

Despite the differences in political systems, a close examination of the major elements of the debate on the relationship between the one-party system and democracy and a look at the workings of many of the political systems that claim to be democratic, not just in Africa but elsewhere too, would reveal some basic characteristics that appear cardinal to democracy as a political system. On the basis of these characteristics and as defined elsewhere in this volume we define democracy as a political system which encourages and makes possible the free and voluntary involvement of the people in the political life of the nation. An important aspect of this involvement must include the right to make such critical decisions as the determination of the type and nature of the government to be established and the right to comment freely on important public issues that may confront the nation from time to time. In other words, important national decisions must emanate from a synthesis of the views of the people, including those of the minority.

Democracy is therefore a system of government in which individual interests, rights and freedoms such as the right to free association, political or otherwise, and the right to be heard, that is, to express oneself freely, and other human rights, are not only recognized and respected but are also protected by the state.

In the complex modern world, democracy requires the existence and use of certain institutions through which the people can participate in their governance. Such institutions include parliament, the executive, the judiciary, political parties and the electoral process. In addition to being used as a means of popular participation, such institutions must also serve as checks on the possible abuse of power by any one of them. The relationship between these institutions and the manner in which they operate rather than their mere existence or forms are therefore central to the determination of whether a system is democratic or not.

Democracy therefore rests on voluntary popular participation in the political process, accountability of the rulers to the ruled and the sharing of power. Situations or political systems, whether they are one-party or multi-party, in which power is concentrated in the hands of a few people, one person or institution and where the principle of accountability is compromised will tend to undermine democracy and democratic politics.

THE AFRICAN ONE-PARTY STATES AND DEMOCRATIC POLITICS

National politics, whether democratic or not, takes place within the context of the state. It becomes imperative therefore that the nature of the state and especially the interests and ideology of those who control the state machinery are taken into account when discussing any political system and the political processes therein. This is because it is those people who control state power who determine the direction of politics and every other process in society. This consideration becomes particularly necessary and relevant in situations such as prevail in African one-party states, where it is quite apparent that the interests and ideologies of those who control political and therefore state power, and the interests of those they rule do not coincide. In such countries the rulers have tended to use their power and the institutions they control not only to promote their own individual and group interest as rulers — and in some cases, sectional as opposed to national interests — but also to manipulate and undermine the rights and freedoms of the rest of the society. This problem has arisen partly because the state in Africa has been unable to satisfy the legitimate demands of society due partly to the insufficiency of resources available for distribution. Faced with the dilemma of choosing between popular demands and their own interests, African rulers have chosen to use state institutions to promote their interests rather than those of the ruled.

One startling political phenomenon in the African one-party states arising partly from the failure to satisfy the various demands of the people, is the sensitivity of regimes to any expression of or attempt to exercise individual rights and freedoms and the resultant tendency on the part of the state and those who control it to interpret any societal or group demands on the system as intended to undermine and subvert its interests, stability and security. In fact their fear is that these demands pose a threat to their own interests as rulers, resulting in feelings of insecurity.

The reaction of the state to such demands has been to control all social and political sources of actual potential opposition to the regime and the interests of those in power. This control is often carried out in the name of creating and maintaining political order. In Mali, for example, before the *coup,* the Union Soudanais Party maintained strict control over voluntary associations and most groups were either extensions or integral parts of the party and subject to party directives at every level.[7]

In Tanzania too the ruling party (CCM) has brought under its control the trade union movements, co-operative organizations, women's organizations etc. The party in such cases dominates all other institutions in the society thus making the principle of division and sharing of power irrelevant. There have been cases in which, because of the excessive concentration of power in one or two institutions or people, the distinction has been difficult to make between actions performed by people in their individual personal capacities and actions peformed by them in their official capacities. A case in point was the barring of the former post-independence opposition leader in Kenya from taking part in the 1979 General Elections as a candidate — on the grounds that he and other members of the party had sued the ruling party. The leader in question had filed a legal suit against KANU's Secretary-General for calling him and other former members of the opposition "security risks". No distinction was made between KANU as a party and its Secretary-General as an individual.[8] The fact that the Secretary-General had been sued was used to bar these people from contesting the elections as if it were the party that was sued and secondly as if it were unconstitutional to sue the party. Earlier these people had been barred from contesting elections on other gounds even though they had rejoined the ruling party.

By taking such repressive actions, African one-party states not only violate the rights and freedoms of individual politicians but also the democratic rights of the electorate to vote for candidates and policies of their choice. This tendency causes major concern particularly because of the absence of alternative parties through which these individuals may articulate their political ideas and seek popular support. Thus it is clear that those in power in the African one-party states regard it as their duty to make decisions, sometimes on very important national issues, without regard to the demands, wishes and interests of the people and their representatives. The result of such repressive tendencies, prevalent in many African one-party states, has been for the states and those in power to increasingly alienate themselves from those they rule and from whom they claim to derive their legitimacy.

The drift and growing gap between the rulers and the ruled, common to many African one-party states, has made those who control state power to become increasingly insecure, sensitive, repressive and less responsive to the wishes of society. The mass of the people in turn begin to regard the state and its organs with fear, suspicion and cynicism because as far as they are concerned, they are no longer legitimate.[9] As a result of the feeling of insecurity on the part of the state, those who control state power no longer regard the various state institutions as instruments for the promotion of the common or national interest but more as instruments of controlling and promoting their own parochial interests as rulers and of those who identify with their policies and programmes. The masses on the other hand, sensing their inability to meaningfully influence the policies of state and the behaviour of those in positions of leadership, tend to develop apathy and to withdraw from participation in the political process. This they do also because as far as they are concerned, and out of experience, it is safer to do so. It is this limitation and restriction of individual rights and freedoms in African one-party states that poses one of the greatest threats to democratic politics in these states. Voluntary popular participation once restricted makes prospects for democratic politics very remote indeed. This unfortunately is the situation in most African one-party states.

ELECTIONS IN ONE-PARTY STATES

The key to mass participation in democracy is the electoral process.[10] Elections represent a way of making a choice that is fair to all — one that leaves each member of the electorate a reasonable hope of having his alternative elected.[11] The use of elections, therefore, implies the existence of several possible alternatives from which to elect, and that, within the electorate, different groups and individuals are likely to hold different political values and preferences. Elections are therefore meant to provide the electorate with the opportunity to indicate their political preferences by voting for one or the other alternative. By doing this, elections and their results confer legitimacy to those who emerge as winners. The winning group will be determined by the number of votes it commands. Such a government can claim rightly that it is ruling for and on behalf of the people who elected it in accordance with democratic principles.

What Makes Elections Democratic?

The mere existence of elections, however, need not make a system of government democratic. This is because as Nsibambi rightly observes, "even some undemocratic regimes which assume power by force, indulge in holding electoral fictions in order to give appearance of being supported by the majority of their victims."[12] And as we have already seen, all governments appear to want to be regarded as democratic. The point we are making is that for elections to be democratic, certain conditions must be present and fulfilled.

The first condition is that the elections must be free and fair. This would require the existence of an independent and impartial authority to organize and conduct them — what J.M. Mackenzie calls an honest, competent non-partisan administration.[13] He gives the other conditions as the existence of an independent judiciary to interpret the electoral law; a developed system of political parties and traditions between which people can choose; and widely accepted rules of the game within which the struggle for power can take place.[14]

By definition a one-party system of government does not permit the existence of alternative forms of political organization. In other words the one-party situation does not permit the fulfilment of the democratic condition that requires the existence of a system of political parties and traditions between which people can choose. Elections in such circumstances are reduced to a choice not between competing political values and governmental systems but between individuals. Rather than provide the electorate with the opportunity and freedom to choose a government of their choice, the government imposes itself on them. The duty of those who participate in such elections is merely to "confirm" the regime in power.

Thus, although it is true that some kind of elections are periodically held in many African one-party states, it must be noted that the absence of alternative political parties, policies and programmes competing for popular support, and upon which the electorate can base their choice, renders the one-party elections largely meaningless as measures of the popularity and legitimacy of these regimes. The elected individuals may claim popularity but since they are operating a government that is imposed on the people in the sense that the people have no alternative in choosing that government, the regime "confirmed" in power must be regarded as illegitimate. Governments whether in one- or multi-party systems, do not consist merely of individuals but rather of policies and programmes that form the basis of and guide the behaviour and actions of those individuals elected or appointed to occupy leadership positions. Such individuals must be seen only as representing particular policies and their election is intended mainly to ensure that they help implement those policies and programmes that they identify with. Their election in the absence of competing alternative programmes **and** policies is meaningless and certainly does not demonstrate or indicate that the system is democratic.

The point being made here is that in the African one-party elections, and indeed in all one-party elections, the electorate are deprived of their democratic right to change governments by electing and choosing them on the basis of policies and programmes of their choice. It is little wonder, therefore, that until the electoral victory of Mauritanian socialists in June 1982, no national government in an independent African state had been transferred to another by electoral means.[15] The absence of the possibility of changing governments democratically due to the absence of alternative political parties has been used in some cases to justify military takeovers, thus prompting the emergence of the military as a major political factor in African politics.

The 1966 army *coup* in Ghana, for example, was justified on the grounds that "the army and the police had used the only means available for removing a dictator . . . and their defence was that only undemocratic methods could be used in the pursuit of the ultimate goal of democracy".[16] We might add that the emergence of the military as a political factor in Africa has made the prospects of democratic politics even more doubtful. Studies[17] on military-led regimes in Africa have shown that in virtually all cases, these regimes have no respect for some of the very basic democratic values and principles such as human rights.

Choosing between Individuals

Even if we were to accept Nyerere's argument in his *Democracy and the Party System* that the most important duty of the electorate in a one-party state is to choose the strongest and most able candidate from among the candidates presenting themselves for election, the experience from the elections held so far in many African one-party states indicates that this has not always been possible. This is because in many constituencies, some candidates are unknown to the electorate, thus causing the electorate to consider factors other than the ability of the candidate which they sometimes cannot judge.

In a study of the 1965 elections in Tanzania, for example, it is reported that the symbols given to the candidates were a factor and an issue in determining the election outcomes in the sense that sometimes a skillful manipulation was necessary to bring out their latent importance.[18] Many voters in these elections voted for symbols[19] rather than the candidates. The importance of the symbol is demonstrated by the fact that out of the 101 contested elections 62[20] of the winners had the hoe as a symbol and used it to convince the voters to elect them to parliament as the hoe had a significant meaning in their day-to-day lives.

Studies[21] of elections in Kenya have also shown that because of the absence of alternative issues and programmes which the voters could use to assess the suitability of the candidates, other factors such as the candidate's clan dominate and determine the outcome of elections. This is particularly so where the candidate's past record is unknown. Candidates elected in one party elections are, therefore, not necessarily the strongest or ablest as all sorts of factors are taken into consideration. As Orwa's study of the 1983 elections indicates, in South Nyanza many incumbent parliamentarians from the district were voted out simply because the electorate wanted a change of representatives. It did not matter who they were replaced with. And as Chikulo also puts it, parliamentary elections (in a one-party system) cannot give us a clear picture about the adherence to or disaffection from the regime.[22] This could only be possible if there were alternative parties and policies competing for public support. These elections only ensure change in personnel but not in government.

The second and third conditions for democratic elections as stipulated by Mackenzie are equally difficult to fulfil in a one-party state. The fact that the party has paramountcy over all other governmental institutions, including the civil administration which in these states is responsible for conducting elections, means that the administration cannot act independently of demands from those in power. Since, as we pointed out, the aim of establishing one-party systems of government has something to do with the desire by the political elite to safeguard their power, one would not expect them to allow the administration to play an impartial role during elections. A good example of this problem was the 1983 general elections in Trans-Nzoia District of Kenya. After the results of the elections were announced, one of the loosers contested them in a court of law. The High Court found that the results were the outcome of massive rigging by the administration officials in charge of polling.[23] That the administration official in question was not disciplined after the court findings indicates that he did not act alone in determining the outcome.

Voter Participation

As we have said before, elections are a means of providing the electorate with the opportunity to participate in the political process and particularly in choosing their government. The voter turn-out at elections would therefore be a simple but objective measure of the extent of participation whether in one-party or multi-party systems — barring, of course, any manipulation of the electoral process.

Although detailed election results in many African states are hard to come by, those that exist tend to indicate that the one-party state elections are generally characterized by low voter turn out. In Kenya, for example, out of the 4,246,682 registered voters for the 1983 general elections, only 46.59%[24] actually cast their votes. Similar low figures were reported in the first elections in Zambia after the establishment of a one-party system of government in 1972. Thus in the 1973 elections, only 39.8%[25] out of the 1.7 million registered voters actually cast their votes.

Although there are many possible factors that may account for the low voter turn-out in any election, it is quite possible that in the two cases cited above, the reason was due to the fact that many voters did not identify with the policies and programmes of the ruling party, and had no other way of indicating their protest. The Zambian case is particularly relevant here if one considers the political activities that preceded the 1973 elections which clearly signified a dissatisfaction with the ruling United Independence Party.[26] If these elections are anything to go by then one can conclude that participation in the electoral process in African one-party states is generally low. One would, however, have to obtain more data on this and compare it with election results in multi-party states in order to arrive at a more conclusive decision.

PARLIAMENTS IN ONE-PARTY STATES

Because of the size and complexity of present-day societies, direct democracy in which every individual citizen participates in major decision-making is no longer practicable. In its place has developed what one might call representative democracy whereby the people elect their representatives to a national parliament. The elected representatives then make decisions on behalf of the electorate. These representatives become the ultimate authority from which national, political and other important decisions derive their legitimacy since democratic governments derive their power and authority from the people. Elections and parliaments consisting of the people's representatives are therefore very vital instruments and institutions for democratic politics in present-day societies.

To serve this purpose effectively, it is imperative and important that the representatives of the people be free to debate and make decisions about policy and to legislate all issues brought before them without a feeling of insecurity and fear of interference from other institutions in society. Their decisions must be respected as they represent the views of the people from whom governmental authority is derived. In other words, representative or parliamentary democracy will only function effectively in a situation in which the concept and practices of parliamentary supremacy are upheld and strictly adhered to.

In most African one-party states, however, parliamentary supremacy is no longer upheld and especially in the conduct of debates and implementation of parliamentary decisions. In some countries such as Tanzania it is clearly stated that the concept of supremacy of the people's representatives has been replaced by party supremacy. Thus as far as Tanzania is concerned, the party (CCM) and not parliament is supreme. In other cases this may not be so clearly or explicitly stated but from practice it is clear that it is either the party or the executive arm of the government as represented by the presidency that is supreme or more authoritative than parliament. In the case of East Africa prior to 1971 Mazrui observed that the tendency was for the presidency to behave as if parliament and other institutions derived their authority and legitimacy from it rather than the other way round.

The powerful position of the presidency in African one-party states and, in some cases, the party, in relation to other institutions and, especially, parliament, has resulted in parliament becoming less effective and almost irrelevant as a source of authority and legitimacy. As a result many members of parliment develop apathy and show very little interest in parliamentary debates as is evidenced by the lifeless and sometimes superficial debates, or the chronic lack of quorum.[27] In some cases very important national issues that have direct effect upon the life of these nations are not debated by the people's representatives. In other cases national parliaments have simply been called upon to ratify decisions or legalize policies. Perhaps the best evidence of the declining role of parliament in a one-party state is Tanzania where national policy decisions are made by the party after which:

"In parliament it is no longer permissible for each member to express his own personal opinion. There is a party line to be followed — the line approved by the party's leaders i.e. the government. And in order to ensure that this is followed, we actually hold a private debate within TANU Parliamentary Party before each meeting in parliament . . . . . . Here it is that they learn from their leaders what the 'party line' is to be, and just how far they may go in criticising any particular bill or legislation when this comes up for debate in parliament."[28]

This practice raises the important question of how responsible, if at all, these regimes are to the wishes of the people whose interest they claim to base their decisions on. It has been observed that in cases where debate is allowed and encouraged, it is often so channelled as to render it inconsequential in terms of the material aspects of a policy.[29] Thus, it is evident that national assemblies in African one-party states are no longer effective institutions through which the representatives of the people can freely and popularly participate in their governance by expressing the popular wishes and demands of the people.

This restriction of the freedom of parliament also renders the institution ineffective as an instrument through which possible excess of the executive, the judiciary and other institutions of state can be checked. The division and sharing of power so central to democratic politics is thus rendered meaningless in one-party states by the limitations of parliamentary powers and privileges. Parliamentary supremacy and the institution's role as a source of legitimacy for governmental decisions cannot be restricted or transferred to another organ of society as has been done in many African one-party states, without detracting from the democratic nature of the system. Under such circumstances, the people's right and power to control and limit governmental power and authority are weakened, thus negating the democratic idea of government by popular consent.

It is of course true that not all public, group or individual opinions and demands are ignored completely in all the one-party states. This would certainly not be possible given the nature of these societies. The important question, however, is the freedom with which these groups or individual demands and opinions are articulated and the manner in which democratic institutions, where they exist, have been used. Generally, these institutions have been used in Africa by those in power not for ensuring popular participation and mediating between governmental authority and the individual, but more as instruments of control and suppression especially of opinion that contradict government policy. Most people have consequently tended to shy away from using these institutions to express their political opinions and beliefs and from participating in their own governance.

CONCLUSION

Despite the many reasons advanced by African leaders for their preference for one-party systems of government, experience derived from the manner in which these states have conducted politics, tends to show that issues of democracy were not necessarily what these statesmen were interested in confronting. Rather they were looking for suitable political institutions and arrangements that would ensure that their control of state power was not threatened by those competing to take over this control. Very few of these leaders have given up power even when it became clear that they had lost their legitimacy and public support. Many have been removed by force or died in office.

Partly as a result of their failure to meet the popular and legitimate demands of the people, the one-party states have not only become sensitive and insecure, but also very oppressive and unresponsive to the demands of the mass of the people whom they rule. They have tended to control and limit the rights and freedoms of the people who would want to voluntarily participate in the political life of the nation. Institutions such as parliaments have been rendered largely ineffective as sources of legitimacy for government decisions. The people, therefore, no longer control and limit governmental authority in the one-party states of Africa.

REFERENCES

1. See Nyerere, J.K., *Democracy and the Party System,* Dar es Salaam, 1962.
2. Cliffe, L., *One Party Democracy: The 1965 Tanzania General Elections,* East African Publishing House, 1987, p. 15.
3. Chikulo, B.C., "Political Parties, Elections and Political Stability in Zambia". A paper presented at the Association of African Political Scientists Regional Workshop on "Constitutionalism and Political Stability in the East African Region", Nairobi, Kenya, January 5 to 7, 1987, p. 1.
4. Cliffe, L., "Democracy in a One-Party State: The Tanzanian Experience". In Cliffe, L. and Saul, J. eds. *Socialism in Tanzania Vol. 1 Politics,* East African Publishing House, 1972, p. 241.
5. Christenson, R.M., *Ideologies and Modern Politics,* Thomas Nelson and Sons Ltd., 1972, p. 178.
6. *Ibid.,* p. 178.
7. Snyder, F.G., *One-Party Government in Mali: Transition Toward Control.* New Haven, 1965, p. 82.
8. *The Weekly Review,* Nairobi, June 15, 1985, p. 5.
9. Anyang' Nyong'o, P., "Political Science as a Social Science". A paper presented at the Organization of Social Science Research in Eastern Africa (OSSREA) Workshop, April 15-17, 1985, p. 5.
10. Hazard, J.N., *The Soviet System of Government.* The University of Chicago Press, 1968, p. 50.
11. Rousseau, Jean-Jacques, *The Social Contract and Discourses,* London, J.M. Dent & Sons Ltd., 1973, p. 251.
12. Nsibambi, A., "The 1980 Elections in Uganda". A paper presented at a Conference on "Constitutionalism and Political Stability in Eastern Africa", Nairobi, Kenya, January 5-7, 1987, organized and sponsored by the African Association of Political Science (AAPS), p. 2.
13. Mackenzie, W.J.M., *Free Elections,* London, George Allen & Unwin, 1958, p. 14.
14. *Ibid.,* p. 14.
15. *The African Studies Review,* Vol. 26, Nos. 3, 4, September/November 1983, p. 4.
16. Rinkey, R., *Ghana Under Military Rule 1966-1969.* Methuen & Co. Ltd., 1972, p. 15.
17. See for example, Decalo, S., *Coup and Army Rule in Africa: Studies in Military Style.* Yale University Press, 1976.
18. Cliffe, L., "Tanzania Election: Its Results and Significance". A paper presented at the Symposium on Tanzanian Elections E.A.I.S.R. Conference, January 1966, p. 16. Other papers on the same subject presented at the same conference include those by G.G. Generya

"Political Development in Sukuma land", and B.P. Mramba "Kiliman-jaro: Chagga Readjustment to Nationalism".

19. Hyden, G., "Buhaya: Selection and Election Processes in Bukoba and Karagwe Districts", In Cliff, L., *One-Party Democracy: The 1965 Tanzania General Elections,* East African Publishing House, 1967, p. 71.

20. Cliffe, L., *op. cit.*

21. See for example, P. Alila, "Luo Ethnic factor in the 1979 and 1983 Elections in Bondo and Gem, Kenya", I.D.S. Working Paper No. 408, June 1984. See also N. Nyangira, "Poverty of Issues in One-Party State by-election: Kenya," Department of Government, University of Nairobi, April 11, 1973. See also D.K. Orwa, "Political Recruitment in Mbita Constituency: A Study in Electoral Politics", Department of Government Seminar Series on General Elections in Kenya, Seminar Paper No. 3, March, 1984.

22. Chikulo, B.C., "Political Parties, Elections and Political Stability in Zambia", a paper presented at the AAPS regional Workshop on "Constitutionalism and Political Stability in East Africa Region", Nairobi, Kenya, Janurary 5-7, 1987, p. 22.

23. *The Weekly Review,* Nairobi, June 15, 1984, p. 4. In *The Weekly Review Election Handbook,* 1979, it is reported that "In 1974 there were a number of cases of the Administration refusing to grant permits for public meetings requested by certain candidates. The most spectacular example of this kind of interference by the administration was in the case of the late J.M. Kariuki who for weeks before the election had not been allowed to address a public meeting in his own constituency even though his opponents were addressing the electorate freely", p. 8.

24. *The Weekly Review,* Nairobi, September 1984, p. 10. See also *The Weekly Review Election Handbook,* 1979, p. 6.

25. Chikulo, B.C., *op. cit.,* p. 20.

26. *Ibid.,* pp. 1-11.

27. *The Weekly Review,* Nairobi, September 1984, p. 10.

28. Nyerere, J.K., *op. cit.*

29. Decalo, S., *op. cit.*

CHAPTER V

THE ILLUSIONS OF DEMOCRACY IN UGANDA, 1955-1966

J.B. Mugaju

INTRODUCTION

A democracy should express the sovereignty of a country's adult population through a system of representative and accountable institutions, competitive party politics, periodic elections and free and open dissent. All parties are supposed to abide by the rules of the game and accept the electorate's verdict.

During the late 1950s and the early 1960s Uganda was supposedly a viable parliamentary democracy. According to Ali Mazrui "Uganda was perhaps the strongest example of a liberal polity still surviving in Africa" because it permitted lively political debate and discussion as well as vigorous litigative constitutionalism.[1] Unfortunately, so the argument goes, this promising democratic start was violently destroyed by Milton Obote in 1966 when he "suspended the 1962 independence constitution he had solemnly sworn to protect" and launched "the Obote revolution."[2] Subsequently, Uganda steadily drifted into dictatorship, political violence and economic chaos — a trend which, needless to say, is yet to be reversed.

This chapter argues that students of Ugandan politics have tended to confuse institutional democratic formalism with actual democracy. Despite the existence of political parties and representative institutions, democracy never functioned in Uganda between 1955 and 1966. On the eve of independence, Uganda not only lacked democratic traditions and culture but the political atmosphere was charged with fear, suspicion and uncertainty. This was not conducive to democratic experimentation. Besides, the new inheritors of the state were of doubtful democratic convictions, their rhetoric and sloganeering notwithstanding. The principles of give and take, reason, moderation and mutual respect, did not appeal to them. On the contrary the Ugandan political elites were primarily inspired by the "winner-take-all philosophy" and the capture of power at all costs was their overriding concern.[3] The bemoaned independence settlement itself was not based on democratic considerations. Rather, it was designed to perpetuate the power and interests of the British-nurtured protestant oligarchy in post-colonial Uganda. Moreover, after independence the conduct of leading politicians in the country proved detrimental to democracy.

THE ADVENT OF DEMOCRATIC FORMALISM

Until 1955 democracy did not exist in Uganda. The Protectorate government was accountable to the British Colonial Office rather than to the people of Uganda. The members of the Legislative Council were nominated by the Governor. Nor were the traditional institutions, which had survived under the British doctrine of indirect rule, any more democratic. However, during the 1950s the British Colonial authorities belatedly began to democratize the political system in preparation for independence. Democratic experimentation began in Buganda, "the nerve centre" of the country.[4]

The Buganda political and constitutional crisis of 1953-55 was resolved when the British government and Buganda concluded the Buganda Agreement of 1955. One of the terms of this agreement was the restoration of Kabaka Muteesa II on condition that he became a Constitutional monarch. The *Lukiiko* (The Buganda Parliament) was to be popularly elected and the government would be formed by the majority party in that assembly. Democratization therefore meant that the Kabaka should be above party politics and desist from day-to-day involvement in the administration of Buganda. But Muteesa was unwilling to play the role of a constitutional monarch. Upon restoration, he was very popular in Buganda because he had apparently challenged the might of British imperialism. His political position was also reinforced by the resurgence of neo-traditionalism in Buganda. As a result Muteesa was determined to play an active part in the politics of Buganda and Uganda contrary to the 1955 Agreement. Although Muteesa was supposedly a constitutional monarch "he retained a great deal of power over his ministers so. . . . the 1955 Agreement achieved the opposite of what it had intended: it had left the Kabaka's power intact while at the same time relieving him of the responsibility of the actions of his ministers."[5] He also surrounded himself with "powerful but unenlightened traditionalist separatists" whose hostility to parliamentary democracy was well-known.[6]

During this period the authoritarian and intransigent regime at Mengo did everything possible to frustrate the development of democratic institutions in Buganda. The Mengo regime persecuted and intimidated anyone suspected of disloyalty to the Kabaka. The *Lukiiko* and the Buganda Administration was purged of all except "the whole-hearted supporters of the post-restoration regime."[7] Nothing illustrates the undemocratic attitude of the Mengo regime in the 1950s better than the famous case of Mugwanya, a prominent Roman Catholic politician.

The religious wars of the 1880s left Buganda divided into rival religious camps. The Protestant elites were the most influential group in Buganda. For example, the post of *Katikiro* (Prime Minister) was held only by the Protestants throughout the colonial period. The majority of the Saza and

Gombolola chiefs were also Protestants. This Protestant hegemony was resented by the Roman Catholics. In 1956, following the launching of the democratic process in Buganda, Matayo Mugwanya stood for the *Katikiroship* against two Protestant rivals, Michael Kintu and Paul Kavuma. The *Lukiiko,* then composed of 3 ministers, 20 chiefs, 60 elected representatives and 6 personal nominees of the Kabaka, constituted an electoral college to choose the *Katikiro.* Pre-election forecasts indicated that Mugwanya might defeat his rivals. This likelihood of a Mugwanya victory was intolerable to the Kabaka and the Protestant oligarchy controlling Mengo. For this reason the Kabaka and his confidants took some measures to block the election of Mugwanya.[8]

First of all, Muteesa instructed all the chiefs to vote for Kintu. The chiefs were warned that failure to do so would be construed as a manifestation of disloyalty to the Kabaka. Paul Kavuma was persuaded to stand down for Kintu. Muteesa also appointed new nominees and instructed them to vote for Kintu. As a result of these manoeuvres, Mugwanya's bid for the *Katikiroship* was blocked. But the controversial victory of Kintu exposed Muteesa's partisanship and compromised the impartiality of his office. Mugwanya's supporters became convinced that the Mengo regime was serving the interests of the Protestant oligarchy at the expense of the Roman Catholic community. Their fears were soon confirmed. After losing to Kintu, Mugwanya won a set in a bye-election in the *Lukiiko* as the member for Mawokota. The Mengo government barred him from taking his seat on the pretext that he was already a member of the East African Legislative Assembly. This vindictive treatment of Mugwanya was clearly detrimental to democratization in post-restoration Buganda.

Mugwanya was not the only target of the Mengo regime. Other independent-minded politicians were also victimized by it. Mulira was barred from taking his seat in the *Lukiiko* because he did not conform to the political orthodoxy then prevailing at Mengo. Joseph Kiwanuka was falsely accused of plotting to assassinate the Kabaka though his real offence was membership of the Uganda National Congress.[9] Throughout the 1950s the Mengo regime systematically obstructed the evolution of party politics in Buganda by "discrediting and destroying parties."[10] According to Karugire, "the Mengo government inaugurated and stepped up a harassment campaign against party leaders and the supporters of national parties lest they secured a foot-hold in Buganda and then threaten their own monopoly of power."[11] This political harassment "took the form of frequently imprisoning the leaders of the parties on trumped up charges and encouraging arson directed against party leaders and supporters alike." *(Ibid.)*

The Mengo Protestant oligarchy also frustrated the democratization process in other important ways. In 1958 the Mengo government boycotted Uganda's first direct elections to the Legislative Council and thereafter refused to nominate representatives to that body. This was a violation of the 1955 Agreement. More importantly, Buganda attempted to obstruct the constitutional preparations towards the granting of self-government to Uganda. In 1959 Governor Crawford set up a Constitutional Committee, under the chairmanship of J.V. Wild to work out a new constitution for Uganda in consultation with all the interested parties.[12] But Buganda refused to work with the Wild Committee. In 1961 when the Protectorate government organized the first general elections, Buganda boycotted them. The registration of voters and the actual voting were frustrated by the Mengo regime through widespread intimidation and violence. Less than 4% of the electorate dared to register and of these only a small proportion were bold enough to cast their votes. The colonial government was forced "to protect African voters against the violence of their fellow Africans seeking to prevent them from exercising a democratic right that colonial governments usually granted reluctantly."[13] Even then the Mengo regime made the 1961 general elections "a mockery of the democratic process."[14]

The intransigence of the Mengo establishment and its hindrance of democracy were reinforced by the tyranny of populism which had a long history in Buganda.[15] In the 1950s populism was a formidable force which enforced conformity. People holding dissenting opinions were often victims of popular violence. Engholm rightly argued that populism was "a dangerous force in Buganda Society."[16] It was certainly not conducive to the evolution of a democratic environment in Buganda.

The populist threat to democracy was illustrated by the activities of the Uganda National Movement (UNM) in 1959. The UNM had many political objectives, but only two of them are relevant here. The movement was determined to frustrate the deliberations of the Wild Constitutional Committee. More importantly, it sought to prevent country-wide parties from gaining support in Buganda. To accomplish these objectives, the UNM launched an eight-month "systematic campaign of intimidation, violence and destruction of property" against real or imagined enemies of Buganda. During the boycott of 1959, coffee trees were cut, houses set on fire and persons assaulted.[17] The UNM campaign made it difficult for politicians to hold a rational and democratic debate about the future of Buganda and Uganda. It encouraged intransigence and contributed to the failure of the democratization process.

The obstacles to democracy were not confined to Buganda. Throughout the country traditional authorities suspected the intentions of the Western educated politicians controlling the newly-formed political parties. To some extent these fears were well-founded. The westernized elites who were about to inherit the colonial state had no proven competence to run the country. On the eve of independence the leading politicians in Uganda were inexperienced young men. None of them had ever held a senior public office. Moreover Ugandan politics in the late 1950s were characterized by ethnic and religious polarization. The spirit of compromise and moderation — of give and take — was (and still is) alien to the country's political life. The Munster Commission Report of 1961 pinpointed this problem when it made the following observations:-

> "No one who examined Uganda's political anmd social life could fail to be disturbed by one dominant characteristic: the unwillingness to compromise. The tension between different religious groups is another symptom of the same trouble"[18]

PARTY POLITICS AND DECOLONIZATION

During the 1950s "the imminence of independence" led to the proliferation of political Parties.[19] The most important of these were the Uganda National Congress (UNC), the Democratic Party (DP) and the Uganda Peoples Congress (UPC). The history of these parties shows that neither the quest for independence nor the building of a new democratic society were major concerns of party politicians. The prime inspiration of party politics was the capture of state power. As Grace Ibingira has pointed out, during the struggle for independence the critical issue was not Uganda's freedom or the foundation of democratic institutions "but who was to inherit the mantle of power from departing colonialists and what security there would be for each of the diverse ethnic groups in the new state."[20] In their bid for power, party politicians did not hesitate to bend or circumvent the rules of democracy.

Nothing illustrates better the undemocratic nature of party politics in Uganda than the manoeuvres that preceded the attainment of independence in 1962. By the end of 1960 it had become clear that the country's progress to independence was contigent on the stance of the Mengo regime. This regime had not only blocked the constitutional preparations for independence. It had also threatened to declare independence from Britain and to secede from Uganda. But given the centrality of Buganda, neither the British colonial authorities nor the emerging politicians could afford to ignore the wishes of that region. Being anxious to formally disengage from Uganda, the British were willing to accommodate the views of the Mengo establishment in order to ensure that Buganda remained an integral part of Uganda.

The attitude of the political parties was rather different. During the 1950s all party politicians were opposed to what they regarded as the Mengo regime's separatist tendencies. Indeed, one of the political parties — the Uganda Peoples Union — was formed to fight Mengo's hindrance of progress towards independence. In 1961 the Democratic Party (DP) and the Uganda Peoples Congress (UPC) contested the elections in Buganda in defiance of the Mengo sponsored boycott of those elections. Although the DP won 20 of the 24 seats in that region, its victory was neutralized by the effectiveness of the boycott. In the rest of the country, the UPC won 35 seats and the DP 24. Thus, the DP emerged as the majority party in the National Assembly and its leader, Benedicto Kiwanuka, was called upon to form the first African government of Uganda.[21]

The elections of 1961 forced the political parties to rethink their strategies and priorities. The Mengo regime and the UPC were determined to dislodge the DP government from power. The Mengo establishment was especially incensed by the DP's defiant participation in the elections. The DP and its leader were regarded at Mengo as traitors who had sacrificed the interests of Buganda. From that year onwards, Mengo "showed an implacable hostility [to the DP] far more bitter than that which had been shown towards the. . . colonial regime."[22] The UPC did not provoke hostile emotions at Mengo because it was led by 9 non-Baganda and it was not a significant political force in Buganda. On the other hand, the UPC, despite its anti-Buganda reputation realized the critical importance of collaborating with Mengo if the DP was to be unseated from power. Hatred of the DP, thus, brought the UPC and Mengo together to form an alliance aimed against the DP. Under this alliance the UPC offered to support Mengo's constitutional demands at the constitutional conference of September 1961. In return the Mengo regime agreed to form a central government with the UPC after the next pre-independence elections. For the purposes of fighting elections in Buganda, the Mengo regime formed the Kabaka Yekka (KY) movement. This movement formally entered an electoral alliance with the UPC which agreed not to contest the next elections in Buganda.

Grace Ibingira, who was instrumental in the negotiations that led to the UPC-KY alliance, has argued that this was "a perfectly legitimate manoeuvre" to capture power from the DP and to accommodate Buganda in a united independent Uganda.[23] Other scholars have argued that the alliance was extraordinarily opportunistic especially in view of the fact that prior to 1961, the UPC leadership had consistently opposed Buganda's political demands for a special constitutional status in Uganda. Nsibambi has argued that the UPC-KY alliance destroyed the opportunity of democratizing Buganda."[24] Even more forcefully Karugire has contended that the alliance "was not an act of statesmanship" but a cynic's delight because of the two parties' divergent views on almost every conceivable subject."[25]

Although the UPC-KY alliance was in the long-run harmful to the fortunes of democracy, it led to the conclusion of the independence settlement. In 1960 the British Colonial authorities set up the Munster Commission to recommend a suitable system of government for Uganda. The Commission submitted a report recommending that Buganda should have a federal status in Uganda. It also recommended a semi-federal status for Ankole, Toro, Bunyoro and Busoga. The rest of the country was to have a unitary relationship with the central government. The Munster Commission Report constituted the basis of the negotiations of September 1961 and culminated in the first constitution of independent Uganda. The Constitutional Agreement was described as "a great compromise" designed to meet "the harsh historical realities" of Uganda.[26] But this great historical compromise had grave implications for the future of democracy in post-colonial Uganda.

The handling of the 1961 Constitutional Conference did not generate confidence among all the interested parties in the independence constitution because the deliberations were actually dictated by the special requirements of Buganda. With the support of the UPC, Buganda achieved most of its constitutional demands. The representations of the DP and the district delegations from other parts of Uganda were simply ignored. For many Ugandans the independence constitution was a partisan document which served the interests of the Mengo regime and the UPC at the expense of the rest of the country. But events were to show that the UPC and Mengo did not have "sufficient determination to make the compromise work."[27] Moreover, the constitutional settlement was not submitted to the country for popular consent through a referendum. Over 80% of the people of Uganda "were largely spectators rather than active participants in the events leading to the granting of independence."[28] This meant that Uganda became an independent state with a political system based on inadequate popular legitimacy.

Some of the provisions of the independence constitution were contrary to the spirit of democracy. For example, the independence settlement provided that Buganda could opt for indirect elections of the members of the National Assembly from that region with the *Lukiiko* acting as an electoral college. In practice this provision disenfranchised the people of Buganda. As Karugire has eloquently put it, the option of indirect elections was "a fraud perpetrated upon the Baganda by their reactionary leaders with the help of the UPC and a pliable Colonial Secretary."[29] At the national level, the constitution provided for the nomination of nine members to the National Assembly by the government on the grounds that this would ensure stability after independence. The result of these provisions was that almost one-third of the first parliament of independent Uganda was not directly elected.

It is arguable that the Uganda electorate implicitly endorsed the Constitutional Settlement of 1961 because the British insisted on holding fresh general elections before granting independence. But how democratic were the elections of 1962? In that year two elections were held: the February elections for the *Lukiiko* in Buganda and the April general elections in the rest of the country. In the *Lukiiko* elections the contest was between the DP and the KY. Elsewhere, it was a straight fight between the DP and the UPC. According to the official results, the *Lukiiko* elections were "a dazzling electoral success" for the KY. The movement won all the seats except three in the lost counties. Immediately after the elections, Abu Mayanja quickly claimed that the KY victory had dealt "a fatal blow at the ugly head of religion in politics."[30]

But the available evidence suggests that the elections were not democratic. Mittelman has pointed out that the 1962 *Lukiiko* elections were marked by intimidation and violence against the DP and their supporters.[31] The Buganda Administration was used to ensure that the KY won the elections. The Kabaka who publicly loathed the DP appointed well-known KY members to supervize the elections. Fred Mpanga, the Chairman of the Buganda Elections Committee, and Abu Mayanja, the Supervisor of Elections, were prominent members of the KY and their impartiality was very suspect. Besides, most of the election officials were active supporters of the KY. During the election campaign itself the DP complained about Mengo sponsored violence and intimidation of DP supporters but their protestations were turned down by the Governor. After the elections the DP submitted a detailed document listing all the irregularities and malpractices which had been committed. These included: violence and intimidation, candidates who also played the role of Returning Officers, cases of declared votes exceeding the actual number of registered voters and voters casting their votes under surveillance of fearsome KY vigilantes.[32] These allegations were simply ignored. The Governor himself conceded that it was virtually impossible to hold genuine elections in Buganda in the absence of international supervision. Clearly with widespread violence and intimidation of DP sympathizers, the *Lukiiko* elections were a mockery of the democratic process. Not surprisingly, the post-election *Lukiiko* was "composed of almost universally like-minded members."[33]

The democratic credentials of the April 1962 general elections in the rest of the country were also highly questionable. The DP had grave doubts about the impartiality of R.C. Pilgram who had been appointed Supervisor of Elections. The DP leadership was also convinced that they were not only fighting the UPC-KY alliance but also the Colonial Office and the Church of England.[34] During the campaign and voting, irregularities and malpractices similar to those in Buganda were reportedly widespread. Grace Ibingira has pointed out that:

"Impersonation was widespread. Extra ballots in bundles appeared in ballot boxes unaccountably. Sometimes after polling in some remote rural areas, some ballot boxes mysteriously got lost. Several electoral districts controlled by the UPC returned minority candidates because electoral boundaries were drawn by pro-UPC officials showing a patent bias against the DP."[35]

These malpractices and irregularities compromised the credibility of the election results. The new government was unsure of its popular support and the DP was convinced that the UPC-KY alliance had won the elections by default. Thus, the first government of independent Uganda was based on questionable democratic legitimacy.

THE AFTERMATH OF INDEPENDENCE

Between 1962 and 1966 several local district elections as well as the lost counties' referendum showed little regard for democracy. There is some evidence, for example, to show that the Bunyoro elections of 1964 were not free and fair. The DP catalogued numerous electoral malpractices and irregularities which were strikingly similar to those of 1962. They included: deliberate changing of the nomination day without notifying all the parties, the physical and psychological intimidation of the DP candidates and their supporters, the disqualification of DP candidates on flimsy technical grounds, and the gerrymandering of constituencies by the pro-UPC Boundaries Commission.[36] Not surprisingly, the UPC won all the seats in the *Rukurato*, Bunyoro's Parliament. This abuse of the electoral process was not confined to Bunyoro. Throughout the country "enthusiastic UPC local officers. . . exceeded their powers and, assured of immunity from above, decisively and unfairly promoted the interests of their candidates."[37]

During the lost counties referendum, the Mengo government tried to frustrate the democratic process. Mengo was apprehensive that Buganda might lose the referendum because the majority of the voters were Banyoro. In the 1962 *Lukiiko* elections, the DP candidate in Buyaga was returned unopposed while in Bugangaizzi the DP candidate won the seat with 83% of the votes.[38] Mengo had hoped that the UPC-KY government would not allow the referendum. Nevertheless, after independence, Mengo took precautions just in case the Uganda government decided to go ahead with the referendum which, according to the constitutional settlement, was supposed to be held within two years after independence.

In 1963 Mengo launched the Ndaiga Scheme to settle many Baganda in the two disputed counties so as to transform the ethnic composition and increase the electoral prospects of Buganda. Muteesa himself moved to Ndaiga on "a prolonged hunting trip" whose purpose was to influence the outcome of the referendum. Vast sums of money, much of it unaccounted for, were spent supposedly on the development of the disputed area. These manoeuvres provoked outrage throughout the country, especially in Bunyoro, and the central government disenfranchised all the residents in the two countries not appearing on the 1962 electoral register. Once the referendum was held the Mengo regime refused to accept the outcome and this contributed to the collapse of the UPC-KY alliance.

The fortunes of democracy in post-colonial Uganda were also irreparably undermined by the politics of "crossing the floor".[39] Between 1962 and 1966 many DP and KY M.P.s crossed the floor and joined the UPC. Although this was not unconstitutional, the UPC gained parliamentary strength which was clearly out of proportion to its 1962 electoral mandate. Since those who changed sides did not seek a fresh mandate the politics of crossing the floor practically disenfranchised many constituencies in the country. Moreover, "the careerism and opportunism" of these politicians eroded public confidence in representative institutions and the National Assembly became a forum of "big-boss-politics".[40]

The chances of democracy were, moreover, impaired by the infancy of party politics. Neither the UPC nor the DP developed mechanisms for ensuring internal party democracy. Nothing illustrates the pitfalls of internal party democracy more than the controversial UPC Gulu Conference of 1964. During this conference the critical issue was the election of a new Secretary-General of the party. John Kakonge and Grace Ibingira were candidates for the post. The Kakonge-Ibingira contest revealed the growing polarization within the UPC and the disregard of democratic procedures. Ibingira wrote that he contested the post because Kakonge had not done enough "to build resistance in the UPC against Obote's tendency to grab all power and promote militarism".[41] If that was the case, then Ibingira and his supporters should have challenged Obote himself. On the contrary, Ibingira's candidacy was tacitly supported by Obote. A more convincing explanation is that the conservative elements in the party wanted to get rid of Kakonge on ideological grounds. He was suspected of communist leanings.

The Ibingira-Kakonge contest was handled in a manner contrary to the rules of democracy. Mujaju has given a vivid account of the manipulation of the Gulu conference to ensure the defeat of Kakonge. Just before the Gulu Conference the UPC Executive Committee changed the basic unit of party organization from *Gombolola* to *Muluka*. This decision constituted some sort of gerrymandering. As a result some districts in the country were over-represented at the Conference since not all the districts used the same methods of choosing delegates. The UPC Secretariat was prevented from organizing the Conference and this task was entrusted to the Acholi UPC branch. The delegates' cards which the UPC headquarters had printed were replaced with new ones on the eve of the Conference. Some of the delegations strongly protested against this. The Ankole and Toro delegations stormed out of the Conference alleging that the elections had been rigged in favour of Ibingira.[42] From then onwards the UPC became a faction-ridden party. The factionalism within it was compounded by the influx of the Baganda into the party during the course of 1965, the aim being to gain control of the party leadership and, through it, the government.[43] Thus, the stage was set for the fateful 1966 confrontation.

CONCLUSION

Despite the outward trappings of parliamentary democracy the political system in Uganda between 1955 and 1966 was not democratic. The country lacked democratic experience and traditions at all levels of society. The problem was compounded by the infancy of party politics and the opportunism of the inheritors of the colonial state. The immediate responsibility for the failure of democracy must go to the Protestant oligarchy which, in the form of the Mengo regime and the UPC leadership, never gave democracy a chance. However, it should not be hastily concluded that the DP was any more democratic.

The experience of independent Africa has shown that seemingly democratic opposition parties have become extremely dictatorial once in power. It is doubtful that the DP would have behaved differently from its rivals if it had gained power in 1962. Indeed the internal politics of the DP in the 1960s indicate that authoritarian and opportunistic propensities were prevalent in the party. The political environment in post-colonial Uganda was — and still is — too backward for the development of sound and durable democratic values, practices and institutions.

NOTES

1. Mazrui, Ali and G.G. Engholm "Violent Constitutionalism in Uganda," in A.A. Mazrui, *Violence and Thought: Essays in Social Tensions in Africa,* London, 1969, pp. 147-148.
2. Uzoigwe, G.N. "Uganda and Parliamentary Government." *The Journal of Modern African Studies,* 21, 2 (1983), p. 253.
3. Ibingira, G.S. *African Upheavals since Independence,* New York 1980 especially pp. 63-243.
4. Karugire, S.R. *A Political History of Uganda,* London, 1980, pp. 162-163.
5. *Ibid.*
6. Ibingira, *op. cit.,* p. 119.
7. Morris, H.F. "Buganda and Tribalism" in P.H. Gulliver (ed), *Tradition and Transition in East Africa,* London, 1969, p. 326.
8. See Gingyera-Pinychwa, A.G.G. *Apolo Milton Obote and His Times, In Uganda, 1952-1962,* Nairobi, 1965, pp. 17-18.
9. Lew, D.A. "Political Parties in Uganda, 1949-1962" in his *Buganda in Modern History,* London, 1971, pp. 190-191.
10. Ibingira, G.S. *op. cit.* p. 30.
11. Karugire, S.K. *op. cit.,* p. 165.
12. Ibingira, G.S. *The Forging of the African Nation,* Kampala, 1973, pp. 89-104.
13. Karugire, S.K. *op. cit.,* p. 178.

14. Dinwiddy, H. "The Search for Unity in Uganda: Early Days to 1966" in *African Affairs* 80, 321 (1981), p. 509.

15. For the advent of populism in Buganda see D.A. Low, "The Advent of Populism in Buganda", in his *Buganda in Modern History,* pp. 133-66.

16. Engholm, G. "Political Parties and Uganda's Independence" in *Transition* 2, 3 (1962) p. 16.

17. Ghai, D.P. "The Buganda Trade Boycott: A Study in Tribal Political and Economic Nationalism", in R.I. Rotberg and A.A. Mazrui (eds.), *Protest and Power in Black Africa,* New York, 1970 p. 757.

18. Quoted in Kabwegyere, J. *The Politics of State Formation: The Nature and Effects of Colonialism in Uganda,* Nairobi, East African Literature Bureau, 1974, p. 190.

19. Rothchild, D. and Rogin, M. "Uganda", in R.M. Carter (ed.), *National Unity and Regionalism in Eight African States,* New York, 1966, p. 351.

20. Ibingira, *African Upheavals,* p. 24.

21. Mugaju, J.B. "The General Elections of 1961, 1962 and 1980: A comparative study", History Department Staff Seminar No. 7, 1982, University of Nairobi.

22. Morris, H.F. *op. cit.,* p. 329.

23. Ibingira, G.S. *The Forging of the African Nation,* pp 201-205 and his *African Upheavals,* pp 29-30.

24. Nsibambi, A. *Intergrating Buganda in Uganda, 1961-1971,* Ph.D. thesis, University of Nairobi, 1984.

25. Karugire, S.K. *op. cit.,* pp. 182-183.

26. Uzoigwe, G.N. *op. cit.,* p. 254. See also Ibingira, *African Upheavals,* p. 35..

27. Morris, H.F. *op. cit.,* p. 337.

28. Karugire, S.K., *op. cit.,* p. 144.

29. *Ibid.,* p. 184.

30. Mayanja, A.K. "What is Kabaka Yekka", *Africa Report,* 7, 5 (1962).

31. Mittelman, J.H., *Idiology and Politics in Uganda.* New York, 1975, p. 75.

32. Karugire, S.K. *op. cit.,* pp. 87-88.

33. Dinwiddy, H. *op. cit.,* p. 509.

34. Welbourn, F.B. p. 37.

35. Ibingira, G.S. *African Upheavals,* p. 72.

36. Southall, R.J., *Parties and Politics in Bunyoro,* Makerere, 1972, pp. 40-43.

37. Ibingira, *op. cit.,* p. 72.

38. Southall, p. 45.

39. For the politics of crossing the floor in East Africa see A. Mazrui and G.F. Engholm, "The Tensions of Crossing the Floor in East Africa" in A. Mazrui, *Violence and Thought,* pp. 122-146.

40. See A.B. Mujaju, "The UPC and Change: An Assessment", a paper presented to the University Social Scíencies Conference at Makerere 18-20 Dec. 1974 and his "The Demise of UPC YL and the Rise of NUYO in Uganda", *African Review,* 3, 2 (1972) pp. 291-307.

41. Ibingira, *op. cit.*, p. 124.
42. Mujaju, *op. cit.*
43. Conen, D.L., and J. Parsons. "The Uganda Peoples Congress Branch and Constituency Elections of 1970." *Journal of Commonwealth Political Studies* 11, 1 (1973) pp. 46-66.

OTHER REFERENCES

1. Apter, D.E. *The Political Kingdom in Uganda,* 2nd. ed. Princeton, 1967.
2. Burke, F.G. *Local Goverment in Uganda,* Syracuse, 1964.
3. Fallers, L.A. *The Kings Men: Leadership and Status in Buganda on the Eve of Independence,* London, 1964.
4. Gertzel, C. *Party and Locality in Northern Uganda 1945-1962,* London, 1974.
5. Gungyera-Pincychwa, A..G. *Issues in Pre-Independence Politics in Uganda 1952-1962,* Nairobi, 1975.
6. Gukina, P.M. *Uganda: A Study in African Political Development,* Notre Dame, 1972.
7. Jorgensen, *Uganda: A Modern History,* London, 1981.
8. Kasfir, N. *The Shrinking Arena: Participation and Legitimacy in African Politics, the Case of Uganda,* Berkeley, 1976.
9. Kasfir, N. "Cultual Sub-Nationalism in Uganda" in V.A. Olorunsola (ed.) *The Politics of Sub-Cultural Nationalism in Africa,* New York, 1972, pp. 51-148.
10. Lee, J.M. "Buganda's Position in Federal Uganda" *Journal of Commonwealth Political Studies,* 3, 3 (1965), pp. 165-81.
11. Leys, C. *Politicians and Policies: An Essay on Politics in Acholi 1962-65,* Nairobi, 1967.
12. Low, D.A. *The Mind of Buganda,* London, 1971.
13. Mamdani, M. *Politics of Class Formation in Uganda,* London, 1976.
14. Muteesa, E. *The Desecration of my Kingdom,* London, 1967.
15. Southall, A "General Amin and the Coup: Great Man or historical inevitability", *The Journal of Modern African Studies,* 13, 1 (1975) pp. 85-105.

CHAPTER VI

BUREAUCRACY AND DEMOCRACY IN AFRICA

Walter O. Oyugi

INTRODUCTION

In this chapter, some thoughts on the relationship between the public bureaucracy and society in Africa are presented. Interest is particularly focused on whether the said relationship can yield practices that could be generally characterized as either democratic or undemocratic. The central issue is whether by its nature and constitution the bureaucracy can and should be expected to be an instrument of democratization of life in society.

It is assumed that the audience is familiar with the key concepts under review — bureaucracy and democracy. No elaborate definitions are therefore offered. Bureaucracy as used here refers strictly to the public service organization and in particular to the civil service. And by democracy we mean no more than the existence of an open polity that is responsive and accountable to the general citizenry. The question we shall attempt to answer is: to what extent can the bureaucracy contribute or be made to contribute to the establishment and institutionalization of such a system in Africa?

THE AFRICAN CONDITION

African societies have gone through major socio-political transformations in the last one hundred years or so. The variations in socio-political cultures and the attendant structures that obtained during the pre-colonial period were destroyed or reshaped by colonial penetration. So were semblances of democratic structures and practices. Indeed, this was the situation regardless of the form of administration the colonial authorities chose to apply. Whether it was direct or indirect administration, the substance of administration was essentially the same.[1] Colonialism had created a new centre that every "governing" institution in society had to relate to and obey faithfully.

The establishment of the colonial administration marked the beginning of the introduction of "modern type" organizations into the African polities.[2] There may have been difficulties here and there regarding the introduction of Western type (i.e. Weberian) bureaucratic principles in the formative years, but by the late 30s in many parts of Africa, the process had established strong foundations. There is disagreement, however, about where in Africa the system operated with relative ease. In his *Bantu Bureaucracy* Lloyd Fallers argues that the societies with hierarchical, centralized political systems incorporate the Western-type civil service structures with less strain and instability than do societies having other types of political systems — e.g., segmentary ones.[3] He comes to this conclusion after observing what he refers to as "the speed and smoothness with which westernization has proceeded in Busoga"[4] (then a centralized polity).

But reporting the findings of a conference held at the then Rhodes-Livingstone Institute (now the Institute of African Studies, University of Zambia) on the adaptation of indigenous African political systems to modern circumstances, Apthorpe states that "it is in the societies which are not hierarchically centralized that Western ideas of bureaucracy can be more speedily adopted".[5] In supporting this position, Apthorpe uses the authority of Fortes and Evans-Pritchard and contends:

> "If the division of African polities made in *African Political Systems* may be expressed as between (a) polities dominantly constituted by competitive relationships, founded on egalitarian principles and diffuse political authority and power, and (b) polities based on ascribed status, hierarchically ordered into a centralized system, then (i) except for the element of non-centralization, the configuration of the former rather than the latter class of polity resembles that of modern bureaucracy, and (ii) to judge from the case studies presented during the conference lack of centralization in an indigenous political structure appears to be less of an impediment to its reception of modern bureaucracy than lack of achieved status ideas and their correlate, an open form of social mobility."[6]

In his final observations he writes:

> "It remains to be discovered whether there is a difference in application of bureaucratic techniques by politically dominant western government in the two types of society."[7]

That was more than twenty-five years ago — in the dying days of the colonial administration.

It should be pointed out that at the time Apthorpe posed the question, there was already enough evidence to suggest that the difference in application, if any, had been minimal. As has been stated above, the application of direct (in decentralized polities) and indirect (in centralized ones) administration differed only in name and not in substance. This was also true of the modernization process as Apter's study of Buganda affirms. Apter found that in spite of its traditional and centralized political structure, the modernization of Buganda, a highly centralized kingdom, went faster than modernization in most parts of Uganda. In his words, "civil service chieftaincy and bureaucratic norms have bolstered the kingdom. The European presence was absorbed and rendered useful".[8]

Against that background the backwardness of Northern Nigeria, for example, cannot be explained in terms of its traditional political structure. Other explanations must be found as Apter did for the Ashanti in Ghana.[9] Therefore, it is suggested here that the bureaucratization of the African polity — in terms of its success and failures could not be directly attributed to the nature of the traditional system. Much depended on the attitude of the colonial authorities *vis-a-vis* the rate at which western type bureaucracies should be introduced in given polities or the rate at which modernization (or westernization as it is sometimes called) should occur.

By the 1950s, colonialism in Africa had developed certain structures and orientations that were capable of being generalized about. Bureaucratic polities had emerged almost everywhere. The administration was the government. Within the framework set in the metropolitan capitals in the west, colonial administrators operated locally with a lot of autonomy and initiative. A similar situation characterized the relationship between the capital of a colonial state and its field agencies.

The bureaucracy that emerged was neither wholly modern nor traditional. It was a carrier of both values. It was "prismatic" in Riggsian terminology.[10] Indeed, its structure and orientations reflected both the modern and the traditional social configuration. According to Dube, it existed in the twilight zone of cultures, partly traditional and partly modern. It could and did in fact choose from the elements of both.[11] He proceeds to identify the basic characteristic and orientation of the bureaucracy in the colonial territories on the eve of independence:

1. It constituted a special sub-cultural segment — the high prestige strata of the society. It had class bias and tended to have a stratification of its own.
2. Bureaucratic positions carried vast powers . . . . the powers gave the functionary prestige, prerequisites and privileges.
3. Within the framework of the overall policy laid down by the imperial power, in day-to-day administration, the bureaucratic machine enjoyed considerable freedom from interference.
4. Its main preoccupation was the maintenance of law and order.
5. It was carefully trained in formal administrative procedures and routines.
6. It resented and resisted innovation.
7. Its attitude to the nationalist forces within was most ambivalent.

A new bureaucratic culture had thus emerged.

If **Dube** is right (and there is no evidence to the contrary) then we must arrive at the uneasy conclusion that colonial bureaucracy was a social monolith, acting mainly on its own impulses, free from any form of control. This relative strength of bureaucracy over the other institutions in the society meant that colonial bureaucracy tended to arrogate unto itself all political functions, always acting to suppress organizations whose activities were manifestly political. The colonial bureaucracy was a "political organization" without a legitimate constituency. It was both unrepresentative and unresponsive — the two hallmarks of undemocratic social systems. It lacked respect for competitive politics, which in many colonial states were never allowed to operate until on the eve of independence. That in itself created problems.

The problems had to do with the poor relationship between transitional bureaucracy and the burgeoning African political leadership. The bureaucrats related to the African politicians like officials that had to be recognized and respected. This attitude was to survive in the period after independence.

What we witness here then is a situation in colonial Africa where the bureaucracy acted politically but pretended to be apolitical. Colonialism promoted the growth and development of the civil bureaucracy at the expense of competitive politics. Thus in Africa, the bureaucracy developed before competitive politics through which it could be controlled. This, we are told by administrative historians, was not the case in the democratic industrialized countries of the West.[12] Nor was it the case in the United States as revealed in the four-volume administrative history of the United States.[13] In both cases "the pluralist political system developed first, and the bureaucratic system arose in response to it". Politics came before administration.[14] Therefore, in the Western democracies, bureaucracies emerged in response to and to serve the demands of the various "political" constituencies.

The underdevelopment of politics in the colonial state was later to have a lasting effect on the nature of the relationship between the civil bureaucracy and the political leadership in Africa. The basic characteristic and orientation of the colonial bureaucracy were inherited at independence by the bureaucracies of the new states. In fact in the first decade of independence, the key actors in the bureaucracy were those men and women who had been crash-trained on the eve of independence by the departing colonial authorities. They had been the instruments of the colonial authority in suppressing competitive politics. Now they were being required to operate within a nascent competitive political system. It was difficult to fit in the "unfit situation". The civil servants had been used to serving a regime not the public as such. And yet the new political order increasingly called for more service to the people. How did the civil service respond?

As would be expected, they continued to serve the master i.e. the man in authority at the centre. They did not pay any regard to the relationship between *them* and the governed. The business was to govern regardless of how the game was played. What mattered was the correct reading of the rapidly unfolding political arena. In many countries the centre was soon captured by a single, often dominant ethnic group or a combination thereof. At once the bureaucracy was transformed accordingly, especially at strategic points to give meaning and service to the group's interest. In the post-colonial state, therefore, the bureaucracy continued to subscribe to the unequal treatment of peoples within the state as much as had been the case during the colonial period.

At this point, a number of salient points should be emphasized. There are fundamental structural problems which limit the possibility of either establishing a democratic administration or an administration that could be used as an agent for propagating democratic principles and practices in Africa. These problems have roots in Africa's colonial past and they include:

1. The problems of the "new culture" raised by Dube above.
2. Problems of underdevelopment and dependence.
3. The absence of a "democratic" ethos in the body politics of many nations in Africa.

AN ENEMY OR FRIEND OF DEMOCRACY

The key question here is whether we can discuss the role of the bureaucracy in the establishment of a democratic society without at the same time addressing certain critical factors which influence the nature of the relationship between the bureaucracy and the society.

One such factor is the presence or absence of a dominant political culture, i.e. the aggregate of cognitive orientations that have direct bearing on the political behaviour of a people.[15] The state in Africa has been described as a "soft state"[16] precisely because it lacks such aggregation. There are several, often parochial, power centres that tend to pull away from the centre in terms of "interest aggregation". Thus, cultural pluralism instead of enriching the political system, tends to perpetuate solidarities that negate the cultivation of a common cultural centre.

Zolberg had this state of affairs in mind when he decried the tendency toward power centralization in Africa. The state, he said, centralizes power for fear of disintegration.[17] That was about two decades ago. The situation has not changed. If anything, the centralization of power has gathered momentum with the decline of competitive politics since the mid-60s. The situation has affected the bureaucracy directly and fundamentally.

As "loyal" servants of the regime in power, the bureaucracy in the post colonial state has continued to play manifestly political roles. The situation is neatly summed up by Eisenstadt:

> "There is high involvement in politics by the new bureaucrats . . . their as effective executive or a component thereof. . . the bureaucracy has emerged as one of the principal instruments of political regulation — one of the main channels of political struggle in which and through which different interests are regulated and "aggregated". . . They are also major instruments of social change and of political socialization in their respective countries."[18]

If the governments in most African countries have been repressive as many observers tend to believe, the bureaucracy has been a major partner, if not the sole actor, in the game. This writer knows of no country in Africa where central control of the villages is not exercised through the bureaucratic controls, whether civil or military or a combination of both. In this regard, it may for example, be stated that even in a country like Tanzania, what has for a long time been regarded by observers as political control is more bureaucratic (meaning it is exercised through public servants) than was first believed.

The decline of competitive politics, it has been observed, has resulted in the emergence of governing coalitions that tolerate no political dissent; yet dissent is a major ingredient of democracy. It was Peter Blau and Marshall Meyer who once observed that the perpetuation of democratic processes depends on permanent factions   that is, "opposition parties" within the organization. Opposition parties, they said, create the organizational conditions necessary for a democratic process to prevail. Bureaucratization of life, they said, concentrates power in the hands of a few men and curtails the freedom of individuals that is essential to democracy.[19] What one observes in many African countries today is the virtual absence of the democratic practice. The role of the political police at once reminds one of how little freedom one has to advance views contrary to those associated with the regime in power.

There is then the problem of underdevelopment and dependence. The culture of poverty creates a pattern of interaction between the governors and the governed that limits the freedom of action of the governed. A dependent person is never free in his relation with the patron. He survives at the mercy of the patron. Poverty in Africa is therefore a factor which militates against the establishment of an open society in which the governed enjoy the freedom to question the manner in which they are being governed.

Because of the high degree of dependence on government beneficience by the citizenry, it has become possible for the government through its bureaucracy to penetrate the life of the governed. Even organizations once started and controlled by the local people in many parts of Africa have since been taken over by the bureaucracy and are now being run on norms centrally determined. Thus, whereas in industrialized democracies of the West interest groups provided a fertile ground for the germination of democratic ideals by articulating the interests of the members, in Africa and the Third World generally, such interest groups as may exist operate on the whims of an administrative fiat.

In a widely quoted paper, Fred Riggs observed that in the Third World, the creation of interest groups "follows a bureaucratic initiative." They are not, he says, spontaneous products of citizen demands in response to felt needs. He says further:

> "The growth of state sponsored interest groups augments bureaucratic control without necessarily strengthening any centres of autonomous political power capable of bringing bureaucratic machines under political control."

All this simply leads to "big government" and therefore to less freedom for the citizenry.

The irony of development is that it creates more specialized organizations that give meaning to it. These organizations among the poor are unavoidably controlled by "outsiders", meaning the government bureaucracy. It means less input in decision-making by the clientele. Therefore, accelerated economic and social development contributes, again in the words of Riggs, to bureaucratic power, and lays the foundation for totalitarianism, weakening the prospects for democratic controls over the government.[20] What prospects then are there to establish democratic structures in Africa in the face of development crises that are being experienced presently?

But even where old organizations already exist, poverty has driven them into the hands of the central bureaucracy. The experience of local government authorities in Africa is a case in point.

In most African countries, these institutions were established in the early phase of colonialism. By the mid-twenties they were in existence in many parts of the colonial empire. Relatively speaking, local governments during the colonial period had some meaning in the life of the people. However, with independence, they began to decline so steadily that by the end of the first decade in many countries their problems had reached crisis proportions. As would be expected, the central government had to intervene by removing essential services from them as well as the power to make decisions regarding their provision. At the same time, central control over local authorities was increased as the latter could not survive without subventions from the centre. In the process, the people lost their say in the governance of their local communities as the central bureaucracy assumed the task of controlling the behaviour of local political institutions.

Indeed, the culture of poverty if examined at the global level means that the African states cannot be *free* to decide their own destinies. There is a limit to the degree to which the countries that are economically dependent can challenge the rich ones. The best example is Tanzania's principled stubbonness in dealing with the IMF and the World Bank. The fact that Tanzania finally yielded to IMF's traditional prescriptions (i.e. devaluation, cutting down on subsidies, reducing government expenditure etc.), shows how difficult it is for poor countries to be independent. The irony then is that the culture of poverty does not only limit the freedom of action at the local and national levels but also at the international level.

Poverty and democracy in the contemporary world are therefore strange bed-fellows. A hungry stomach has an angry mind that has no time for popular participation in decision-making. The concern of a hungry stomach is not how decisions are made but whether the decisions made will put something in it. How they are made is not the principal concern. If the bureaucracy is the provider, the hungry stomach will do nothing that will antagonize the decision-making situation. There will be loss of the "voice" in order to gain access to the essential need — food.

At this point we can answer the question that was posed at the beginning of this paper: whether bureaucracy (i.e. the civil service) is an enemy or a friend of democracy? To do so, we must return to the examination of the basic characteristics of the bureaucracy raised by Dube above. These were, by and large, anti-democratic. The class bias of the bureaucracy meant it was a closed system, to be penetrated only by members of the privileged group (however defined). Possession of vast power often leads to abuse of it. Too much freedom from interference turns the bureaucracy into a "governor" rather than a tool in the service of the people — the "sovereign people". Its preoccupation with the maintenance of law and order suggests authoritarianism and anti-democratic tendencies; its orientation to routines makes it unresponsive to popular demands; its resentment of innovation implies an inability to change with the times; its self-image as a government is a (false) construct that can only destroy democratic practices.

From the foregoing, one can conclude that bureaucracy in Africa cannot be an instrument for the propagation of democratic practices without itself undergoing fundamental structural and behavioural changes. To act as an agent for the creation of an open and participatory system, the bureaucracy must itself be an open social entity. It must be democratized if it has to be a democratizing instrument. The question is: can this be done?

The need to open up the bureaucracy as a process of democratization was first recognized by M. Weber. Writing about bureaucracy and democracy he stated:

"The political concept of democracy deduced from the 'equal rights' of the governed, includes these postulates:

(1) prevention of development of a classed status group of officials in the interest of universal accessability of office and

(2) minimization of the authority of officialdom in the interest of expanding the sphere of influence of public opinion as far as practicable."[21]

He proceeds to suggest that the most decisive thing is the *levelling of the governed* to the ruling and bureaucratically articulated group, which in its turn may occupy a quite autocratic position, both in fact and in form.[22]

Weber's "universal accessability of office" suggests an open recruitment system according to which recruitment is based on the merit principle. Since merit as used here knows no class or caste barrier, it is seen as the most rational way of providing for equality of opportunity. If Weber were living in Africa today, he would be greatly disappointed at the frustration to which the merit principle has been subjected. The persistence of socio-cultural groups around which interests are aggregated suggests ascription, hence the cry about tribalism, ethnicity, clanism and nepotism that we hear and read so much about in the popular press in Africa. The problem exists everywhere. It is the degree that is different. How to remove them is the problem, since such practices are merely manifestations of under-development and poverty. In situations of abundance, there would be no need for preferential appropriation of resources. Indeed, as Victor Thomson points out, administrative self indulgence inevitably leads to the conflict between administrative interest and public goals.[23]

An alternative approach to the quest for openness in the bureaucracy is to introduce a quota system in the recruitment process so that bureaucracy becomes a "microcosmic reproduction of total society". The supporters of this view suggest that "because of its size, government service can be a good index of the degree to which a society is open to talent rather than a vehicle of restricted group power".[24] But there are problems here. A quota system in recruitment smacks of patronage which is inherently ascriptive. It runs contrary to the ideals of bureaucracy as Weber outlined them in his *ideal type*. Indeed, if bureaucracy exists to serve the public interest (in principle) it must be seen to be doing so *efficiently* and effectively. Only the merit principle guarantees that. The fear about the merit principle is that in some societies it favours the relatively developed groups. The fear would not be however where people of a given polity are committed and are loyal to a common centre. They would in that situation serve the system well regardless of where they were posted to serve the society. The reality however is that the "dual" nature of the society remains a negative influence, acting against the creation of such a centre.

Weber's second question deals with how to control the controllers. How do we minimize the authority of the officials? What role can public opinion play? How can the citizens control the behaviour of the bureaucracy?

The answers to these questions touch on the nature of the political system — whether "open" or closed. In Western democracies public opinion expressed openly in a free press is a major device for controlling the behaviour of public officials. But a free press exists only in a democracy which most African states are not.

Citizens as such also have little or no mechanism through which they can control and stop the arbitrary actions of public officials. In Western bureaucracies, the mechanisms for such control exist. In the Scandinavian countries, notably Sweden, the institution of an ombudsman enables the citizens to lodge complaints against the arbitrary actions of government officials. In France and Germany, administrative courts exist in addition to other devices.

In Africa the attitude has been that the legality of administrative actions should be challenged in the common law courts. Efforts to establish special institutions for such controls have often been resisted on the grounds that they would lead to witch-hunting. That was the position of the Kenya Government in responding to the recommendation of the Ndegwa Commission Report (1971) calling for the establishment of the institution of an ombudsman in Kenya.[25] Similar reactions have been reported in other African countries. The bureaucracy in many parts of Africa, therefore, still enjoys a lot of freedom of action in its relationship with the citizenry. In many respects the said freedom often infringes the freedom of the people.

It may be affirmed here that far from being a friend of democracy, the bureaucracy in Africa has been and still is a carrier of anti-democratic practices. These include the preferential treatment of clients on ascriptive criteria, self indulgence, which has tended to lead to conflict of interest and to the subordination of public interest to those of its own, lingering myth about its self importance which has made it less and less responsive to public opinion, its insensitivity to the problems of inequality in society and finally its "deadened insensitivity" to what the public interest is all about. It is not alone here, for it would not continue to be what it is in the absence of the support that it enjoys at the higher reaches of the political system.

CONCLUSION

We can only arrive at tentative conclusions here. Firm conclusions require a wealth of primary data which we have not been able to present. Nevertheless, the available evidence so far suggests that it is difficult in a poor agrarian society to expect the bureaucracy to be an agent for the propagation of democratic practices. This cannot be so for a number of reasons which we have discussed.

The culture of poverty extends to the political arena, thereby making people associate political office-holding with wealth. There is therefore a tendency to hang onto power even where the democratic practices would dictate otherwise. This happens through a system of political control which ensures continuation in power. Because the bureaucracy is a tool of the regime, it becomes the facilitator of such undemocratic practices. The politico-economic environment in which the bureaucracy operates in Africa, therefore, renders it impotent as a facilitator of democratic behaviour. This is what we called broadly the "African condition" (using Ali Mazrui's terminology in his Wreith lectures on BBC in a somewhat different context).

There is also the problem of the bureaucracy's self image. By its own constitution it is hierarchical and monocratic, and therefore undemocratic. The quest for monolithic efficiency which is its *modus operandi* is a contradiction of dissent, the hallmark of democracy.

Indeed, the whole idea of democracy does not make sense in a situation where a peoples' major preoccupation is survival. One would agree with those who have argued before that in contemporary society, it is virtually impossible to establish democratic practices in a polity which is technologically underdeveloped. Industrialization and the attendant diversification of the economy that accompanies it is, therefore, a basic prerequisite for the establishment of democratic practices in the contemporary world. In the circumstances of Africa it is unfair to expect of the bureaucracy that it can be a "friend" of democracy.

REFERENCES

1. Kiwanuka, Semakula has written extensively on this point. See for instance his — *From Colonialism to Independence*. East African Literature Bureau, Nairobi, 1973.
2. See Apthorpe, Raymond 'The Introduction of Bureaucracy into African Polities' in Nimrod Raphaeli (ed) Readings in *Comparative Public Administration*. Allyn and Bacon. Inc. Boston, 1967, pp. 269-282.
3. Fallers, Lloyd A. *Bantu Bureaucracy*. The University of Chicago Press (1965 edition) p. 242.
4. *Ibid.*
5. Apthorpe Raymond, "The Introduction of Bureaucracy in African Polities" op. cit. p. 277.
6. *Ibid.* p. 279.
7. Loc. cit.
8. Apter, David. "The Role of Traditionalism in the Political Modernization of Ghana and Uganda" in Gable, Richard W., and Finkle, Jason L, (eds) *Political Development and Social Change*. John Wiley & Sons, Inc. New York 1966 pp. 65-81, p. 79.

9. *Ibid.*

10. Riggs, Fred, *Administration in Developing Countries.* Houghton Mifflin Company, Boston, 1964.

11. Dube, D.C., 'Bureaucracy and Nation Building in Transitional Societies' in *International Social Science Journal* Vol. 16, No. 2 (1964) pp. 229-236.

12. See e.g. Chapman, Brian, *The Profession of Government* George Allen and Unwin, London, 1959; Barker, E., *The Development of the Public Services in Western Europe* 1660-1930 Oxford, 1930.

13. White Leonard: *The Federalists: A study in Administrative History: 1789-1801* New York, The Free Press 1965; *The Jaffersonians: A study in Administrative History: 1801-1829* New York, McMillan 1951; *The Jacksonians: A study in Administrative History: 1829-1861* New York, The Free Press 1954; *The Republican Era: A study in Administrative History: 1869-1901* New York, McMillan 1958.

14. Thomson, Victor, 'Bureaucracy in a Democratic Society' in Rascoe C. Martin (ed) *Public Administration and Democracy.* Syracuse University Press New York 1965, pp. 205-226, p. 208

15. A crude reformulation of S. Verba & G. Almond, *The Civic Culture.* Little Brown and Company, Boston 1965, especially pp 12-14.

16. Hyden, Goran, *Beyond Ujamaa in Tanzania* Londin, Heinemann 1980 and *No Shortcuts to Progress:* African Development Management in Perspective Berkeley, University of California Press 1983.

17. Zolberg, A., *Creating Political Order: The Party States of West Africe* Chicago, McMillan, 1966.

18. Eisenstadt, S.N., "Problems of Emerging Bureaucracies in Developing Areas and New States' in N. Rahaeli *Readings in Comparative Public Administration* op. cit., pp. 220-232, see especially p. 226.

19. Blau, Peter and Meyer, Marshall, W., *Bureaucracy in Modern Society* (2nd Edition) Random House, New York.

20. Riggs, Fred, "Bureaucrats and Political Development: A Paradoxical View in Joseph Lapalombara (ed) *Bureaucracy and Political Development.* Princeton: Princeton University Press, 1963, pp. 120-167.

21. H.H. Gerth and C. Wright Mills. *From Max Weber: Essay in Sociology.* Oxford University Press, New York, 1958, p. 226.

22. *Ibid.*

23. Thomson, Victor, "Bureaucracy in a Democratic Society" op. cit.

24. See, e.g. Krislov, S., *Representative Bureaucracy.* Prentice Hall, Inc., Englewood Cliffs, New Jersey p. 81.

25. Republic of Kenya, *Sessional Paper* No. 5 of 1974.

CHAPTER VII

WOMEN, DEMOCRACY AND DEVELOPMENT IN AFRICA

Maria Nzomo

INTRODUCTION

Central to any conception of democracy are the principles of freedom, equality and social justice. However, democracy, both as a concept and as a social, economic and political system, has, throughout history, been variously defined and interpreted both by theorists and practitioners. Clearly, democracy is one of the most overused and often misused terms.

Historically, as well as in the contemporary era, it has been used to justify revolutions, counter revolutions, as well as a whole array of socio-economic and political organisations of society. The French, American, Russian and Chinese revolutions, for example, were all executed and justified in the name of democracy. In 1917 U.S. President Wilson took his country into the First World War, with the imperative of making "the world safe for democracy".

It was in the ancient Greek city-states that the term "democracy" was first conceptualized, from the Greek word, *demos,* meaning, *people.* These ancient city-states, however, were strange examples of democracy as their version of it only benefited those who had inherited full citizenship, constituting only about 10% of the total population of a city-state. The rest of the people, who included women, children, resident aliens and slaves, were excluded from Greek citizenship. This despite the fact that it was these non-citizen groups who produced all the city wealth, while the citizen "class" simply engaged in leisurely and political activities.

The Greek conception of democracy and their practice of it then, only makes sense if viewed within the context of the slave type of political economy that then characterized those ancient societies. In that regard, the hierarchical division of labour and socio-political organization that existed was deemed to be just (and hence democratic), in as far as each person was seen to be performing the task(s) one was naturally fitted to do. Similarly, equality in this context was interpreted to mean equality for those who were equal, rather than equality for all.[1]

While acknowledging that the primitive structure of Greek democracy has over time been replaced by more "progressive" and "modern" versions of democracy, one is still struck by the gap between theory and praxis, even among the so called "liberal" (Western) democracies. Indeed, a close look at the historical development of societies clearly indicates that all class societies, dating back to those ancient slave societies, have in one way or other fallen short in their practice of democracy. The class nature of these societies dictates that whatever the democratic arrangements existing at any one time, they serve, first and foremost, the interests of the economically dominant class, which has always been a minority. This defeats the majoritarian principle of democracy. Thus, just as under Greek slave society democracy served the interests of the ruling oligarchy, in modern capitalist societies, democracy is really a bourgeois democracy, serving the interests of the owners of the means of production, the bourgeoisie. Thus, all the rhetoric about constitutional guarantees of freedom for all and equality and social justice before the law becomes highly questionable in the face of what one observes in all capitalist societies today, namely, gross inequalities between the wealthy few and the poor majority, sexual and racial discrimination and unfair division of labour.

The main proposition in this chapter, then, is that democracy in a class society is an ideological weapon that serves the interests of the dominant class; that the dominated classes have, through history, been subjected to varying degrees of exploitation and oppression, depending on such intervening factors as the historical period, sex and cultural identity. It is argued that women, as an intra-class sexual category, have historically suffered and continue to experience the worst forms of oppression and exploitation, despite the central position they occupy in the production process of current and future wealth and labour.

In this connection, the development of democracy (or the lack of it) in post-independence Africa, given its Western capitalist origins, has not manifested itself in a significantly different manner from that of contemporary Western societies. If anything, due to the special problems arising out of Africa's colonization and incorporation into the international capitalist system, even the "standard" of democracy attained in the Western capitalist countries have yet to be realized in Africa.

In line with the above propositions, we examine in this chapter, (i) the historical origins of gender inequalities and consequent loss of freedom and social justice for women, (ii) the forms and manifestations of women's exploitation and oppression in Africa, with a view to demonstrating that, like many other contemporary societies elsewhere in the world, Africa is far from achieving genuine democracy on the continent, and, finally, (iii) some possible strategies for eliminating the existing structures that perpetuate inequalities and injustices.

ORIGINS AND NATURE OF CONTEMPORARY STATUS AND ROLE OF WOMEN

In *The Origins of the Family, Private Property and the State,* Friedrich Engels[2] argued that the monogamous family developed out of an older matrilineal form of family relationship as the economic wealth of males within the society increased. By the time of the Roman Empire, the monogamous marriage relationship based on the domestic slavery of women was fully developed. The woman was classified among the private property of the male head of the household and was fully subject to his demands. Her position as property included the condition that she was the sole sexual property of the male. Engels saw this right of sole sexual access as developing out of the desire by the man to guarantee that his wealth be inherited by his true children. If the woman remained chaste until marriage and faithful thereafter, the certainty of such lines of inheritance was guaranteed.

Engels' thesis then views the historical process by which women became subordinated to men as one characterized by the emergence of the monogamous family structure and the development of a class society. In this connection, it was the emergent class structure that shaped the nature and pattern of evolution of the family, which was to become the central arena for women's oppression and exploitation as women, regardless of their class position. In turn, the emergence of a class society was itself triggered by the evolutionary development in technological capability of the existing communal societies, who could now produce more than the groups needed for consumption. At this stage the surplus goods produced acquired an exchange value, and henceforth could be exchanged for other commodities produced by neighbouring communities. More significantly, since (within the gender based division of labour in the household) men were directly responsible for making the tools — productive forces which were used to produce the goods for exchange, it was they who became the owners of the means of production.

Thus began the era of the institutionalization of private property and the establishment of the patriarchal family system. In other words, those who controlled the means of production used their newly acquired power to also gain control over reproduction. From then on, the woman became, for all practical purposes, part and parcel of private property, valued only for her ability to produce and sustain current and future labour and heirs, to whom control over property was to be passed.

Broadly speaking then, the historical origins of contemporary inequalities between the sexes and all forms of exploitation and oppression of women in society, can be traced to the beginning of the class society and the institutionalization and privatization of property and family relations.

Thus, it is proposed here that the view which claims that men are by nature superior to women is not only fallacious but ahistorical, and only serves to justify the existing gender, racial, class and other types of inequalities and injustices that characterize most of the contemporary world, all which are neither inherent nor natural. They are the product of the same history that generated the class structure of societies. It is within this historical framework, that the nature of oppression and exploitation of women should be examined and analyzed.

THE NATURE OF WOMEN'S OPPRESSION AND EXPLOITATION

Beginning with the slave society, one finds that the economic basis of slavery gave rise to a social superstructure which defended private property and exploitation of all women, both slaves and non-slaves. In other words, despite the fact that the whole society was divided into two distinct classes: masters and slaves, all women, regardless of their class, suffered some kind of exploitation.

First the slave woman suffered the exploitation all slaves suffered. In addition, in her domestic environment, she had already been pushed to a second position behind her husband, in accordance with the patriarchal family set up. Furthermore, under the new division of labour arrangements, the domestic labour of women had ceased to have the importance it held in communal society. It was increasingly becoming relegated to a position of invisible, unproductive labour, as it was oriented toward direct consumption, rather than production. Even the slave men who did not own the means of production or any meaningful property, regarded slave women as their property. In this context, the slave women had often to endure exploitation and oppression in the form of sexual harassment from both the masters and her fellow slavemen. Similarly, while the woman in the slave-owning class suffered comparatively less exploitation than her slave counterpart, she however was also subordinate to her husband, as she also did not own any property. Indeed she was viewed more as a mother to heirs than another human being.

The situation hardly changed in the feudal era which superseded the slave economy. Characterized as it was by lavish and conspicuous consumption among the lords and absolute exploitation of the serfs, the women in this society fared no better. For the serf woman was subjected to long hours of unpaid labour in addition to sexual exploitation by both her fellow serfs and the lords. The woman in the landlord class also continued to experience subordination to her husband, mainly by being treated as a reproduction machine and an item of luxury consumption, deprived of any role in *social production*.

Under capitalism, the exploitation and oppression of women, though less crude and overt, has in many ways been just as severe as that experienced by women living under previous modes of production.

However, compared to the feudal order, capitalism brought with it a technological and scientific revolution which has to some extent enabled women, particularly in Western capitalist countries, to achieve and to exercise fairly effectively such rights as the right to vote and run for public office, the right to own and inherit property, the right to divorce and many others. Modern technology has also, to some extent, simplified the burden and drudgery of domestic tasks for women by making available (to those who can afford), labour and time-saving domestic devices and gadgets (laundry and dish-washing machines, vacuum cleaners, microwave ovens, and so on). In addition, the establishment of such social services as day care centres has reduced the burden of childcare. Capitalism can also be viewed as being more "liberal" than previous modes of production in that it gives "freedom" to the working class (both men and women) to sell or to refuse to sell its labour on the capitalist labour market.

However, a critical look at women's position under capitalism reveals these rights to be more illusory than real. For example, the labour- and time-saving technology such as the one cited above, is beyond the financial reach of the majority of women, particularly those in under-developed capitalist societies. Hence the problem of double workload, and the domestic exploitation of women, is not solved by the availability of these modern technological innovations. Indeed, under capitalism, women's role as domestic labourers increasingly becomes the site of their subordi-nation. In this regard, capitalism even more than previous modes of production finds it necessary to legitimize and institutionalize women's role as unpaid domestic labourers and their subordinate status to men. This legitimization and institutionalization of women's domestic role and status, is vital for capitalism because it is through family structures and domestic labour that workers are reproduced and it is these same structures that reproduce a reserve army of labour that is necessary to ensure a regular supply of cheap labour. In other words, under capitalism, the sexual division of labour assigns to women not only the task of reproducing future labour on a regular basis, but also many of the activities required to reproduce living labour on a day-to-day basis. Even when women are drawn into socialized production outside the home, they are not thereby released from their domestic "duties", nor are they necessarily given shorter working hours in recognition of these duties. Wage discrimination which involves unequal pay for equal work is also often hidden in the segregated labour market which relegates women to lower jobs.

Further still, due to the capitalist need to maintain the domestic role of women, education for females, both formal and informal, has deliberately been structured in a manner that makes its quality and quantity generally inappropriate and/or inadequate to gain access to powerful (in social, economic and political terms) positions in public enterprise. These points are examined in greater detail in the following analysis of the position of African women in their society[4] and its implications for the development of democracy on the continent.

AFRICAN WOMEN AND PROPERTY OWNERSHIP

In power terms, those who own and control the means of production can and do exercise control over those who do not. In a predominantly agrarian continent such as Africa, land is the basic means of production. Hence land ownership is used by those who possess it to dominate, exploit and undermine those who do not. In this respect, under contemporary land ownership patterns and customary laws operating in most African countries, women in general do not own land, although they may have usufructory rights over their husband's or father's land. This, in a sense, means that although rural women bear the heaviest burden of sustaining the rural (and urban) economy, they are, for all practical purposes, a highly exploited rural proletariat, stripped of even the right to a wage commensurate with the long and strenuous hours of domestic and agricultural work that they put in. This position of rural African women has grave negative implications for the development of democracy and Africa's political economy generally.

In the first place, despite the existing male-dominated patterns of landownership, the actual managing of the land is often left to the females as more and more men migrate to urban areas in search of other sources of wealth. Under these circumstances, the female heads of household are deprived of the necessary power and autonomy to plan and determine the production process on the land. They can only participate in the physical labour involved in agricultural production, often with meagre resources and limited skills.

Thus even if the female household heads wanted to borrow money to develop "their" land from a lending institution, they would be unlikely to succeed as most banks would demand collateral in the form of property. Similarly, due to the general assumption that households are headed by males, many rural households which are *de facto* female-headed are ignored and discriminated against when it comes to the provision of government extension services and credit facilities. This position was revealed by a study conducted in rural western Kenya.[5] It found that women farm managers experienced a persistent and pervasive bias in the delivery of government agricultural services to which they were entitled. This bias, it was observed, tended to increase in intensity as the value of the service required increased. In its concluding remarks the study warned that if the existing discriminatory patterns were not altered, the prospects for women's productivity and for increasing agricultural productivity in general appeared limited.[6]

Jennie Dey arrives at a similar conclusion in her study[7] of the lack of involvement of Gambian women in the rice development projects of that country:

> "Agricultural development projects usually channel inputs to male household heads on the assumption that they control the land, labour, crops and finances. Failure to involve women in rice development schemes has not only increased their economic dependence on men but is also a major reason for deficiencies and low national rice production."[8]

This particular system of land ownership not only has negative implications for rural economic development, but also enhances women's dependence and loss of autonomy. This trend is hardly conducive to the promotion of the freedom and equality of the genders. Pat Caplan in her study of the position of women in rural Tanzania concludes:

> "Because many policies are based on the assumption that productive and consumption units are households headed by males, ... there is the possibility that women will be redefined as dependants and thus lose much of their autonomy."[9]

Indeed, among some African communities, the position of women on land has been shown to be deteriorating. In a study conducted among the rural Luo community of Kenya, Achola Pala[10] observed with concern that under the post-colonial individualized land tenure system, women's usufructory rights on the land were diminishing, particularly for childless or widowed women with only daughters.

The fact that women do not own landed property also means that they cannot acquire, as easily as men, businesses and real estate forms of property. Again the major constraint is the collateral required. In Kenya, for example, both public and private lending agencies such as DFCK (Development Finance Corporation of Kenya) and ICDC (Industrial and Commercial Development Corporation), look into such factors as land title deeds, liquidity and social status of the applicant. Consequently, many women do not qualify as applicants in their own right, as they have no land title deeds and very few possess jobs that give them the kind of liquidity and social status required.

It would then seem from the above that women's continued inequality, dependence and powerlessness, derives in large part from their propertylessness. Despite their central role in the production and sustenance of Africa's rural economy, they are held hostage by a reactionary patriarchal land tenure system that obstructs them from participating and contributing more effectively in productive activities and their countries' economic development. If therefore it is accepted that women in Africa need to be full participants in Africa's development, then a democratic environment should be created whereby women's participation will not only be in the arena of physical labour but also in that of decision-making and planning.

This in turn means that the existing social, economic and political structures which discriminate against women must be changed in a manner that enhances the equal treatment of the sexes in terms of access to opportunities, services and control of the economy.

This change is necessary because development can only occur in an atmosphere where the majority of the people exercise freedom and control over their destinies. As President Nyerere once put it:

> "both political and economic power has to be held by the people . . . . if development is to be in the people's interests. People are the best creators and defenders of their human rights — including the right to eat. Freedom is essential to development and not just a product of it."[11]

"Freedom" in this context, must mean much more than freedom to work. It must include freedom for all to acquire and control property. Freedom can also be enhanced through formal education and productive employment. But in these two spheres as well, inequalities persist.

AFRICAN WOMEN: EDUCATION AND EMPLOYMENT

> "(Human beings are) often respected because of (their) achievement, ... Their occupancy of (certain) positions is justified on the basis of possession of relevant knowledge concerning the position and ability to execute what in their judgement rightfully constitutes the duties and responsibilities of the position. Any person, regardless of sex, may, therefore, aspire to any role and status and claim to have earned the right to aspire to it . . . . on the grounds that the requirements relevant to the role are appropriately met."[12]

What position they occupy and what role and status women are accorded in contemporary Africa is to a significant extent determined by the quantity and quality of formal education they have access to. Indeed, that women remain underprivileged and underrepresented in all important authoritative and decision-making positions in the African society is primarily a function of the institutionalized and structural bias in the educational system, which ensures that the amount and type of education made accessible to the majority of them is inappropriate and/or inadequate for participating or occupying hegemonic positions in public life.

Opposing this view, many African leaders and defenders of the male-dominated *status quo* have argued and even produced statistical evidence to demonstrate that female education has been very well taken care of in post-colonial Africa. As evidence, they show the high rates of quantitative increase in female education since the colonial era.[13] Nevertheless, much as one would want to applaud the African post-colonial leadership for making formal education available to more women than was the case previously, the fact remains that the educational structural bias favouring men against women has not changed significantly. Furthermore, African countries continue to reward and allocate societal roles in relation to the *type* and *level* of formal education achieved.

In this regard, it is important to note that it is only at the primary school level that some kind of "equality" has almost been achieved in post-colonial education on the continent. The proportion of primary school enrollment in most African countries is almost 50:50 for boys and girls.[14] But the proportion of illiterate female population continues to be much higher than that of men. Thus for example, while in 1980, 72.8% of African women were illiterate, only 48% of African men were.[15] Moreover, the percentage of female school enrollment gets smaller as one goes up the educational ladder, reflecting the high drop-out rate for girls, particularly at the primary school level. Some of the common factors contributing to this include:

(i)   The patrilineal family system, whereby, when confronted with limited opportunities or resources for provision of education, parents generally favour the education of male children. Linked with this is the traditional belief that women's proper place is in the domestic environment and therefore, much formal education is irrelevant for them.

(ii)   Poor performance due to the fact that after school, girls have to help in domestic chores and hence have no time to study and, lastly,

(iii)   Pregnancy due to lack of sexual education or miseducation.

Thus, in Kenya, for example, only 27% of those enrolled in the final two years of secondary education in 1979 were female.[16] Apart from parental and societal bias in favour of male education, a similar inclination by the government has been observed in regard to the quality and quantity of education provided, particularly at the secondary school level. Thus, by 1979, there were only 107 government aided girls' schools in Kenya, as opposed to 200 government aided boys' schools.[17] The implications of this educational structure which favours boys has meant that, as government aided schools tend to provide a higher quality education than unaided schools, the secondary school level of education received by most female students tends to be of much lower quality than that received by their male counterparts at the same level. Secondly, educational opportunities for women are much more limited than those of men and, thirdly, since the level and quality of performance in the final examinations determine entrance to higher education institutions, training programmes and job opportunities, women are clearly at a disadvantage in all these respects.

In addition, as our educational institutions still retain to a large extent the sexist curricula inherited from the colonialists, female education is still oriented towards domestic roles and low status professions such as nursing, typing, primary school teaching, and the like, while legal and medical professions, scientific research, management and technical professions are still patronized by men. In preparation for these professions, most boys' secondary schools emphasize science and mathematics,[18] while girls' schools continue to lay emphasis on home economics, cookery, needlework and religious studies. Furthermore, despite the fact that most African women end up as agricultural labourers, their school curricula do not include courses in agriculture. It is therefore hardly surprising that the few women who find their way to university are enrolled in the liberal arts subjects and only a handful venture into the more technical, science-oriented fields, such as engineering, medicine and architecture. Recent research has shown, for example, that while there are, on average, seven male students for every female student at a university in Africa, the average number of men for every woman studying engineering is seventy. In the natural sciences the number is ten and in medicine seven for every woman.[19]

Given the shrinking labour market for liberal arts degree holders in most African countries, if the current educational orientation continues, more women graduates than men are likely in future to be either unemployed or forced to accept lower paying jobs than their fellow male graduates. This is all the more likely given the fact that there is already an existing tendency to discriminate against women in employment. Indeed, it is not uncommon for employers to subject female employees to lower wages than their male counterparts doing the same type and amount of work, by, for example, clothing the same job with different names. Thus, for instance, a woman worker is termed a "clerk" and the male counterpart a "clerical officer" while, in actual fact, the two employees are both clerks.[20]

In any case, as indicated earlier, the majority of African women who gain access to formal education do not manage to go beyond primary school level, and, hence, their chances of getting any wage employment are extremely slim. Many are therefore forced to wind up in unpaid domestic labour as wives and mothers. Eliou has rightly observed that, "The road that leads (girls) to school is in fact only a detour which leads them back to the home."[21] And as Claire Robertson has aptly pointed out, the education received by the majority of African women is not only economically dysfunctional, but does no more than prepare them for subordination:

> "If the substantial progress towards universal primary education has become dysfunctional for men, it has become a disaster for women both in terms of reducing labour force participation and increasing subordination to men."[22]

Apart from the bias in the educational structure, parents in many African countries still play a critical role in molding their daughters' attitudes in a manner that leads them to aspire to domestic roles and low status professions. Furthermore, in some African countries, notably Zaire, it has been shown that formal education has not only reinforced the differential treatment of the sexes, but has also facilitated the imposition and the legitimization of Western sexism regarding women's roles. Thus while President Mobutu Sese Seko of Zaire claims to be a fervent believer in the improvement of the position of the Zairean woman, he at the same time insists that such changes in the female's position as should occur must be within the framework of male dominance, which women should accept without question. In his words:

> "This integration of the woman, we want it at all levels .... we wish to give to the Zairean mother the rights that her capacity of equal partner to man gives her.
> But, everything considered, it still remains of course that there will always be a boss in every household. And until it can be proved otherwise, the boss in the home is the wearer of trousers. Our female citizens should also understand this and accept it with a smile and revolutionary submission."[23]

In a nutshell then, one of the major drawbacks to the development of democracy in Africa is the inherited colonial educational system. Apart from its Western orientation, its structure favours men against women. To this extent, it fosters rather than reduces gender inequalities and subordination of women to men. In particular, the inadequacy and/or inappropriateness of the education accessible to the majority of African women hinders their ability to participate on an equal basis with men in public employment, thus reinforcing the already existing discrimination in job placements and remuneration. A similar scenario can be observed in the political sphere.

AFRICAN WOMEN: POLITICAL PARTICIPATION AND LEADERSHIP

"In a largely patriarchal world . . . brain and brawn are assumed to be bedfellows. Moral and physical courage are often conveniently confused. *The heroic in man is presumed to be a male quality. Great leadership is usually exemplified as a product of tough manly life.* Political leadership as we have in recent decades seen in Mrs. Gandhi, Mrs. Bandaranaike, Eugenia Charles and Mrs. Thatcher is a comparative novelty in modern society. A lot of excited and noisy surprise is made of the fact that the U.S. Vice-Presidential candidate for the Democratic Party (in 1984) . . . (was) a woman almost as if being female is incongruous with the position she (was) contending."[24] (Emphasis added).

As pointed out earlier, those who control the economic domain invariably exercise similar control over the political arena as well. Thus, political leadership and important decision-making in Africa, as elsewhere in the world, continue to be dominated by men. Despite the fact that female political participation at the level of voting is generally much higher than that of men, all available evidence points to extremely low female participation at the level of holding public and decision-making positions. A 1985 report on women's position in Africa[25] noted, for instance, that in Zambia there has never been women Cabinet Ministers, university professors or directors of big companies, while only four women sit on the twenty-five member central committee of the ruling party two of whom are restricted to women affairs.

A similar situation was found to prevail in most other African countries, including Botswana, Cameroon, Djibouti, Malawi, Rwanda, Somalia, Uganda and Kenya. In the latter case, women constituted less than 3% of the Parliament whose term ended in 1983. Out of 28 Cabinet Ministers, there was not a single woman and there has never been one since independence in 1963. Out of about 54 Assistant Ministers there was only one woman among 158 elected members. In addition, out of 26 Permanent Secretaries, there has never been a woman.[26] (a) Indeed, none of the many government corporations in Kenya had ever been headed by a woman prior to the 1986 presidential appointments.[26] (b)

Even in the few cases where a few token women have held important leadership positions in post-colonial Africa, their tenure in those positions has tended to be short-lived, depending, as it were, on the whims of the head of state or corporate body that facilitated the appointment. Thus, for instance, the appointment in 1975 of a woman Minister by the then Emperor Bokassa of the Central African Republic was nullified a year later. A similar fate befell Uganda's first woman Foreign Minister and roving ambassador who was appointed to the two posts by the then President of Uganda, Idi Amin, and was dismissed and publicly humiliated shortly thereafter, for alleged promiscuity in her personal life.

One of the arguments often put forward to explain the apparent low participation of women in decision-making positions, particularly in the political arena, is that women are generally apathetic and demonstrate little or no interest in this regard. It is thus argued that they have no one but themselves to blame if they are not adequately represented in public decision-making positions. It is further pointed out that their countries' constitutions guarantee them equality with men. To the extent, therefore, that women are under-represented in public positions under such circumstances of equality, it is argued that this is particularly due to the fact that few of them offer themselves as candidates and, when they do, their credentials may be of a lower quality than those of their male competitors.

Viewed entirely from a theoretical standpoint, the above argument does have some validity. But then we are dealing with practical situations where, for example, constitutional guarantees of equality of all before the law do not count for much. Similarly, public positions are not always occupied by the most qualified persons. This is particularly true of electoral political positions where an individual's economic clout, and hence ability to employ illegal means to manipulate the electoral process to one's advantage, may be the only "qualifications" the victorious candidates have over the losers. In this respect, most women candidates are likely to be at some disadvantage. Apart from the fact that the female socialization process does not generally prepare them for "cut-throat" politics, they are unlikely to be wealthy in their own right — given the property ownership and employment hindrances noted earlier. Consequently, they may be unable to display the same kind of aggressiveness and patronage as fellow male candidates. It is indeed partly due to financial and socialization constraints, rather than political apathy, that few women present themselves as candidates for electoral positions. Otherwise, if women were that apathetic, how would one account for the fact that many more of them than men turn out to vote?

Another factor that militates against women holding decision-making positions is the images and ideologies society has caricatured about women's roles. As it has been pointed out, each epoch in the history of a class society has based its justification of women's subordination and exploitation on certain superstructural social practices and beliefs. In this respect, the social attitude that regards women as being incapable of effective decision-making and as being the "weaker sex" (both physically and mentally) continues to persist despite the legal equality of the sexes. Indeed, this belief is widely shared by African leaders. A Kenyan minister, for example, in his closing remarks to an International Women's Year Seminar, found it quite appropriate to tell a female audience the following:

> "I am forced to believe that the woman is lazy in her mind. She is too lazy to think. You women think and believe that you are inferior to men. This is what it is all about. It is a psychological problem and 99.9% of women suffer from it."[27]

Thus, whereas a man may enter a political or any other public office without much scrutiny as to his physical and intellectual fitness, a woman would first and foremost have to prove to all concerned that she is the exceptional one among her female kind. Furthermore, she is likely to meet with resistance from her husband, family and friends, who may feel that the game of politics too "dirty" and hazardous for a woman. Again, this reflects on the general paternalistic association of women with physical weakness and a moral innocence — traits that quite clearly are not unique to any one gender.

Given the fact that potential female candidates for political office encounter so much resistance and disapproval from the male-dominated society, one would expect the existing women organizations to sponsor and provide full backing to women candidates. But this is not the case. Part of the problem here lies with the structure and goals of these organizations themselves. Kenya, for example, has over 16,000 registered women's groups.[28] All of them are constitutionally non-political bodies and hence cannot legally engage in politics or behave in a manner which could be deemed to be political. According to Jane Kiano, the ex-chairperson of one of the leading women's organizations in Kenya, Maendeleo ya Wanawake,

> "We at Maendeleo would like to actively support all the women candidates we feel deserve to go to parliament. But as Maendeleo, *we are non-political and cannot therefore be involved.* I can only support candidates as an individual and my lone vote cannot do much."[29] (Emphasis added)

Mrs. Kiano was therefore of the view that Kenyan women needed a political pressure group, which would not only educate them on their political rights and responsibilities, but also initiate lobbying for issues that affect women and which male politicians never take seriously. But the ineffectiveness of Maendeleo Ya Wanawake and other women organizations in voicing support for women's rights is not entirely due to their non-political nature. Another problem lies with the organization's leadership, which tends to be divided between, on the one hand, those who have adopted an accommodative relationship with the government and, on the other, those who appear to be dedicated to the struggle for the rights of women.

This division and its implication for the Kenyan women's liberation struggle was clearly revealed in an incident[30] that occurred in September 1984, following a Kenyan women leader's conference, held in August 1984, in preparation for the July 1985 International Conference to end the United Nations Women's Decade. At the end of the former conference, the women representatives presented a memorandum to the Kenyan government, listing a number of social, economic and political reforms that they felt should be effected to allow greater women participation in decision-making and improvement in their quality of life. The list included the following resolutions:

(i)   All unionizable women workers should join trade unions;
(ii) Women should be involved in decision-making processes;
(iii) Discriminatory practices against women in employment should be corrected.[31]

As it turned out, the Kenyan government was not amused by this list of demands. Indeed, through the Minister of Culture and Social Services, it issued a warning to Kenyan women, "to avoid making statements and demands that could create problems for them". It also reminded them that "it was not wise to continue talking about (their) rights as indeed all Kenyans have their rights but do not talk about them". Furthermore, according to the Minister, "women had little to complain about as they were adequately represented in various fields in the country".[32]

Apparently, the government's reaction to the women's resolution scared off a section of the women leadership, with the result that the latter completely diassociated itself from resolutions reached at the conference, arguing that they ridiculed and wrongly accused the Kenyan government of discrimination against women.[33]

Quite clearly, then, Kenyan women seem unable to stick together on issues that directly affect their basic human rights in their own society. It is indeed the conflict within the women's movement that is one of the major obstacles in their struggle for the equality of the sexes. One of the Kenyan women leaders summarized this problem as: "Failure by women to support one another is what denied them chances in decision-making bodies."[34]

Factionalism among women groups derives from the contradictions inherent in a class society. In this context, it has to be remembered that women are not in themselves a class or a monolithic group, as they belong to various social, economic and political backgrounds. There are, for example, vast differences in the aspirations and needs of the urban as opposed to the rural women. Indeed, for the illiterate rural women, the urbanized women leadership is as far removed from them as the national government itself. Given these differences among them, when women attempt to unite around issues that affect them as women, they become easy targets for manipulation and suppression by the dominant economic and political class, which quite understandably, is dedicated to the preservation of the *status quo*.

Another obstacle arises primarily from the high rates of illiteracy and miseducation among the majority of African women. Many years of societal indoctrination and psychological conditioning have led many African women to accept the inferior and subordinate status accorded them, thus inhibiting them from challenging the male-dominated *status quo*. Indeed, some of the African women are aware that they have the same rights and responsibilities as men in society, but they just do not have the courage and self-confidence to exercise these rights. It is this acquiescence, built sometimes on ignorance and sometimes on lack of assertiveness, that to a significant extent helps to perpetuate the paternalistic attitudes African men continue to have towards their fellow women citizens.

Women's exclusion from decision-making positions then is not only a function of the existing social and economic structures that discriminate against them but is also due to the prevailing political structures that manipulate and divide them by co-opting some and terrorizing the rest into silence or submission and which outrightly deny women the right to organize as a political pressure group. This denial is justified in the name of equality of all before the law, regardless of sex, thus making it unnecessary for women to struggle for an equality they already have.

The law, particularly constitutional law, is an aspect of the political superstructure that gives legitimizing force to the whole state machinery and consequently to many of the social practices that discriminate against women including marriage, divorce, property ownership, inheritance, education, employment and many others. Conventional law has also helped to reinforce certain customary beliefs and practices of African societies in regard to women. The belief, for example, that women are inferior to men is reinforced by a law that exists in many African countries and which lumps women together with minors, thereby implying that they are still something less than responsible adults.

In a nutshell then, the laws, in as far as they give legitimacy to the existing political and social practices that discriminate against women, cannot effectively guarantee or defend the rights of female citizens. As one scholar has pointed out: "The laws are based on a formalistic and mechanistic ideology of equality which is oppressive to women by making their functions private . . . . and their movements and solutions non-political."[35]

Thus, although in theory the safeguards of democracy are supposed to be embedded in law, to the extent that the legal system legitimizes inequalities and injustices in gender relationships, the law can hardly be said to be promoting democracy.

RECOMMENDATIONS AND CONCLUSIONS

Much as Africa is characterized by democratic rhetoric, one is hard put find democracy in operation here. Instead, one is faced with glaring inequalities, injustices and the absence of freedom. On all the three counts, women have experienced most intensely the effects of the absence of democracy. And yet, it is an indisputable fact that no meaningful development can occur as long as more than half of Africa's population continues to be denied the right to be full and equal participants in that process. The attainment of democracy in regard to the role and status of women in African society should therefore be treated as a necessary step and instrument in the struggle for national and continental development. It is imperative, in the interests of Africa's political and economic future, that women's contribution to the development process be fully recognized and rewarded and a conducive democratic environment be established to allow for greater female participation in public life. Towards this end, the following structural changes are suggested:

Firstly, since the institution of private property is the root cause of all types of exploitation and oppression in a class society, women's emancipation and restoration to their rightful place in society can only be fully realized under conditions where, at the very least, this institution is greatly reformed or, at best, abolished altogether. It is only then that women can become fully integrated in social production and realize their full potential in a democratic atmosphere. In this connection, one of the major changes that should be effected within the institution of private property is the abolition of the individual family as an economic unit. This process of change, which undoubtedly would be long and arduous, would culminate in freeing more than half of Africa's population (women) from the drudgery of privatized domestic work, thus making them economically independent and more effective participants in national development efforts. The vicious circle, whereby if a woman engages in public activities she cannot perform her household "duties" effectively and vice-versa, will have been removed. Furthermore, democracy, at least on this issue of domesticity, would also have been realized.

Here it is important to point out that, although what is being recommended here is a socialist transformation, it is also being acknowledged that a socialist revolution does not automatically create equality of the genders. Indeed, most of the countries that have undergone socialist revolutions such as the Soviet Union, China, Cuba and others have not yet succeeded in abolishing inequalities within their domestic structures. This in itself is a glaring indication of the incompleteness of these revolutions. In fact, Cuba's Fidel Castro is on record as having openly admitted that the Cuban socialist revolution is not yet complete since "in practice, women's full equality still does not exist", particularly within the domestic arena.[36] Nevertheless, socialist societies have made substantial progress towards the emancipation of women through the removal of class oppression generally as well as through legislation and the establishment of programmes aimed at achieving real equality of the genders, especially within the household, by the time the implementation of the socialist transformation is complete.

In addition to the struggle for the elimination of domestic tyranny, African women need to strive for the total abolition of such reactionary African customs and traditions as betrothal, abduction, dowry, early marriages and domestic male supremacy — all of which keep many African women in a state of subordination and exploitation. These customs and traditions would be replaced by a programme of reintegration of the affected women into public life and social production by uplifting their educational and professional positions, thereby assuring them of a full participation in their country's political and social life. Towards this end, a political environment would also have to be created in which women can freely form political pressure groups and other organizations that would unify their struggle across the class, racial and ethnic divisions that often keep them apart. These organizations would have to be strong and revolutionary enough to resist co-optation and sabotage by reactionary forces.

As the changes suggested here are enormous and difficult and may take a prolonged struggle to achieve fully, it would be necessary to have a committed, dedicated and persevering leadership. In this connection the major part of the struggle would have to be vanguarded by the women themselves. In preparation for this role, African women would need to engage in their own inward battle for psychological liberation from the servile and defeatist mentality that most of them have come to acquire and

127

assimilate. Thus they will need to acquire self-confidence by first recognizing that there is nothing inherently inferior (physically or mentally) about them. That they perform heavier tasks and for longer periods than men is enough demonstration of their great physical strength as well as endurance.

Furthermore, women's military prowess has been historically demonstrated in such countries as Vietnam, Cuba, Mozambique, Angola and elsewhere, where women have proved to be as efficient in handling machine guns and anti-aircraft weapons as their male comrades. It is historical examples such as these that should inspire self-confidence in women and replace a servile, defeatist and sometimes fatalistic attitude with assertiveness and aggressiveness, both of which are essential in the struggle for democracy and development. They would then be at the forefront, particularly in combating and exposing the falsity of the widespread belief that domestic work is only fit for women. Victory in this particular "battle" is important in that, for as long as domestic work and the care of the household is considered to be a private affair relegated to them, women cannot engage effectively in social production and public life, let alone pursue self improvement activities.

It would, however, be foolhardy and unrealistic to expect women to go it alone in this struggle. Indeed, all progressive men who are committed to the total emancipation and development of the African society, would have to join hands with women in the course of the liberation of the latter. This should be the case, since the liberation of women is necessary for the total emancipation of society to be achieved:

> "The problem of ultimately transforming world capitalist society is so vast, so enormous — that to consider it seriously, calls for the recognition of the need to combine the special drive for liberation of half of humanity, women as women, with the drive of women and men as workers and as members of the oppressed races and nations."[37]

It also needs to be recognized that, because women's oppression is so deeply embedded in the entire economic, political and social structures of a capitalist society, if they organize themselves around the problems they face, they can unify the diverse struggle for class, race and national liberation.

This interrelatedness between national and women's liberation has indeed been acknowledged by a few African leaders, notably the late President Machel of Mozambique, who, in one of his speeches, observed that:

> "The emancipation of women is not an act of charity, the result of humanitarian or compassionate attitude. The liberation of women is a fundamental necessity for the revolution, the guarantee of its continuity and precondition for its victory. The main objective of the revolution is to destroy the system of exploitation and build a new

society which releases the potentialities of human beings, reconciling them with labour and with nature. This is the context in which the question of women's emancipation arises. . . . If more than half the exploited and oppressed people consist of women, how can they be left on the fringe of the struggle?. . . If it is to be victorious, the revolution must eliminate the whole system of exploitation and oppression, liberating all the exploited and the oppressed. Therefore, if it must eliminate the exploitation and oppression of women, it is forced to liberate them."[38]

Thus, the women's struggle for domestic rights and freedoms is not antagonistic to men as such, since the major contradiction in class society is not between the two genders but between both of them and the exploitative system of private property and the domestic institution. Women's struggle for democracy and development should be waged against this system and its ideological and cultural mechanisms which maintain women in subordinate positions and condition them to accept subordination.

REFERENCES

1. See for example, Barker, Ernes (ed.) *The Politics of Aristotle,* London, Oxford University Press, 1972, p. 117.
2. Moscow, Foreign Languages Publishing House, 1891.
3. See for example, Safa, Helen, "Women Production and Reproduction in Industrial Capitalism", paper presented at the Institute for Development Studies (I.D.S.), University of Sussex, England, 1978; Deere, Carmen "Rural Women's Subsistence Production in the Capitalist Periphery", in *The Review of Radical Economics,* (Vol. 8, No. 1), pp. 9-17 and Beneria, Lourdes, "Women's Participation in Paid Production under Capitalism: The Spanish Experience", *Ibid.,* pp. 18-33.
4. The literature on the role and status of African women is increasing rapidly. The following are but a few examples:
Hafkin, Nancy and Bay, Edna, *Women in Africa: Studies in Social and Economic Change,* Stanford University Press, 1976; O'Barr, Jean F. (ed.) *Perspectives on Power: Women in Africa, Asia and Latin America,* Duke University, Center for International Studies, 1982; Boserup, Esther, *Women's Role in Economic Development,* New York, St. Martin's Press 1970, and her *Integration of Women in Development, Why, When, How?* (UN Development Programme, 1975); Nelson, Nici (ed.), *African Women in the Deve-*

lopment Process, London, Frank Cass, 1981; Obb, C. *African Women: Their Struggle for Economic Independence,* London, Zed Press, 1980 and Rogers, B. *The Domestication of Women: Discrimination in Developing Countries,* London, Travistock Publications, 1980.

5. Staudt, Kathleen, A. "Inequalities in the Delivery of Services to a Female Clientele: Some Implications for Policy", I.D.S., University of Nairobi, Discussion Paper (DP) No. 247, January 1977.

6. *Ibid.,* p. 21.

7. Dey, Jennie, "Gambian Women: Unequal Partners in Rice Development Projects?" in Nelson, N. (ed.) *African Women in the Development Process, op. cit.* p. 99.

8. *Ibid.,* p. 109.

9. Caplan, Pat, "Development Policies in Tanzania: Some Implications for Women", in Nelson, N. (ed.) *African Women in the Development Process.*

10. Pala Achola, O. "Women's Access to Land and their Role in Agriculture and the Farm: Experiences of the Jaluo of Kenya", I.D.S., University of Nairobi, DP No. 263, April 1978.

11. Nyerere, J.K. *On Rural Development: International Foundation for Development Alternatives,* Geneva, Dossier II, September 1979, pp. 8-9.

12. Miranda, Eveline, O.Y. "Educating Women for Development" in *Canadian Journal of International Education,* Vol. II, No. 1, 1982, p. 9.

13. See for example, Oyugi, W.O. *The Role of Women in the Political Process in Kenya.* Paper presented at a Conference on Women and Development in Africa, Nairobi, Kenya, September 1984, p. 8.

14. See for example, Robertson, Claire "Women's Education and Class Formation in Africa, 1950-1980" *(Ibid.);* Eshiwani, George, S., "Women's Access to Higher Education: A Study of Opportunities and Attainment in Science and Mathematics Education" *(Ibid.),* pp. 4-5 and Maitum, Mary I.D.I.E. "Women, The Law and Convention" *(Ibid.),* p. 10.

15. Robertson, Claire, *op. cit.,* p. 8.

16. Eshiwani, George, S. *op. cit.,* p. 8.

17. *Ibid.,* p. 8.

18. *Ibid.,* pp. 17-24.

19. *Ibid.,* p. 1.

20. Gutto, S.B.O. *The Status of Women in Kenya: A Study of Paternalism, Inequality and Underprivilege,* I.D.S. University of Nairobi, DP No. 235, April 1976, p. 64.

21. Robertson, C., *op. cit.,* p. 24.

22. *Ibid.,* p. 26.

23. Newbury, M.C., *Ebutumwa Bw'emiogo: The Tyranny of Cassava: A*

Woman's Tax Revolt in Eastern Zaire; paper presented at the Annual Meeting of the Canadian Association of African Studies. Universite Laval, Quebec, May 1983, p. 30.

24. *The Weekly Review,* (Nairobi) October 1984, p. 31.

25. Nabwire, S., "Discrimination Against Women", *The Express,* (Nairobi) Vol. 2, No. 1, 1985, p. 36.

26. (a) The first woman permanent secretary in Kenya, was appointed by President Moi, in June 1987. For further details, see *The Weekly Review,* June 5, 1987, pp. 7 and 12.

26. (b) On January 16th 1986, President Moi announced that he had decided that he would appoint women to head twenty parastatals previously headed by men whom he accused of embezzling public funds from those corporations. For details on this presidential decree and some of the appointments he has since effected, see, *Daily Nation,* January 17, 1986, p. 1 and p. 34, *The Weekly Review,* January 24, 1986, pp. 4-13 and *Daily Nation,* February 1, 1986, p. 1 and p. 24 and February 28, 1986, p. 1 and p. 36.

27. "Women, d'you believe that?" *Sunday News* (Dar es Salaam), May 25, 1975, p. 1.

28. This was the total number of women's groups registered by the Kenya Women's Bureau in 1985.

29. "Women in Power" *The Standard* (Nairobi) September 16, 1983, pp. 12-13.

30. This incident was reported in the *Daily Nation* (Nairobi) September, 18, 19 and 20, 1984 and *The Weekly Review,* October 5 1984, pp. 11-12

31. See, *Daily Nation,* September 20 1984, p. 21.

32. *Ibid.*

33. "Ogot Disowns Top Jobs for Women Campaign" *Daily Nation* September 18 1984, p. 4.

34. See, *Daily Nation,* September 19 1984, p. 3.

35. Schirmer, Jennifer, G. "Women and Social Policy: Lessons from Scandinavia", in Obarr, Jean F. (ed.) *Perspectives on Power,* p. 87.

36. Norma Peachcock, "Family, Class and Modes of Production: Notes on the Material Bases of Women's Oppression", in A. Imam *et al.,* (eds.), *Women and the Family,* Dakar, Codesria, 1985, pp. 44-45.

37. Leacock, Eleanor, "Women, Development and Anthropological Facts and Fictions" *Latin American Perspectives,* Issues 12 and 13, Vol. IV, Nos. 1 and 2, (Winter and Spring 1977), p. 8.

38. Isaacman, Allen and Barbara, "The Role of Women in the Liberation of Mozambique", *Ufahamu,* Vol. XII, Nos. 2 and 3, 1984, p. 174.

CHAPTER VIII

EXTERNAL RELATIONS OF THE AFRICAN DEMOCRATIC EXPERIENCE

Franz Ansprenger

INTRODUCTION

Linkages are nothing to be ashamed of. Africa and the outside world are linked together, in a mutual experience with Democracy. This experience is no violation of national dignity. Linkage means interdependence of Africa and Europe and will not disappear in our century, or during the next one. Concern is caused, and correctly so, only by the many facets of *asymmetric* interdependence in world politics and in the global economy: hence the Latin American theories of *"dependence"* — again linking Africa to still another outside continent. Colonialism is at the root of these asymmetries, and colonialism of the African kind is only one printout of the more general program: a modern world system has been established through capitalism, whose core or centre oscillates among European and Northern American nations — including Japan — since 1945.

The great leaders of the liberation struggle in colonial Africa were not ashamed of their intellectual contacts with Europe. *"Assimiler, non être assimilés"*, was Leopold Senghor's slogan as early as 1945. *"We may borrow useful ideologies from foreign ideologies, but we reject the wholesale importation of foreign ideologies into Africa,"* was one of the articles of "Our Creed" in the South African ANC Youth League Manifesto, issued in March 1944.

FACTS OF HISTORY

The fuel of those linkages in the more than 50 African countries cannot be reviewed here. Such a review would face methodological problems. We quote easily from political documents written by or in the name of African statesmen, most or all of whom were educated in formal school systems full of "wholesale imported" European ideas. So the linkages become evident. Democracy, on the other hand, has something to do with the people, all the people. What do we know, how can we learn something about the political perceptions, the articulation of interests, the sets of priorities of ordinary people in Africa? In how many countries are opinion polls being conducted? How many African newspapers publish political letters to the editor? Can we trust, as sources for political ideas of the people, certain novels written, again, by African intellectuals educated in Western-type schools? Without proper data, social science quickly degenerates into social imagination and romanticism.

Transfer of Constitutions during the Decolonization Process

This is a story well documented and known to everybody. Wherever independent statehood was achieved after a non-violent liberation struggle, the constitution resulted either from a sort of round-table-conference between the colonial government and "recognized" African leaders in British colonies, or the new African administrations copied on their own initiative the French constitution. Many writers have written about this "import of Westminster democracy", and how it did not work and why. A very similar debate is presently going on in Zimbabwe in spite of the fact that independence for that country was the result of a *violent* liberation struggle.

But there was a large element of deliberate choice by Africans, even in the transfer of the early days. Did the leaders of French colonies, for example, really just copy the French constitution? They definitely rejected a constitutional model quite familiar to those among them who had for years been elected to the National Assembly of the *Fourth* Republic. Nobody even thought of importing the *Regime d'Assemblee* into Africa; this would have meant concentrating state power in the shifting parliamentary majorities. But Africa did not simply copy the constitution of the *Fifth* Republic either. De Gaulle ruled France in a highly delicate balance between presidential power, the executive responsibility of a Prime Minister, and the residual powers of Parliament. French-speaking Africa consolidated presidential autocracies.

Or did the British really want to implant the Westminster model in Africa? Whereas Britain's constitution has never been codified, independence constitutions of countries like Ghana or Nigeria fill books. Britain has always refused to accommodate Scottish and Welsh nationalism (or tribalism), and the present-day economic dissatisfaction in the English Midlands, by introducing federal political structures. In Africa, the British did market federalism wherever they found a buyer. Nkrumah had to struggle hard to kill this scheme in Ghana.

Transfer of Ideologies after Independence

The most important set of political ideologies imported into Africa from overseas, during the 1960s and early 1970s, was *Socialism*. Rather, it came as a controversial bundle of very different kinds of Socialism. Not all the varieties arrived in Africa at the same moment, not all in all the countries of Africa.

Some writers draw a sharp distinction between a type of moderate "African" or Populist Socialism presumably derived from Western Europe's Social Democracy, and "Scientific" Socialism of Afro-Marxism or Afro-Communism or Marxism-Leninism derived from the Soviet Union's state ideology. It is necessary, however, to stress the continuity between all these concepts. Socialism of all persuasions became popular in Africa because it promised some form of economic independence, the lack of which was bitterly felt immediately after the hoisting of so many new flags. The particular brand of Socialism chosen by an African leader, depended more on his personal "state of mind", his decision how fast his people should "run", and on his loss of illusion about previous experiments rather than on a fundamental choice between Western democracy and the Soviet political system.

Certainly, Marxism-Leninism was not imported into Africa straight from Moscow. In Brazzaville, in Cotonou, in Luanda it bears the marking of the left bank of the River Seine — in the (apocryphal) words of Felix Houphouet-Boigny: "If I want communists in the Ivory Coast, I shall send my students to Paris; if I want anti-communists, I shall send them to Moscow..." More authentic quotations can be reproduced from present-day Soviet writers showing reluctance by African governments to commit themselves fully to "socialist" orientation. For them, too many ambiguities remain.[1]

We are not concerned here with Socialism (or Capitalism) as a path to economic development. We are interested in the political systems compatible with, or linked necessarily to, Socialism and Capitalism. In Africa, historical reality often goes against established European patterns of political thought. There are some "capitalist" African states — all the successful ones, it seems, where the government not only is planning the economy, but acts as the biggest, or the only indigenous capitalist investor and entrepreneur. We have at least one Socialist State (Ethiopia) of the "Scientific" brand, where it took many years after revolution, and some persuasion from abroad, before a "proletarian" single vanguard party emerged.

Evidence indicates that many African leaders and would-be leaders who opted for Socialism, and particularly for Leninism, did so, not so much because of the influence of economic textbooks, but out of admiration for the efficiency of government in Warsaw Pact countries. At their time, they probably admired the success of the Soviet experience more than Mr. Gorbachev seems to do today.

Transfer of Political Techniques

The political technique developed to a certain perfection in post-colonial Africa is that of the *coup d'etat*. Was it actually transferred from elsewhere (that should have been Latin America)? Or did African army officers invent it themselves? Compared to the bad performance of German army generals in July 1944 and of French colonels in Algiers from 1958 to 1961, we can hardly speak here of an African import from Europe. But the art of the *coup* has only peripheral importance for Africa's democratic experience.

Transfer of New Academic Ideas

Lenin's concept of "democratic" centralist rule by a single vanguard party is not really a modern idea: it dates from 1905. Since then, quite a number of new ideas have emerged in the West, some of them coined by academics. While Africa lived through the failure of "Westminster democracy", and subsequently got disappointed over doubtful achievements of single-party and military systems, while African liberation policies in South Africa were deadlocked, intellectual exchange between Europe and Africa continued. Another blueprint of democracy started to make its way from theoretical books of political scientists into (for the moment) programmatic speeches of (mainly South) African politicians: the blueprint of *consociational democracy*.

It is offered as a possible solution for the evil of African "tribalism"; minority groups would be protected against arbitrary political measures backed by a "majority tribe", beyond the individualistic protection of a Human Rights bill. The minorities would not only be permitted to deal with their "internal" affairs autonomously, but certain positions in government would be reserved for them constitutionally.

Indeed, this is a fascinating perspective for states still engaged in the difficult process of nation-building, for poor countries unwilling to waste human resources in "sterile" opposition politics and for people of a political culture favouring broad consensus over the "game" of majority decisions. But, on the other hand, it is pure illusion to run a political system completely on the basis of the rule observed by Guy Clutton-Brock and according to which ". . . the Elders sit under the big tree, and talk until they agree . . .". That was impossible already in 1963 when Julius Nyerere chose these words as the motto for his pamphlet introducing the single-party system. Such a system cannot work in the modern world.

It is wrong to tie up consociationalism too closely with the multi-ethnic character of nearly all new African nations. It makes funny reading for a European when eminent American political scientists, in an effort to recommend consociational democracy to Africans, present Austria as a multi-ethnic state.[2] True, the most famous European showcase of this kind of democracy, Switzerland, is composed of four language groups. But in Austria, the two "tribes" sharing power during the reconstruction period after 1945, were the Socialists and the Catholics-Conservatives. Power-sharing between them was a good idea because their civil war mentality after 1918 had ruined the prospects of the First Austrian Republic. Their common coalition government became outmoded, and was abolished as soon as an ordinary civic consensus "to play the (majority) game fairly" had been established. To day Austria lives happily with a competitive "football democracy" as Nyerere polemically called it in 1963.

The Netherlands, home of the standard-bearer of consociationalism,[3] are not really a multi-ethnic nation either. Political divisions there run mainly between Catholics and Protestants, and again between Conservatives and Socialists.

Consociational democracy may be recommended to iron out misunderstandings and entrenched confusions about the proper role of political parties, on the one hand, and interest groups on the other. Popular support for political parties must be flexible, unstable, if democracy is to survive. The floating vote is good and necessary. Interest groups are, and must be, more permanent. They must very often *share* responsibility ("power") in one and the same institution, as it is obvious in the case of work force and capital. Therefore, conflicts among interest groups must normally be solved by compromise. Competition among political parties must be solved, for a limited period of time, by a majority decision, and "winner takes all" is a perfectly fair rule of *that* game. The need for consensus and stability as a fundamental rationale of any political system, arises from the limitation of time: all parties concerned must trust each other that the winner will respect this rule enshrined in the constitution or the electoral law. If this trust disappears, not even the most elaborate consociational *Pacte National* can save the country from bloodshed. That is the sinister lesson of Lebanon.

QUESTIONS IN THE BACKGROUND

When considering the different stages and different sorts of intellectual transfer between Africa and the outside world that are relevant for Africa's democratic experience in the post-colonial period, we can pull them together analytically and ask a certain number of background questions of a more general nature.

How Sincere are the "Exporters"?

We ought to be puzzled by the sudden philanthropy of colonizers leaving behind their own blueprints for democracy when they left Africa around 1960. Colonial administration — British, French, or other — had never been an exercise in democracy. It was sheer authoritarian government, in a way similar to the absolutist and feudal European past. We know that some colonial conquerors and administrators (Peters, Lyautey) went to Africa because they preferred to live in those "good old days" at home, rather than in a "decadent" democratic polity.

Were the democratic independence constitutions introduced in order to *strengthen* the new African leaders through well organized popular support, or to *weaken* them through entrenched opposition groups and/or feudal complications? Clearly, Zimbabwe's constitution was drafted not to safeguard Joshua Nkomo, but Ian Smith. Fortunately, this constitution enables Zimbabwean whites to turn away from Smith and elect better representatives!

Does Moscow really support progressive governments and liberation movements in Africa for the sake of internationalism (proletarian or other)? Or is it simply looking for bases to accommodate its growing battle fleet? Are American congressmen or the French government anxious about the oppression suffered by Blacks in South Africa, when they both are only starting now (a bit late!) to put pressure on Pretoria for power sharing or do they simply join H.P. Oppenheimer in his fear of economic disruption?

How Prejudiced are the "Importers"?

A similar set of questions must be asked on the African side. When African leaders choose among "useful ideologies" from which they may "borrow" in the words of the African National Congress Youth League, what do they have in mind? It is not enough to confront the *bonum commune* of the nation with the private bank account of its President in Switzerland. Even in a perfect democracy safeguards against this kind of corruption do not always work.

Is there a "political technology" appropriate for Africa and adaptable to the African condition, comparable to an appropriate technology in the economic field? All political experience tries to "assimilate" (Senghor's word) and amalgamate foreign blueprints with traditional African political systems. But how genuine is a leader's image of the "traditional" political system (or systems) of his own nation? Did he learn about it from his elders, from his school teachers or out of the book of a European anthropologist? It is reported that certain religious people in Zaire wishing to draw from authentic sources rely instead on Father Tempels'"discovery" (better: invention) of "Bantu philosophy".[4] Are there no parallels in the political kingdom?

There is no such thing as a "natural" political system for any nation. There is no such thing as a "natural" boundary — islands excepted. There is no such thing as an "artificial" nation: all nations are artificial creations of human political endeavour and all political systems are constructs of the human mind — of the *one* human mind common to the human race. It was Robert Sobukwe, founder of the South African Pan Africanist Congress (PAC) who used to say that in his vocabulary, the word "race" did not possess a plural form.

True, forms of thought are different between human beings. Of the great philosophers, Plato did think differently from Aristotle, and Hegel differently from Kant. But Whites as a group do not think differently from Blacks as a group, not about politics or anything else.

If this contention is accepted, then the transfer of political ideas and blueprints and, therefore, the transfer of democracy from one continent to another, becomes, not only normal, but, desirable. The Ricardo formula for optimal mutual benefit in this "trade", however, remains to be discovered.

By definition, exchange can never occur on a one-way basis. Time is soon coming when some African democratic experiences and ideas are going to be discovered as being beneficial for Europe. Europeans certainly are not sincere if they tell their African friends that "our own political system is perfect for us" — would it be the one working in West Berlin or the other one working in East Berlin! There are many challenges Europe does not yet know how to find responses for. Pollution is one.

Some Eastern European systems even try to learn from African experiences in "One-Party Democracy" — Tanzanian, Kenyan, Algerian or others. We all know about the shortcomings of these African models, about nepotism in the competition of candidates for office and how administrations paralyze their nation's parliament when protest candidates have been elected. But all shortcomings included, this African one-party democracy is still a lot better for the learning capacity of the system than the "democratic" centralism of the Stalinist model. African one-party democracy deserves to be considered seriously among the *democratic* experiences of Africa and of mankind.

How "Populist" can Democracy Be?

This is one of the questions which Africans, Americans and Europeans can discuss in common. Africa, but not Africa alone, is full of personality cults. A cynic may say that literacy was essential for the emergence of bourgeois democracy in Europe, because only people capable of reading programmes could choose between competing parties, and that as this art is getting lost in front of the TV screens, democracy in Europe could go down the drain and be replaced by acclamation for the most pretty or impressive face. One may observe, however, that, so far, not a single truly *good* actor has been elected president in a Western democracy.

The choice between personalities, as leaders, has always played a legitimate role in all democratic systems. Traditional Western democratic thought went so far as to ignore political parties, or to reject them as "factionalist". This was always an unrealistic view. But it remains true that democratic movements in Europe, and in particular successful democratic revolutions (successful in actually stepping forward to democracy), were triggered by the personal incompetence of the individual monarch.

Napoleon Bonaparte is not the only one who emerged from the ranks as an alternative leader on account of his personal charisma.

A strong "populist" leader elected democratically who preserves his country as a democracy is not easily to be found in history. Napoleon seems to be more the rule than the exception, if we think of Julius Caesar or Juan Peron or Adolf Hitler or Sekou Toure. But there are examples: De Gaulle in France, Konrad Adenauer in West Germany, Nehru and his daughter in India. Among African "populist" democrats of this generation let us only mention by name the one who has already stepped down from office — Leopold Senghor.

Democracy will not survive in a TV world without personalized "populist" appeal. Charisma must be rationalized, studied, demystified and reconciled with the traditional checks and balances of democracy.

SOME ESSENTIALS OF DEMOCRACY

In an international perspective, a few remarks on democratic essentials can be submitted for discussion.

The State

Democracy is a political system, that is a system appropriate for a "body politic" aspiring to be independent of others, to be a sovereign unit. This is an essential notion. It used to be happily ignored among European new-left radicals around the year 1968. They wanted to "democratize" all branches of society, from the nuclear family where children would exercise self-determination about their education up to churches, factories and universities. The result was not better democracy, but bureaucracy, for the simple reason that social groups of this kind are never independent of each other. If "everybody concerned" should have a vote in a university, for example, this would include not only the actual student population, faculty and technical staff but many other people outside campus equally "concerned" about the success or failure of a university: parents of future students, employers of future graduates, etc. Democratic rule presupposes a relative degree of autonomy, of distinction of the body so ruled, from other bodies. Traditional thinking calls such a relatively independent body a "state", and distinguishes it clearly from subordinate social bodies within a state.

Of course, it is a fact that states today are no longer sovereign units. They are asymmetrically independent in the global "political" system, as we all know. The pertinent question therefore is not if subordinate social bodies could be "democratized", but if democracy still makes sense for a "hostage" state — like Botswana, for example, strongly dependent on a foreign government. But as long as the legal claim to independent statehood is upheld, and can even sometimes be enforced under happy circumstances, the answer to that question would be, that for the people in such a state, it is still better to exercise internal democracy than to enjoy no political rights at all.

Regarding Africa, the old European debate of 1968 ought to be taken up again. The question arises as to whether "the state" is the only body politic conceivable. Under European conditions, democracy can only apply to a state. But Africa has had plenty of experience with "stateless societies". To be sure, politics were conducted, and "constitutions" existed in all those stateless societies. Is there anything relevant to democracy which could be saved from this particular tradition and employed usefully to respond to the challenges of the future? How "democratic" were politics in the stateless African societies of the past? Is the establishment of an "independent state" the only conceivable solution for political conflicts around the globe? This last question may be more relevant to the people of certain islands of the Pacific (Nouvelle Caledonie, for example, or to the Palestinians, than to those of Africa which is fairly completely subdivided now into "sovereign" states.

The Nation

The right of peoples to self-determination is now firmly anchored in international law, definitely since it was included in the two Human Rights Covenants of the United Nations. But neither the law nor political science have yet answered clearly the question: what is a "people"?[5] If we admit, referring to the essential question above, that a state remains today the normal expression of a political system, we are well advised to keep in mind, as contended earlier, that there are no "natural" nations. Fortunately, the bitter dispute between France and Germany is now closed: whether the inhabitants of Alsace *"truly"* belong to the German nation (because they speak German and because their ancestors belonged to the old German Empire), or to the French nation (because they *want* to be French rather than German). The founding fathers of the Organization of African Unity (OAU) were wise enough to opt for a straightforward principle. By declaring Africa's inter-state boundaries sacrosanct and the integrity of every African state to be unshakable, they supported Ernest Renan's definition of the nation as a *plebiscite de tous les jours* against Herder's and Stalin's ideas that there exist objective criteria for membership in this or that nation.

The OAU decision of 1963 was clear, and it remains a consensus in political Africa. But is it always well understood? Any *plebiscite* is an instrument of democracy, that is, if it is not a fraud. A dictatorship can determine the "objective" nationality of its subjects and may even leave some room for cultural "autonomy" of different nationalities within one state. Voluntary decisions about nationhood cannot be made without democracy; not without respect for the rules of democracy.

Let us not overlook the logical follow-up: human beings, as long as they live, can change their decisions. Nations are not permanent. The decision of people in the Western Sahara to belong to Morocco or to establish a Sahroui nation, whatever may actually happen, is not for eternity. It can always be changed. This is another essential of democracy. It is one of the "strategic deterrents" a people possesses against tyrannical rule.

Legitimacy and Consensus

For the European historian, democracy and legitimacy are contradictions. The French Revolution was a democratic revolt against legitimate royalty, and Metternich restored legitimacy wherever he could, by fighting democrats. But then we have to consider the famous words at the beginning of the American Declaration of Independence: it was for their old legitimate rights that these people started to go to war.

A successful democratic system must be based on consensus about what is legitimate: which Human Rights are inalienable; to what extent individual freedom must be protected against governmental interference; how the people are supposed to control government. If and when consensus on these essentials withers away, the door opens for civil war (as in Spain in 1936, in Nigeria in 1967). If and when the rigid claim to respect consensus is pushed too far, democracy is lost.

Consensus, in a democracy, must exist on fundamental political values and on procedure. It cannot exist on group interests or on specific political strategies and decisions. To draw reasonable lines between these two realms is, indeed, essential.

What sort of political consensus can be found in Africa today that may be suitable as a valuable base for democracy? The strongest attachment is still to be found on the consensus for national *liberation*. It has been said that this commitment to a specific kind of collective freedom has not prevented many African nations from falling from the White man's domination into a Black man's misrule. But consensus on national liberation remains an important prerequisite for the exercise of other political freedoms (of groups and individuals). The Polish people's experience shows that this is not so only in Africa. The German people have been brought to accept a consensus on democracy, by the experience of Hitler's tyranny, despite the fact that this was an indigenous tyranny and that liberation came out of the barrels of foreign guns.

To the extent that, in retrospect and in the teaching of colonial history, Africans will understand colonialism not simply as *foreign* government but as *bad* government, the liberation consensus will provide a suitable base for African democracy. Opinion polls among Black South Africans conducted in the 1970s indicated that a 50 to 80 per cent majority of this oppressed people held firm democratic beliefs.[6]

Other issues of broad consensus in Africa may still be the contention that there are no antagonistic class interests in Africa, or that some form of African unity is desirable, or that Iron Curtains must not be lowered between African states of different ideological persuasions. These ideas are achievements from the common struggle against colonialism (the liberation consensus for example), and they can probably provide a useful contribution to a fundamental value system of democracy. But with the passage of time and with rich Africans becoming richer in some countries and the poor staying very poor, with wars and subversion and an impotent OAU, these common values are in danger of becoming obsolete.

Social Bargaining

Europe has learnt the hard way that conflict among organized interests, lobbying of pressure groups and bargaining for sometimes untidy compromises are not only a corruption of democracy and a public scandal, but necessary ingredients of a democractic political system. When city workers go on strike and dust bins are not emptied for two weeks or so, even seasoned democrats start to complain. But what is true remains true and Americans have always been better prepared to live with this ugly side of democracy. There is a wide range of possibilities as to what extent the state should intervene — by fixing minimum wages, by compulsory arbitration of strikes and so on — and still remain democratic. One thing is certain: as soon as a government totally prohibits interest groups from consolidating themselves and bargaining freely, that political system ceases to be a democracy.

In Africa group interests are often perceived in tribal terms and ethnically based (traditional) political systems tend to act as interest groups, exercising pressure on the "national" system. The trouble is not that ethnic pressure groups exist: this is a natural thing whenever individuals experience social security and solidarity on an ethnic level. It is that other interests are not organized adequately and that very small groups wield disproportionate pressure power. This is not, however, a purely African problem. There are a few really big capitalists in Europe and they carry a lot of social and political weight. Everywhere in Africa, peasant farmers form the broad majority of the people but are hardly anywhere organized for efficient bargaining or carry any weight. Every instance of emerging interest groups ready to bargain — be it market women, university students, or a small "labour aristocracy" — should be encouraged as a necessary prerequisite for democracy. One may even include soldiers as long as they are willing to bargain for better pay and to refrain from plotting a *coup*.

142

Criticism, Flexibility and Change

This is the heart of the matter. Democracy needs the free flow of ideas, the free expression of criticism, the floating vote, the crossing of the floor in Parliament, the noisy electoral campaigns, victory and defeat, in one word: *instability* in important spheres of political life. This experience is always painful for somebody but it cannot be helped. The only assurance necessary is the existence of a fundamental consensus that the loser may try again next time.

Africa has a bad record here. For a German observer, all the derogatory remarks of dictators or would-be dictators on Members of Parliament ("they are just talking nonsense"), on the endemic corruption in democracies (while the same corruption by ruling cliques in a dictatorial regime is just pushed under the carpet), on the financial waste of electoral campaign, and so on, sound quite familiar. Germans heard all this talk from Fascists and Communists alike during the short years of the Weimar Republic (1919 to 1933).

As the saying goes, you cannot have the cake and eat it. If Leninism, in the strict sense of "democratic centralism", according to the Soviet model, is to be included among the democratic experiences of Africa, then anything could be included and the issue becomes completely diluted. Leninism has never intended and is not intended to establish a political system or *rule by the people,* with its essentials of open criticism, flexibility, reversibility or choices and change. Leninist single parties do not even rule "in the name of (all) the people" — which is the populist form of a single-party system — but rule in the name of a politically conscious vanguard, presumably for the benefit of the people. In some respects people have benefitted from Leninist rule, but they did this equally from enlightened absolutism in Europe, from intelligent emperors in China or from colonialism in Africa. To call such a system democratic is to call all political systems of this globe democratic, from Paraguay to Iran and Saudi Arabia.

The Importance of Playing Games

Another standard derogatory remark about democracy ridicules its procedural complexities, its bureaucracy, its game content. It may be ridiculous to throw a coin when two candidates for an office obtain an equal number of votes. In some countries, electoral structures are so complicated that nobody understands them, not even university graduates. It was certainly not a good idea of the Western "Gang of Five" to prescribe (in 1981) such a system for Namibia.[7] But in general, these silly procedures and games are another essential for democracy.

Here, paradoxically, we return from a sphere of flexibility, of built-in instability, to the fundamental issues on which consensus is needed. The big moral values and the rules of the game seem to be essentially different. A democracy, however, will not work without the two of them.

This interrelationship applies to the field of Human Rights as well. There is no doubt that they are a corner-stone, a very fundamental value, for democracy, and that consensus about them must exist. But the finest Bill of Rights is politically useless if procedures and "games" to enforce these Rights are not developed and protected. A Human Rights Charter proclaiming, for example, that "every individual shall have the right to free association provided that he abides by the law. . ." may eventually find the consensus of a certain group of governments. But the procedure directly recommended here, that is, to ban all unpleasant associations by law, makes it unsuitable for a democratic experience.

AFRICA'S INTERNATIONAL RELATIONS AND DEMOCRACY

Has democracy been instrumental for the establishment of friendly relations between the new nations of Africa, and governments or societies overseas?

This is not the case. True, racist South Africa has been coerced out of the Commonwealth. But no responsible statesman in London, or in Paris, or in Washington, or in Bonn has ever *acted* on the presumption that democratic political systems in Africa are better partners for his country than dictatorial ones. Instead, the governments of the Western world seem to choose their African friends and priorities on such shaky basis as investment opportunities or arms sales. This is a leftover of colonial racist arrogance. Some people up North think that Africans are incapable of ruling themselves democratically. At any rate, they prefer a solid dictatorship, whose actions they believe they can anticipate, to the incalculable flexibility of democracy. Hopefully Africa will prove them wrong and show that in the long run, democracies make more solid friends than dictators.

The Soviet leadership takes political systems more seriously. Among their African partner governments, the Soviet leaders do not only invest in profit-making industries (they do this too, where they can!), they also invest in the recruitment and education of political cadres and Soviet academic writers say openly that the political participation of communists is necessary for successful socialist orientation, in Africa as elsewhere. But socialism of the Soviet type and democracy exclude each other. The development and active life of democracy in Africa needs other transmission belts of international solidarity. The belts will be useless if democracy does not grow out of African soil, as a basically self-reliant plant. Irrigation may help. For the rest of this century, and probably for the coming one as well, democracy is the only known political road to social and international peace, to rational bargaining among serious interests, to some sort of world order that will not be so oppressive as to force us all into emigration.

REFERENCES

1. Cited from a German-language article published in common by two scholars from the USSR and GDR: Revmira Ismailova and Ursula Padel, "Zur Widerspiegelung der gegenwartigen Etappe der nationalen Befreiungsrevolution in der Sowjetwissenschaft. Literaturbericht," *Asien-Afrika-Latein-amerika,* Berlin (GDR), 1982 no. 2, pp. 217-224. See also Young 1982, INFRA, pp. 258 SS.

2. Jackson and Rosberg, 1984, INFRA, p. 182.

3. Arend Lijphart himself defines the Plural Societies for whom he advocates Consociational Democracy, not just as multi-ethnic societies, but more broadly (with Harry Eckstein) as societies ". . . divided by segmental cleavages . . ." These can be ethnic in character, but also of a different nature. Lebanon gives an example of religious denominations having become, over centuries of self-isolation, ethnicities for all practical purposes. See Lijphart 1977, INFRA, p. 3.

4. See Pladice Temples, *La Philosophie Bantou,* Paris, 1949, 125 pp. Tempeles "discovered" astonishing harmony between beliefs of Black Africans in Zaire, and his own Thomistic school of thought.

5. The African Charter of Human and Peoples' Rights is not more explicit. It says in Art. 18: "All peoples shall be equal . . .", and in Art 20: "All peoples shall have the right to existence. They shall have the unquestionable and inalienable right to self-determination . . ." But the Charter does not hint at any definition of the term "people".

6. A question was: "Think of an independent African country, like Tanzania, Zambia, or Botswana; what would be in the best interest of such a country: (a) a government listening to criticism and trying to satisfy the people who do not agree with it, or (b) a government that does not tolerate too much criticism and prefers to keep order and unity?" 17.5% of the respondents choose (b), 79.9% (a). Another question was: "What would be in the best interest of such an African country: (a) a single political party with a single plan for the future, or (b) more than one party while every party has its own plan for the future of the country?" 49.4% choose (b), 45.4 (a). See Hanf *et al.,* 1981, INFRA, p. 342 of the German original edition.

7. See *Africa Research Bulletin* (Political series), December 1981, p. 6293: "The West now says that half the seats in the assembly should be elected by proportional representation, with parties being represented in exact proportion to the number of votes they receive, and the other half on the basis of single-member constituencies containing as nearly equal a number of inhabitants as is practicable . . . The Western five say that this will mean that each voter will have two votes . . ." ARB was wrong to add that "the model for this scheme is clearly the West German electoral system". In fact, such a model was considered only

briefly by Chancellor Adenauer in the 1950s when he wanted to threaten the small Liberal Party with electoral extinction.

Further Reading

African Charter on Human and Peoples' Rights. Appendix 4 to: Sesay, Amadu *et al., The OAU after Twenty Years,* London, 1984, pp. 109-124.

Dumont, Rene and Marie-France Mottin, *L'Afrique Etranglee,* Paris, 1980, p. 265.

Hanf, Theo *et al., South Africa. The Prospects of Peaceful Change,* Cape Town, 1981.

Ilunga, Kabongo, La Science Politique Africaniste ou les Culs-de-Sac des Modeles d'Analyse ethnocentriques. In (Alf Schwartz, ed.), *Les Faux Prophetes de l'Afrique ou l'Afr(eu)canisme,* Quebec, 1980, pp. 161-178.

Jackson, Robert H. and Carl G. Rosberg, "Popular Legitimacy in African multi-ethnic States", in *Journal of Modern African Studies* (Cambridge) 22 (June 1984) 2, pp. 177-198.

Lewis, W. Arthur, *Politics in West Africa,* London 1965, p. 90.

Lijphart, Arend, *Democracy in Plural Societies: A Comparative Exploration,* London, 1977, pp. x + 248.

Mandela, Nelson, *The Struggle is my Life,* (including ANC Youth League Manifesto, 1948), London, 1978, p. 209.

Nyerere, Julius K., *Democracy and the Party System,* Dar es Salaam 1963, p. 27.

Person, Yves, "Le Socialisme en Afrique Noire et les Socialismes africains", *Revue Francaise d'Etudes Politiques Africaines,* (Paris) no. 127 (July 1976), pp. 15-68.

Senghor, Leopold Sedar, "Vues sur l'Afrique Noire, ou Assimiler, non etre assimiles", in *La Communaute Imperiale Francaise,* Paris, 1945, pp. 55-98.

Young, Crawford, *Ideology and Development in Africa,* London, 1982, pp. xvii + 376.

PART III

DEMOCRACY AND NATIONAL DEVELOPMENT

INTRODUCTION
Walter O. Oyugi

If the second section of the volume succeeded in demonstrating that there is limited democratic practice in Africa today, this last section reminds us that there has not been much development either.

A good starting point in discussing the relationship between democracy and development is to be found in the arguments advanced in Meddi Mugyenyi's essay. The basic argument is that the likelihood of developing countries enjoying both democracy and development at the same time is limited. Either of the two must be sacrificed in favour of the other. In the author's view, development appears to be the major concern and democracy only comes in to give protection to it. He then proceeds to observe that in Africa, where there has been concern with the democratization of the society, there has been a correspondingly poor performance of the economy. Therefore, for him, a scramble for democratic credentials can only undermine the prospects for development. He cites examples to support his position.

Mugyenyi's theoretical expose finds empirical support in what is presented here by both Michael Chege and Nick Wanjohi. Using some of the most recent data on economic conditions and performance in Africa, Chege presents a rather gloomy assessment of the situation. A continent that was once a net exporter of food in the 1960s is now a net importer; and in many countries, the food shortages have reached crisis proportions. The explanations are readily provided: the pursuit of ideas that cannot be operationalized; the failure of African governments to pool their resources in the face of mounting crises; the tendency to look for scapegoats where none exist instead of grappling with the problems at hand, etc.

The irony, Chege laments, is the failure of fashionable paradigms and models such as modernization, political development, etc. that were expected to lay the foundation of economic development. Thus, the optimism of achieving economic development with democracy, which saturated African nationalist rhetoric in the 1960s was both misplaced and unrealistic. What has happened instead is the disappearance of political liberties accompanied by the decline in the standard of living — a phenomenon that is best depicted in the term: "development of under-development".

The essay by Nick Wanjohi carries the democracy-economic development debate yet a step further, by raising a number of questions about the comparative performance of Kenya and Tanzania in the fields of development. The historical roots of the problems have been addressed as well as the factors currently affecting performance.

In summary it can be stated that the issue of the relationship between democracy and development in Africa still needs a more systematic investigation. After more than a quarter of a century of independence for many parts of the continent, there should by now be enough data to enable scholars to come out with a more detailed and comprehensive analysis. This volume does not claim to have made the start. But it can claim to have revived the issue in the hope that others will take up the challenge.

CHAPTER IX

DEVELOPMENT FIRST, DEMOCRACY SECOND

A Comment on Minimalist Democracy

Meddi Mugyenyi

Developing countries are committed to development and democracy. On which of the two should they lay the greater emphasis? In the comments that follow, we recommend that it be laid on development.

Democracy may be understood simply as government by popular consent. But popular consent does not imply a particular origin or structure or form of government. We propose to conceive popular consent as a sufficient sum of supportive people in the population to outweigh serious challenges to the government. This sum need not be a majority. It only needs to be effective. The concern is for effective government which is not actively threatened by dissent involving significant portions of society. Such a government requires active support by a few and abstension by the majority from active dissent. It requires effectiveness in maintaining order and providing goods and services to win endorsement by the people. This form of democracy has no illusions about appealing to the liberals.

The more common view of democracy is what we describe as maximalist. It is more generous. It is also phenomenally popular. It centres around popular participation in the allocation of values. But it also incorporates majority government, rights and freedoms related to speech, assembly, dissent, intellect, life, property, dignity, liberty, office, opposition, opportunity, movement and the press. In this way, maximalist democracy implies certain forms, structures, institutions, and procedures of government.

Development may be understood as the process of increasing the capacity to cope with internal and external demands. It includes increasing the capacity of individuals and collectivities. The concern with increasing capacity is a persistent theme in the study of developing countries. For this discussion, we are not concerned with normative values such as equality and justice. The normative aspects of development are important, but even more so is the universal quest for increasing capacity. The world we live in is saturated with debate about ideologies and their diversity, about cultures and their mysteries. But the same world subscribes to a fundamental consensus about development. There is no country today whose objective is to reduce its capacity, although there may be countries whose policies are accomplishing just that.

DEMOCRACY AND DEVELOPMENT

We have recommended the greater emphasis to be laid on development. The likelihood of developing countries enjoying both democracy and development at the same time is limited. In the short run, they must sacrifice some of one for the other. They must decide which of the two is more urgent. That is their challenge. Yet it is not such a tricky challenge. Our proposition is that democracy, however defined, comes in small instalments behind development. We suggest that democracy comes in to protect the accomplishments of development. From this perspective the sequence is straightforward. Development first, democracy second.

In the reality of social change the sequence above is not easy to calibrate. There is interpenetration between development and democracy. It is possible that this increases in depth and scope as the two processes take root in society. But the sequence does not thereby run into trouble. Causality is not nullified by mutuality. Predominant causation can be established in complex social situations involving thousands of variables. Processes can be evaluated in causal terms and their sequences can be elaborated. In short, interpenetration between social processes does not foreclose the elaboration of causality.

The history of various countries at different levels of development suggests conflicting evidence for the sequence proposed above. Some countries may have developed most significantly during their most democratic epochs. Democracy and development may have proceeded hand in hand. Some may have experienced their most significant development during their most autocratic times. Indeed there have been times when liberalism has been considered a danger to development. Socialist and communist thought on development is suspicious of liberalism even today. It is concerned less with liberty and more with discipline. In short, significant development changes have not always appeared in step with democratic epochs.

From development studies arise suggestions about the difficulty of marrying democratic politics to the conditions of low capacity in the developing countries. A substantial portion of works with relevance to this subject proceeds from the assumptions of maximalist democracy. This is in part because the studies are rooted in the cultural background of the Western world where democratic traditions are well established in society. Democracy in the Western world has its share of dogmatism and idealism, but there is no question that it is sufficiently established to the point of being taken for granted in many countries.

Studies of developing countries which predicate analysis on maximalist democratic tenets start from a high level of expectations. Almost invariably, they wind up with pessimistic conclusions about the prospects of democracy in those countries. Attempts to escape accusations of Western ethnocentrism may have had the effect of under-playing the conditions in which democracy tends to blossom. Development may be a necessary, though not sufficient, precondition for democracy. But to elaborate that precondition, we may have to entertain data that are culturally offensive and politically unpleasant.

Analytical problems notwithstanding, democracy has maintained its appeal. Few fancies of man enjoy the same levels of universality. Countries of vastly different circumstances proclaim commitment to democracy which continues to engage philosophers, politicians, behavioralists, ideologues and even simpletons. The magnetism of democracy suggests that many people perceive the good society in its tenets. There is nothing especially outrageous about the basic tenets of maximalist democracy. Besides, there is a case for setting ourselves high standards in our quest for improving the quality of our life. Democracy sets pretty high standards.

Ubiquitous as it may be, democracy is not so rosy. Part of its glorification arises from overzealous propagation which stands in the way of reason. In common with other ideological formulation, democracy has creative advocates to rescue it whenever it stumbles. For every breakdown as it traverses our globe, there is a breakdown service to rescue democracy with a dexterity of intellect that is truly remarkable. For every democratic accident there is fantastic rationalization.

FROM MAXIMALITY TO MINIMALITY

Maximalist democracy suffers dilution when it is adopted to different environments. Yet democracy, any way you like it, survives because it is terribly adaptable. Variations in democratic practice are as numerous as they are baffling. The variations practiced and rationalized around the globe make it seem coreless. Virtually every country somehow fits its unique credentials into the democratic bag. But the accommodation of immensely different political systems has a gain in quantity and a loss in quality. Given what we can see passing for democratic government, we have no business being uncritical about democracy. What we are seeing, especially in the developing countries are variations on the theme of minimalist democracy.

In the absence of a developed society, only minimalist forms of democracy can be attempted. Many developing countries have come to such a conclusion but will probably not admit it. We can deduce from their political practice. Practice has so violated the expectations of maximalist democracy that reformulations of its tenets have become necessary. And developing countries have become expert at rationalizing their brands of democratic adaptations.[1] Developing countries have become adept at presentations of minimalist democracy that are clever enough to elicit system support from the populations. The policies and courses of action which governments justify to the people in terms of democracy are as diverse as they are curious. The fact that the people accept what they are told by their governments, and proceed to provide support for them, throws some light on the efficacy of minimalist democracy.

The minimalization of democracy is understandable. After all, political management boils down to handling realities rather than ideals. Developing countries have discovered from experience that they must adapt to their environment whatever they elect to apply. They are basically right about that. But critics may feel that the massive adaptations in democratic practice run the risk of wiping out any traces of democracy. Adaptations can wipe out essence. Democracy can be adapted to death.

In a sense the life and death of democracy are intimately related. Its life depends on its adaptability. But so too does its death. Its appeal transcends diversity, but in the diversity of the social conditions of man lie the fuel of its self-destruction. It is the diversity of the human condition which has forced a magnitude of adaptations that have left the cherished ideals of democracy compromised. Democracy has become uncertain. Its core is no longer clear.

The wailing of idealistic academics and naive politicians about un-democratic politics in developing countries is at once instructive and useless; instructive, because it draws attention to the prospects of democracy in diverse conditions; useless, because it seldom pursues the matter to a detached analysis of the circumstances that make democratic adaptations imperative. By predicating lamentations implicitly or explicitly on classical democratic tenets, the wailers erect maximalist democracy as a priority above the conditions of the developing countries. And yet it is the conditions of a society, not the elegance of democratic theory, that embody the most critical variables which give a society its special political style.

On the other hand, if it can be shown that in developing countries democracy has been adapted virtually to death, we may be looking at the ultimate evidence that developing countries do not yet have the capacity to handle democracy in its maximalist form. The resources required to operate a democracy are among what is missing in those countries. Overall development will probably accummulate such resources in due course, and make it increasingly possible for developing countries to adopt more and more of the democratic style of politics. But for the time being, the conditions of low capacity, which define the state of being underdeveloped, also mean poor prospects for democratic politics.

DEVELOPMENT AND MINIMALIST DEMOCRACY

Can it then be argued that democracy depends on development? **Maybe** yes, maybe not. The assertion implicit in the argument would be too categorical. Social scientists advise that claims about dependence must be founded on empirical study. Even the most tantalizing propositions must be subjected to empirical verification. Verifying a hypothesis of democratic dependence on development would run into various methodological problems.

One of them would be the controversial nature of historical data. Whether quantitative or qualitative, much of these data have been afflicted by rather disturbing levels of uncertainty. Historians have wrestled with this problem and continue with the struggle. Students who have tried to build models around the stages of development and growth have run into problems such as questionable assumptions, chaotic data, over-generalizations, shoddy variable definitions, doubtful variable relations, uncertain comparabilities, questionable causal propositions and damaging simplifications.[2]

At the most ambitious level of analysis, causal relations would be most useful for our understanding of development and democracy. But the ambitions of this short essay are humbler than that. We suggest that *development leads with democracy in tow*. For developing countries, the democracy in tow must be of the minimalist variety regardless of their political sloganeering and other democratic pretensions. Given the allocation of resources between development and democratic demands, development should take precedence over democratic demands. Rural electrification and access roads should take priority over expanding the participation of rural folk in major policy decisions such as those affecting the infrastructure and industry. Facilities and incentives for increasing production should take precedence over demands for lifting curbs on the freedom of the press. Public order should take precedence over the freedom of dissent.

The suggestions above constitute no apology for repressive governments. But they could offend the merchants of dogma and the hawkers of Utopia. Even so, government has always been essentially about order in society. There is nothing too Hobbesian about that.[3] The development of man's resources blossoms in environments which are orderly and, therefore, predictable. In the pursuit of order, governments have always played a balancing act between authoritarianism and compromise. Within compromise are fancy gimmicks of control such as democracy. Within authoritarianism lies the ultimate insurance for order in the event of breakdowns in the efficacy of compromise. Every system of government pushes people around. And every government persuades the people to the contrary. The former is reality, the latter, rhetoric. And yet government remains a necessary evil in human society.

Let us shift our discussion to Africa. How have African countries handled development and democracy? Over the last three decades of independence, some of the African countries which have emphasized democratization have also tended to perform poorly on important indicators of development. As they have worked hard on politicization, participation, activism, equality, socialism and humanism, they have sacrificed improvements in development performance. Tanzania is a case in point.

Tanzania, at any rate President Julius Kambarage Nyerere, believed in socialism and democracy as the dynamo of development. Tremendous drama was made of that belief. Tanzania proceeded to implement what it believed in. A highly activist posture was fostered. Politicization was accelerated. Participation was expanded. Equality was socialized. Rural habits were re-arranged. Collective production was instituted. Communal services were provided. *Ujamaa* villages were established. Commercial and industrial organizations were nationalized. Enterprise was circumscribed. And centralization was adopted. It was a massive experiment in development which excited the attentions of the leftists and the curiosity of the rightists.

But the Tanzanian development approach, launched formally by the Arusha Declaration of 1967, quickly ran into problems. While the political music played, progress fell rapidly behind objectives. Production declined rapidly. Services collapsed. Infrastructure suffered. Incomes tumbled. Taxes increased. Supplies fluctuated or vanished. The cost of living jumped. Bureaucratic bottlenecks multiplied. Efficiency nose-dived. Foreign debt mounted. Self-reliance wobbled badly. Disillusionment set in. International philanthropists were running out. Bankrollers for expensive national experiments were becoming scarce, and mother nature found Tanzania a soft punching bag. The country simply found its overall performance suffering multiple failures. And, mark this, the political music played on.

From the perspective of this essay, the Tanzanian experience is understandable. Tanzania put the cart before the horse. The result has been disaster. From 1985 President Nyerere began to admit that his government had made some serious policy mistakes. It sure had. Unfortunately, it took a couple of decades for the blunder to be recognized for what it was. Tanzania is now trying to resurrect private enterprise, to interest foreign investors, to promote the tourist industry and to loosen controls here and there. Nyerere, now no longer President but still Chairman of the ruling party, has realized that certain enterprises should not have been nationalized. Some things should have been done differently.

By contrast, next door, Kenya steered clear of populist experimentation. It maintained a relatively humble political profile. It did not make too much drama of its political wisdom. It certainly made less political noise than Tanzania. And yet it was Kenya, not Tanzania, which had shown Africa the way by fighting colonialism. It was ironic that independent Kenya did not go out of its way to hold on to the mantle of· anti-colonialism. But that irony fitted well into the political stance which Kenya chose to adopt after *Uhuru*. Kenya was concerned less with democratic show business and more with development.,

Kenya saw her priorities differently from Tanzania. The country sought to develop economic capacity. Kenyans were encouraged to engage in self-improvement. Enterprise was fostered. Private enterprise blossomed side by side with co-operative enterprise. From the start Kenya built flexibility into its policies. Some social processes were permitted to take their own course. Production was boosted. Infrastructure to facilitate economic and social development was steadily improved. The spirit of self-reliance and communal development enterprise was facilitated through Harambee which has become one of the most significant forces of development in the country. Few innovations in voluntary development mobilization in the developing countries have built up as much capacity, momentum and efficacy in their countries as Harambee has done in Kenya. Although colonial policy bequeathed some advantages to Kenya by developing it as the industrial centre of the regional economy of East Africa, there is no doubt that Kenya's post-independence policies have helped to develop capacity that is unequalled by any of her immediate neighbours.

Kenya has not become paradise. It has had its share of omissions and commissions. It has ran into difficulties in such areas as land distribution, food policy and social services which have come under tremendous pressure due to a rapidly rising population. It has had its share of unemployment. But Kenya's social and economic problems are minor compared to those of her neighbours. Moreover, Kenya has remained relatively stable in spite of her low profile in the political field. Kenya put the horse before the cart.

But the policies which have tended to foster capitalism in Kenya have drawn fire from critics. Essentially the critics insist that Kenya has become a neo-colony insured by underdevelopment and dependency.[4] Academics and policy-makers cannot afford to ignore the critique because it is a constructive input into our understanding of development. For our part, we find it incompetent. First, the critique needs to be argued more rigorously with comparative and quantitative data. Until then, it is not particularly articulate. Second, the point at which a country becomes a neo-colony or something else has not been specified either for Kenya or for any other countries. We must assume that point to be arbitrary. The omission is most disturbing.

The third problem with the critique is that it pretends to universal applicability without establishing basic measures for the purposes of verification. It can be carelessly flung all over the developing countries, but it will tend to fall apart at the point of verification. Fourth, underdevelopment and dependency thought has tended to be repetitive and speculative at the expense of sharpening its assumptions and testing its hypotheses. There has been too much taken for granted, too little subjected to the test of reality. Fifth, students from non-economics backgrounds could use some help from economists before risking categorical statements about the world economy and the dynamics of economic change. Together, these problems have helped to create a club of excited people who specialize in sweeping critiques but avoid rigorous verification.

Returning to democracy, it is not obvious that Tanzania has become more democratic than Kenya next door. The two countries are probably more similar than different in their modest democratic achievements. Both countries have remained stable over the last couple of decades. In 1978 Kenya executed a smooth succession from Jomo Kenyatta to Daniel arap Moi who became both President of the Republic and of the ruling party KANU.

In 1985 Tanzania executed a transition in which Hassan Mwinyi took over the presidency from Julius Nyerere who, nevertheless, remained the boss of the powerful ruling party CCM. Maintaining stability is important but not enough for development to occur. Continuous capacity building is required. Kenya is credited with both stability and continuous capacity building since independence. Tanzania has maintained stability but neglected capacity building. Both countries have their opportunities and constraints, but what will weigh most heavily in the end is the capacity they will have built over time. It is that capacity which will moderate the prospects for democracy.

Through history, it would appear that most countries preferred what amounted to minimalist democracy in their early phases of development. This inclination arose out of circumstances rather than calculation. There are no grounds for excepting developing countries. The political language of developing countries may scream routinely about democracy. But rhetoric and practice can be far apart. Developing countries understand what democracy involves, and they are nervous about letting it loose on their territory, at least for the time being. They do not reject democracy out of hand. They are trying to build it their own way, at their own pace, to suit their conditions. We have depicted the brand they can afford to practise as minimalist democracy, which leans more on effective government than on democratic government. Some of our critics may reject our position as a euphemism for dictatorship.

Among the most abused democratic practices in developing countries are elections. Originally designed as a means by which the people would control their governments, leaders, policies and destinies, elections have deteriorated into a controversial farce. For some observers of politics, that is a terrible thing. We are not so sure. We suggest that elections can be bad for development. They can produce leaders who will do havoc to it. This is partly because the qualities that determine electability are not always relevant to the performance of development roles. Electability is not the same as capability in handling public policy and management. Social assets can secure one an elective public office or a seat in a legislature. But they do not confirm the possession of skills for effective participation in development decision-making.

Elected politicians tend to be populist but development decision-making tends to be technical. The role of consultants and expatriates in developing countries has often been decried. But it must be considered in the light of the capacity of politicians to process demands and prescribe competent solutions that continually add to national development. Politicians are possessive about their political legitimacy, but they are often short on technical legitimacy. Incidences of politicians forcing decisions down the throats of technocrats in developing countries are common, and their implications for development have not always been encouraging.

Developing countries love to justify their actions as if they have a contract to impress democratic countries in the industrialized world. We think there are sound reasons for the adaptations of democracy in non-industrial societies. These reasons are tied to the levels of capacity, the state of nationhood, the condition of statehood, the psychology of the people and the overall fit between the political system and the environment. Consider, for example, that developed countries conduct their political contests within a settled basic consensus. Their fights are about secondary matters. Against a political, social, economic and cultural consensus, democratic contests can be undertaken without threat to the foundations of society.

By contrast, developing countries are touchy because they are wobbly in their foundations. Basic consensus is usually non-existent. People there may not be agreed on being countrymen, on their identity, on their language, on their culture, on their governmental institutions and structures, on the rules of the political game and on economic direction. In these conditions, open democratic politics can be divisive and destabilizing because society lacks social cohesion.

When African countries adopted the one-party state shortly after they became independent, there was consternation and disapproval from liberal democrats in the Western world. There was reluctance to accept that the conditions of society shaped its political options. There was suspicion about innovations emerging out of the political game in developing countries. Politicians spent much of their time justifying their innovations to the Western audience. Fortunately, over the years, there has emerged a greater willingness to evaluate democratic practice in terms of the constraints imposed by the government.

Given their shaky foundations, developing countries are too easy to throw off balance. Petty issues tend to loom gigantic. Destabilization by minor issues is possible. Fancy democratic practices cannot be accommodated where social cohesion and basic consensus are still weak. Hence the need for drastic democratic adaptations to the environment, a shift to minimalist democracy. To aggravate a bad situation, a developing country is often faced with demands for both development and democracy. Both demands require relative stability in the first place. How can a developing country break out of this dilemma of demands and preconditions? This essay proposes that the way to go is to adopt a minimalist democratic stance and put the greater emphasis on development.

The point is that development can occur in the absence of democracy, but democracy cannot operate in the absence of development. It is possible for an enlightened monarch to foster development without making too many concessions to democracy. Not all development histories have been positively correlated with democracy. The early phases of state-building in history were generally managed in undemocratic styles. Once the state was secure, it was possible to take on the developmental tasks of increasing general capacity in society.

History seems to suggest that the establishment of a secure state is more crucial to development than the building of democratic political cultures. And current trends in the developing countries suggest that a scramble for democratic credentials can undermine the prospects for development. They have not rejected democracy. But they imply that resorting to unbridled democracy prematurely can be dangerous. It is a matter of timing and adopting only those facets of democracy which entail no more risks than their fragile conditions can handle. After all, the majority of the people in any country are not bothered by the particular form of government in control of their society, provided their life, security, property, services, food and similar basic needs are taken good care of. When the chips are down, what matters to most people is whether a government delivers the goods.

In Africa the pattern of going easy on democracy has been evident over the last two decades. Some brief comments about this de-democratization are useful.

At the time of decolonization, African elites shouted their democratic ambitions on rooftops all over the continent. In a relatively easy struggle for independence, African elites swore to create nations and political systems with which the Western world would be happy. They spoke of nations very much in the cultural mould of Western civilization. And at independence African countries' constitutions and political vocabulary were made in the West.

Immediately after independence, African countries were confronted by the rigours of state-building, nation-building and development. They realized they had a challenge to hold together discrete people, to sustain fragile statehood, to foster a sense of nationhood, to develop socio-economic capacity and to evolve political capacity. It was imperative to do all those things at the same time while also minimizing disruption to society. As they got down to tackling those tasks, it became clear that the expectations they had raised during the drive for independence could not be satisfied quickly enough. Demands exceeded capacity. Gaps between promise and fulfilment became too clear. The stage was set for trouble.

Confronted with the prospect of disintegration, it was the commitment to democracy which suffered rapid blows. Few of the democratic practices to which African countries had committed themselves at independence remained unassaulted. Frightened by the convulsions of low-capacity countries suddenly let loose from rigid control, African governments groped for strategies of control to hold fragile societies together. Gears shifted quickly from liberalism to control techniques. In doing so, the governments ran away from the cherished ideals of maximalist democracy.

The list of betrayed democratic promises was long. It included popular participation,[5] freedoms, dissent and the peaceful resolution of conflict. The supremacy of the people became increasingly hollow. Elections to fill public office became infrequent. Opposition parties were banned or induced to wind up. The one party stepped in, claiming superior facility for promoting nationhood, development and democracy.[6]

The one party state was singleminded. Freedoms of speech, dissent, assembly and petition were severely circumscribed. The masses took the back seat as political elitism got institutionalized. Political coercion increased as consultative norms fell by the wayside. The fragile state became more unilateral as the ethos of compromise gave way. Military establishments were politicized as civilian political elites got fragmented. Presidentialism rose as the representative role of parliaments subsided. The African continent quickly got accustomed to government by acquiescence as the distrust of democracy got consummated in less than a decade. By the mid-1960s soldiers were shooting their way to State Houses and walking all over the civilians. It was a costly statement about the prospects of democracy in low-capacity countries.

The proposition of minimalist democracy does not reject democracy. It suggests that if the developing countries adopt forms of democracy that are rather weird, we should try to understand why. If these countries find some utility in democratic rhetoric alongside nondemocratic practice, we must not react with shock and fury. In their circumstances they can best partake of democracy by applying it as a dependent variable that comes in small instalments behind development.

Implicit in this recommendation are reservations about overzealous critiques of the propensity for nondemocratic politics in the developing countries. Critiques which proceed from the assumptions of maximalist democracy fail to do justice to the link between development and capacity for democracy, not to mention other social variables which come into play. Democracy, like any other political style, must be adjusted to the conditions of the countries that choose to practise it. Such conditions are complex and diverse. And the countries which opt for democracy are under no obligation to adopt a particular version of it. Some of the tenets of democracy may fit many countries, but it is unlikely that they could fit all countries in the same way. One of the variables moderating their fit is the level of development. This variable ought to be elaborated and investigated more carefully than has been the case to date.

Before closing the chapter, we comment briefly on equality in the context of development and democracy.

In discussing democracy one is often reminded of the central place of equality. It seems to us that man is a long way from equality in any but the philosophical sense. Development increases capacity. But it also generates hierarchy by increasing complexity. It proliferates groups, interests, demands. Populist demands for development and democracy which includes equality overlook a contradiction.

Development produces inequality, democracy secures it! Social inequalities produced by development are protected, sanctified, insured, perpetrated and institutionalized by democracy. Nowhere has democracy produced equality. For one thing, it has often come either in tow behind development (read inequalization), or pretty far behind it in historical time. To demand development is to demand inequality. To demand democracy is to demand insurance for inequality.

Regardless of official ideology, every developed country is also inegalitarian. For the developing countries, inequality is a condition which calls for creative handling as it changes its characteristics through the course of development. There is no chance that they will eliminate it on the way or when they have finally arrived. Even so, they may wish to blunt some of the sharper edges of inequality, provided they make sure not to do so at the expense of their development.

What has happened in Africa and other developing countries is a movement from idealism to pragmatism. The language of idealism may continue. But the actions of these countries now show a greater concern with development realities than in the past. There are still difficult decisions to be made about courses of action that will enhance development. But there is no doubt about the urgency of development and the utility of pragmatism. The transfer of emphasis from idealism to pragmatism is confirmed in our comments about democracy and development.

The journey of development is frustrating in its own right. It need not be made additionally frustrating by indiscriminate inputs of dogma. It is possible for development to travel light by leaving behind a large portion of the dogmatic baggage it has tried to travel along with. The only baggage that ought to be carried is what a traveller cannot do without. This essay has recommended minimalist democracy in which the allocation of resources is guided by the principle of development first and democracy second.

REFERENCES

1. Nyerere, J.K. *Freedom and Socialism,* London, Oxford University Press, 1968; *Freedom and Development,* London, Oxford University Press, 1973; *Freedom and Unity,* London, Oxford University Press, 1967.
2. Relevant works include those of Karl Marx and his interpreters; Rostow, W.W. *The Stages of Economic Growth,* London, Cambridge University Press, 1960; *Politics and the Stages of Economic Growth,* London, Cambridge University Press, 1971 (*Ibid.*); Robert Nesbit, *Social Change and History,* London, Oxford University Press, 1969.
3. Hobbes, T. *The Leviathan.*
4. Leys, C. *Underdevelopment in Kenya: The Political Economy of Neo-colonialism,* London, Heinemann, 1975.
5. Kasfir, N. *The Shrinking Political Arena,* Berkeley, University of California Press, 1976.
6. Nyerere, J.K. *op. cit.*

CHAPTER X

THE AFRICAN ECONOMIC CRISIS AND THE FATE OF DEMOCRACY IN SUB-SAHARAN AFRICA

Michael Chege

INTRODUCTION

At the height of Ghana's struggle for independence, the late Dr Kwame Nkrumah implored his countrymen and Africans in general "to seek the political kingdom." "The rest" he said, "shall be added unto you". As Harold Macmillan's "wind of change", independence and nationalism, swept over most of the continent in the 1960s, there was a strong faith that most of the new states would succeed in consolidating territorial integrity, promoting economic growth and development and reversing the trends of political and racial oppression associated with colonialism. Self-rule, democracy and prosperity appeared co-extensive.

Nearly three decades after Ghana acquired independence from Britain the first territory in Sub-Saharan Africa to do so — a spirit of gloom and despondency hangs over the continent. Political chaos and disorder have become commonplace. Leading economic indicators tell the tale of a generally declining economic growth and productivity in the last two decades leading to a crisis of serious dimensions. The continent has moved from the status of food exporter in the 1960s to that of a net food importer. Between 1980 and 1984 alone, per capita income fell by 10%. The United Nations Economic Commission for Africa, which has deliberated at length on "Africa's economic and social crisis", notes that "the food situation has deteriorated so drastically that in the 34 drought-striken countries, the imports of cereals have increased from about 4 million metric tonnes in 1970 to over 23 million metric tonnes in 1982".[1] A full 24 of these 34 are incapable of financing food imports.

Industrial growth has varied by country. But it has generally been hit by shortages of inputs, occasioned by foreign exchange shortage arising from the depressed earnings of Africa's traditional exports. This is because Africa's industrial capacity is heavily dependent on external inputs. Production of non-energy minerals has been depressed by international demand. Copper prices for instance fell by 18.7% between 1970 and 1980. Production decreased for most minerals excepting gold, zinc and diamonds. In manufacturing, after some growth in the 1970-75 period, the Africa region has registered either little growth or stagnation in the 1980s.

In the field of international trade, Africa has experienced declining terms of trade, the singular exception being the oil producers. The most precipitous shortfalls have been recorded by leading mineral producers like Zambia, Zaire, Liberia and Mauritania. Current account deficits in external payments have hence become commonplace. Only one or two African states had a positive balance of trade in 1982.

Although this problem could be corrected by capital inflows, there has been falling official development aid to Africa and a sharp increase in external debt servicing caused by rapid appreciation of Western currencies — principally the dollar — and skyrocketting interest rates in the West. As a matter of course, African states have been borrowing largely to finance inputs of consumer goods, principally food, and also energy.

The net social result of all this has been governments with slim financial bases, invariably operating on large deficits and thus fuelling domestic inflation. Since domestic rates of inflation invariably exceed those of the West, there are many overvalued domestic currencies, and domestic import shortages, promoting black-marketeering and smuggling. This in turn has tended to erode confidence in government and regimes in power. The path has thus been paved for recurrent military *coups d'etat*, intolerance, political repression and intensifying human misery. Democracy has fallen victim to economic capriciousness.

Nowhere is the drop from the political effervescence and optimism of the 1960s to the economic and social disaster of the 1980s better exemplified than in Ghana itself. In 1950, Ghana had the highest per capita income in Africa south of the Sahara.[2] Compared to the rest of the colonial dependencies in Africa, she came to independence with a sizeable corpus of skilled indigenous manpower, some local capital and adequate foreign exchange. Agricultural resources were in local hands as opposed, for instance, to Kenya and Zimbabwe. In comparison with her neighbours, Ghana inherited a sophisticated transport network of rail and roads.

In 1982 by contrast, the Ghanaian social and economic situation could be described as follows:

> "A survey of international costs of living showed that it was over 100% more expensive for a Briton to eat in Ghana than in the U.K. Ghana's inflation rate was said to be the highest in the world, and its official exchange rate about 15 times less than the reported black market rate.
> Dr. F.W.A. Akuffo, national president of the African Youth Command declared that Ghanaian society was becoming more and more rotten because no one was able to survive without breaking the law; those who are not corrupt depended on the corrupt ones for survival".[3]

In a recent assessment of the external origins of Ghana's economic problems, Robert M. Price, has remarked:

"The optimistic expectations that surrounded the independence celebrations in 1957 could not contrast more dramatically and tragically with the reality that surrounded Ghana's silver jubilee, the anniversary in 1982 of twenty five years of that independence. Production in all sectors was abysmally low. Food production had not kept pace with population increase and cocoa production was approximately half of what it had been two decades earlier. Mining was performing at a similar standard; production of most manufacturing industries, if occurring at all, represented only a marginal utilization of capacity and the timber industry was at a standstill. Economic deterioration had eroded Ghana's once impressive economic and social infrastructure. The systems of health care, education, transportation and communication were in disarray."[4]

The food supply system had become erratic and non-dependable. The flight of skilled sections of the middle class to other African states and abroad accelerated. One regime after another seemed incapable of reversing this trend.

After toying with left-leaning populist ideas blending popular mobilization, "inculcation of a new social morality" and opposition to exploitation by multinational corporations, the Rawlings government had by 1985 gone full circle to work out an economic stabilization programme with the IMF and the World Bank. This opened the road for negotiation of loan funds from Britain, West Germany, France and the United States. Signs of economic recovery were widely publicized. Yet Rawlings had initiated a *coup* on New Year's Eve of 1982 against the democratically-elected Hilla Limann government which was contemplating precisely those very same measures.

Ghana's road from hope to collapse and from democracy to left-wing dictatorship is in no way unique. Variations of this have been replicated elsewhere, only this time, under right-wing autocracy. This chapter outlines the extent, magnitude and growth of the contemporary African economic crisis. It also attempts to sketch the political consequences thereof and to explain why democratic government in Africa is so imperilled by parallel regimes of economic catastrophe.

THE EXTENT AND GROWTH OF THE ECONOMIC CRISIS IN AFRICA

There are various interpretations of the origins and causes of Africa's economic and social crisis of the 1980s. We shall look at some of these in our quest to explain whence the current social and economic crisis facing the continent. For the moment, it is necessary to demonstrate the principal areas in which African economies have faulted and thus become dependent on external support.

Food

Food is the most basic of human necessities. It is also a political and social issue upon which governments the world over have fallen, and upon which social insurrections have arisen.[5] Charley Tilly has (in the early modern European context) demonstrated the close relationship between state-formation and food supply, and how public order was affected by disruptions in food supply.[6] Food is also a strategic weapon by which food-deficient nations become politically beholden to the providers. Finally, imported food costs African states foreign exchange. But food is most expensive of all to the hungry who cannot afford to pay cash: in return for food handouts, they forego their human dignity. On the whole, the average annual growth rate of agricultural production per capita has been negative (-1.1%) between 1970 and 1982 and a similar situation is observed in food production where the figure is -1%.

The result of declining food production per head has been malnutrition and attempts to meet food deficits by food imports and food aid. Table 1 below shows quantities, in thousands of metric tonnes, of food aid to Sub-Saharan Africa between 1975 and 1982. It is apparent that food aid more

TABLE I: FOOD AID IMPORTS INTO SUB-SAHARAN AFRICA

Year	'000 Metric Tonnes
1975	957.3
1976	752.0
1977	868.6
1978	1,237.2
1979	1,124.9
1980	1,552.6
1981	2,346.7
1982	2,168.6

Source: World Bank, *Towards Sustained Development in Sub-Saharan Africa,* p. 76; and *Accelerated Development in Sub-Saharan Africa,* p.166.

than doubled between 1975 and 1982. It will have risen yet higher for 1983, and 1984 when the full statistics of food aid to Ethiopia and other drought-striken countries in Africa become available. But it is worth noting that food aid recipients have included countries with no history of drought, for example, Zaire, Mauritius and Guinea Bissau. Leading per capita food aid recipients in 1982 were the Sahel drought victims: Mauritania (54 kg. per capital), Somalia (39 kg.), Gambia (34 kg.), Bourkina Faso (13 kg.). Other major food aid recipients however are non-Sahelian: Tanzania (13.1 kg. per capita), Zambia (16 kg.), Lesotho (24 kg.), Liberia (21 kg.) and Guinea Bissau (32 kg.).

Apart from dependence on food aid, there has been a growing importation of food, primarily cereals from Europe and the United States. This is also a reflection of changing consumer tastes (in favour of wheat and rice and against traditional staples) as urbanization and a class of *nouveau riche* spreads. Table II below indicates the trend in agricultural imports into sub-Saharan Africa for leading agricultural commodities.

TABLE II: AGRICULTURAL IMPORTS TO SUB-SAHARAN AFRICA

	Annual Average Metric Tonnes ('000)		
	1961-63	*1969-71*	*1980-82*
Rice	464	480	2456
Wheat	394	1043	3269
Maize	197	385	1686
Other Cereals	123	239	244
Sugar	690	816	1632
Meat	38	42	129
Animal/Vegetable Oils	71	155	710

Souce: World Bank, *Towards Sustained Development in Sub-Saharan Africa,* 1984, p. 79.

It is important to note that oil exporting countries accounted for a substantial (but not predominant) part of these imports only after 1980, when they absorbed 20% of imported rice, 30% of wheat and 25% of maize imported into the region.

Export Dependence, Concentration and Declining Terms of Trade

African states have a high commodity concentration of exports. Nearly all of the continent's exports fall under the category of unrefined minerals, petroleum, "food, beverages, and tobacco". On average, the share of the three principal exports in total country exports went up from 60.6% in 1961 to 79.1% in 1976-8.[7] Fluctuations in earnings as a result of turbulence on the supply side such as droughts, floods, natural catstrophes, etc., or the demand side, for example, recession or technological change in the West, can have tremendous repercussions on states and governments. This is because government revenue structure (customs duties or export taxes) is tied to international trade. A good example of this is Zambia, which depends on copper for 95% of its exports and 60% of government revenue. The drop in copper prices has had tremendous effects on the balance of payments and state revenue.

In addition, risks are heightened by the concentration of exports to a few states, almost predominantly the ex-colonial power. In 1982, 80% of Africa's merchandise exports were sold to the industrial market economies of the West. The consequences of economic recession in the West have had immediate adverse repercussions on Africa. The much-vaunted "recovery" in the West, however, has yet to be felt in most African states.

As is well known and well-established by now, the African international trade scene has been marked by a remarkable deterioration in terms of trade. Even the most conservative observers of Africa's socio-economic problems do not dispute this. As the World Bank recently reported, "Between 1980 and 1982, prices of non-oil primary commodities declined by 27% in current dollar terms. The loss of income due to deterioration in the terms of trade was 1.2% of the Gross Domestic Product for Sub-Saharan Africa."[8] The World Bank counsels diversification of Africa's primary exports and more producer incentives. This is recommended as a short-run solution by the "Berg Report".[9] Since Africa has seen a decreasing share of her basic exports in quantitative as well as proportionate terms, it is difficult to gainsay this argument particularly in the short run. In the medium and long-term, Africa will need to reckon with export diversification and the "new protectionism" in the West.

Declining Foreign Assistance, Investments and Domestic Savings: The Onset of Disinvestment

African states are said to have done comparatively well in attracting official development assistance from the West in the 1970s. However, this is only true when aid is calculated on a per capita basis. Generally, in the period under question, external aid accounted for about 10% of Africa's gross domestic investment. In the 1980s, official development aid fell sharply as leading Western governments cut aid or made it conditional upon domestic policy reforms worked out by the International Monetary Fund. For instance, even the Scandinavians and the Dutch, who are generally sympathetic to the Third World, have been anxious that Tanzania reaches some agreement with the IMF in the 1980s before aid expansion can be undertaken.

At the same time, the net flow of capital from private sources declined by nearly 50% between 1980 and 1982.[10] Against the declining or stagnant levels of economic growth, and hence domestic savings, African states were borrowing capital for import consumption instead of investment purposes. It is now abundantly evident that the majority of states in Africa have been unable to maintain even the little capital equipment and infrastructure built up in the past. In other words, a process of de-capitalization has set in. Roads are not maintained, hospitals and education equipment is often unserviceable and civil servants go unpaid for months in some countries. With this reality, African states have become even more vulnerable to pressures from outside, now and in the future.

168

External Debt Servicing

The headlines have drawn attention to the debt problems of Latin American countries, beginning with the debacle which occurred in Mexico in mid-1982. But, in fact, by the early 1980s, external debt and debt servicing had become a major problem of African states. Considerable external borrowing took place in the 1970s with the onset of balance of payment problems caused by oil price increases. In time these states were also caught up in the spiral of declining domestic productivity, declining export revenue and rising interest rates. Up to 1982, twenty-three of the thirty-one re-schedulings of external loans done by the Club of Paris was for African states. Those facing problems included perennial defaulters like Zaire, but also states like the Ivory Coast which had been praised in the West for its prudence in public spending and capitalist policies and which had serious trade arrears even though it had so far avoided an IMF agreement and a Paris Club re-scheduling.

Science and Technology

One of the most important objectives set out in the Lagos Plan of Action is the harnessing of science and technology in the interests of African development. Major breakthroughs in industry, agriculture and animal husbandry are called for. But these are dependent on the development of new research and technology. The plan sees this occurring in a co-operative pan-African network of research and development institutions. Africans are called upon to support these institutions in finance and manpower. Up to the present there are few indications of success in this direction.

Between 1970 and 1980, the number of research scientists working in Africa is said to have risen from about 1,600 to 4,000. This is just about half the number of those working in Asia. National research and development programmes have been marked by under-financing, discontinuity in projects, inadequate dissemination and under-utilization of research findings. Isebill Gruhn says that only in one African state is the scientist/population ratio in excess of 121 to a million whereas it is 380 per million in Italy, 830 in Sweden and 2,600 in USA.[11]

Between them the Economic Commission for Africa and the Organization of African Unity have established a number of research and training institutions covering the areas of scientific, technological and industrial research.[12] But these have been marked by a poor record of member-country contributions and not all African states have become members. Western donor agencies have therefore continued to provide most of the support for scientific research on a national or regional basis. The continuity and viability of these have been uneven. Notable progress has been made by a few, operating on a regional basis. These include the International Centre for Insect Physiology and Ecology (I.C.I.P.E.), the

International Centre for Research in Agro-forestry (I.C.R.A.F.) and the International Livestock Development Centre for Africa (I.L.C.A.).

The Cost of Militarization

This is the most subtle form of external dependence, perhaps the most deep-rooted and most difficult to tackle. Africa's militarization has gone apace with declining growth and declining political liberties.

In the field of armaments manufacturing, only Egypt has an armament industry to speak of in independent Africa. Thus according to the figures from the United States Disarmament Agency (ACDA) and SIPRI in Sweden, both of which monitor progress about the global arms trade, between 1975 and 1980 African countries received about US$14,000 million worth of military equipment, representing about 20% of the total world trade in military equipment. Between 1974 and 1978 alone, African countries (excepting Egypt) imported 2,224 tanks, 1,500 anti-aircraft pieces, 4,278 armoured personnel carriers, 117 warships, 3 submarines, 19 guided missile patrol boats, 820 combat aircraft, 330 other military aircraft, 320 helicopters and 8,020 surface-to-air missiles.

The main arms suppliers to Africa down to 1980 were USSR (55%), France (12%), West Germany (5%), USA (4%), Italy (4%). The main recipients of Soviet armaments were Ethiopia, Algeria, Libya, Angola, Mozambique and Tanzania. France's main customers are her former dependencies, Madagascar, Morocco, but also South Africa. America's major arms clients now are Egypt, Sudan, Kenya and Somalia.

But these facts and statistics cover only officially acknowledged arms transfers. There is a good deal of arms coming into Africa from private arms dealers in such countries as Belgium and Switzerland, and also Israel and South Africa.

The contours of military dependence closely approximate those of political influence and control. The USA and Britain wield considerable influence in Kenya. France has changed regimes in Africa without the slightest consideration of world, let alone African, opinion (for example in the Central African Republic in 1979), and has intervened in Chad's civil war and in Zaire during the two Shaba uprisings (1977 and 1978). The Soviet Union has got repeatedly into trouble for seeking to influence domestic politics in African states as in the Sudan (1971), Egypt (1972) and several times in Guinea under the late President Sekou Toure.

Many regimes in Africa in fact, arm themselves as much against their own citizens as against external enemies. The internal legitimacy of most African states is shaky. At any one time most African states are under a military dictatorship of one sort or another. Corporatist interests in the military seek newer and better arms each year for prestige and sometimes, strategic military purposes. The cycle is completed when an external power

170

seeking interest and influence in that particular state, obliges and provides arms and training.

But just as important is the configuration of domestic social forces that make African societies succumb easily to dictatorship and state terror, rendering the prospects of democratic government very bleak. Economic vulnerability is the cause as well as the result of political authoritarianism in Africa.

THE ECONOMIC CRISIS AND THE FATE OF DEMOCRACY IN AFRICA

With the benefit of hindsight, one can now observe that the hope of achieving economic development *with* democracy which saturated African nationalist rhetoric in the 1960s, was both misplaced and unrealistic. The truth had by the 1980s sunk in. Not only had Africans lost Nkrumah's political kingdom but nothing material had been added unto them. In contrast, Africans have not just seen political liberties swept away, they have also witnessed a *decline* in the standards of living, including in those African states which had claimed the alleviation of poverty to be their primary social goal. That much is clear from our survey of the contemporary economic situation in the foregoing pages.

But the African economic crisis has just aggravated a political situation which was brittle and fragile right at the onset of independence, for a number of reasons. Firstly, a democratic government has never been accomplished anywhere by proclamation. Rather it is the product of a prolonged political and intellectual conflict between social forces unleashed by industrialization at a given phase in the history of the Western world. Democratic government in the capitalist world came violently and concomitantly with economic liberalization. Thus contradictory as it may sound, Adam Smith at the height of the Age of Enlightenment stood for self-interest and individual gain in the market-place as a means of *maximizing* the public good. John Locke argued for a government accountable to the citizen, which rested on the "consent of the governed" and whose primary objective was to safeguard private property. Of late, Albert O. Hirschman tells us that freedom of commerce and private gain were seen as the ideal social tools in "taming" autocratic monarchies.[13] Somehow, a monarch who engaged in private enterprise was inclined to be less autocratic than the one who did not. But it must be presumed that in this case one is speaking of modern, organized, productive capitalism based on free markets and not what Weber refers to as "booty capitalism".

In sum, therefore, the evolution of a democratic government cannot be dissociated from the social pluralism which economic development creates, and on which democracy thrives. Democratic government essentially rests on toleration of diverse, even conflicting ideas and socio-economic interests. It was John Stuart Mill, in *On Liberty,* who remarked that any insistence on a uniformity of ideas by whatever terms is tyranny.

In Sub-Saharan Africa by contrast, it was assumed at the zenith of nationalist euphoria that there was such a thing as a uniquely African approach to democracy, to economic organization ("African Socialism") and to the domain of culture and thought ("Negritude", "African personality" etc.). All that was required was to resurrect these cut-and-dried artifacts from African pre-colonial societies and use them as foundation blocks for the new state. African intellectuals whose vocation it was to give a systematic and reasoned critique of society abandoned their mission and sank into sycophancy and vulgar nostalgic exercises. The costs which African societies have paid on account of this intellectual folly are enormous.

It was also a way of running away from the bitter political facts: nationalism in Africa served as a medium for ethnic mobilization bringing in its train, ethnic coalitions posing as parties, which could become unstuck at the slightest strain. And this is true of *all* the African states. Elliot Berg reckons that in the nationalist period, political parties based on trade union or specific social class were rare; the possible exceptions being Tom Mboya's NPCP and Sekou Toure's PDG.[14] Secondly, if economic development were to mean the modernization of agriculture and industrialization, there were tremendous social costs to be paid by African societies quite apart from economic costs. It was Barrington Moore who remarked at one point that wherever industrialization had taken place, be it under capitalist or socialist regimes, there was no evidence that peasants and other underlying classes welcomed it, and plenty of evidence that they resisted it and were invariably victims of it.[15]

The construction of industrialized capitalist and socialist societies has been done invariably on the ashes of pre-modern social formations, including their social norms and cultures. The kernel of the problem is that African statesmen claimed they wanted economic and social development while marching in the opposite direction towards tradition. The swim against the currents of history could always be justified by the premise that the African experience and intellectual ethos had a peculiarity which was special to it. Anyone failing to see that is presumed to be brainwashed or neo-colonialist.

It was an intellectual premise for which as already mentioned, the African people, and in particular the peasantry, were to pay dearly. It is by now common knowledge that the dominant paradigm for explaining African political evolution in the 1960s — "modernization" and "political development" — saw the chances of a secular evolution to more representative government spearheaded by modernizing elites. The key assumption here was that political engineering would be done by the new elites to tackle the problems of national integration, the creation of a rational bureaucracy and wide social consensus based on a national "political culture". But with the Ghanaian *coup* of February 1966, the first spate of military takeovers in the 1960s and the failure of the UN First Development Decade, other explanations became terribly urgent.

The "perspective" of "dependency and underdevelopment" came to centre-stage to explain how "underdevelopment" was the product of prolonged integration into the world capitalist system. Africa, said Walter Rodney, was underdeveloped by Europe. In this context, political repression and lack of democracy in Africa was easily explained: the "comprador" agents of international capital had to repress the "masses" because only that way could the pumping out of surpluses continue in economies which stagnated and reproduced themselves in stunted, imbalanced forms.

That may be. What remains to be explained is why countries like Kenya and Zaire which have been recipients of Western capital, have evolved palpably different economic systems (one thriving, the other in decay) and such different political systems. More importantly, dependency fails to explain why a country like Somalia, hardly a haven for multinational corporations had developed such an autocratic militarist regime in contrast to say Nigeria, or Brazil.

After Bill Warren's critique of "dependency",[16] and the writing which has followed it, and, further, the diversity of experiences which African states and the Third World have gone through, it would appear that the popularity of dependency as a concept persists for only two reasons. One is its intellectual nuisance value, and the second is that it is still a powerful political weapon to absolve African elites and their societies from their own shortcomings by heaping all of these on "imperialism"

A more accurate picture would be presented if due consideration were given to the interface of international forces and domestic social forces. This would require that we train the analytical spotlight on economic evolution and social conflicts *within* African states and their interraction with external forces. In the end, we may learn something about Africa's internal deficiences and the reasons why we have proved so vulnerable to external predators and to consistently authoritarian regimes. In the remaining part of this chapter we focus on the impact on domestic politics of the African economic crisis.

Essentially, when in the 1980s African states found themselves in a spiral of declining agricultural productivity, large budget deficits and balance of payments problems, they were inclined to blame the international capitalist system and the weather. To begin with, a new so-called international economic order will never appear simply because heads of governments have summoned it. Further, the effects of weather are an admission of failure to translate agricultural surpluses of the good year into the agricultural reserves of the bad year.

Since, as Goran Hyden, among others, has recently said, the transformation of pre-capitalist social formations were never really a part of Africa's political agenda,[17] economic progress was arrested by recourse to populism: government based on some mythical "ordinary person" who is victimized by immorality, exploitation and esoteric intellectual ideas. Populism is not just part of the intellectual baggage of ruling elites, it is the most common paradigm for social analysis among African academics.

Garvin Kitching has brought out the lineages of populism in the Third World and demonstrated similarities with economic ideas prevailing in most of the now industrialized states at the early periods of industrial and agricultural change.[18] Kitching does not say so but populism has ironically been the handmaiden of authoritarian governments of left and right, not excluding fascism.[19] And this is the nemesis of democracy in Africa; not so much because its value premises espouse the dignity and welfare of the "common man", rather because it stands on cause-effect relationships which are factually untenable.

As its basic objective populism seeks a regeneration of basic rural, country "folk" virtues which have supposedly been corrupted by the materialism and individualism of modern society. It is anti-intellectual through and through, since it assumes the enemy has already been defined and all that matters is combat. The enemy is seen essentially as anything foreign be it in the forms of ideas or institutions. Its ideal person is the "ordinary" or "small" man battling big bureaucracy, traders, businessmen and alien institutions, lumped together as "suckers" or "exploiters" of the people.

Left-wing populism in Africa identifies the enemy as foreign private capital and its domestic auxilliaries, "the comprador" bourgeoisie. By definition no internal structural changes need be made except to weed out the morally corrupted, the smugglers and those who overcharge. High prices are never seen as the logical consequence of diminishing capability to produce. Smuggling across borders is never viewed as the logical product of over-valued domestic currencies and a balance of payments crisis, instigated in the first place by declining agricultural productivity. The inert and counterproductive state institutions in agricultural marketing and distribution are never viewed as a source of concern. Anyone who urges that the government budget deficit be halted because it generates inflation is branded an "anti-people" renegade or an agent of the IMF.

The political effect of such policies is to drive trade underground where goods become even more expensive because of the higher risks entailed. The governments turn to rationing foreign exchange and scarce consumer goods. Trotsky is reputed to have said that those who ration, allocate themselves first, and in this case it is understandable that bureaucrats and party officials seldom appear in the food lines. From Tanzania, Ghana (under Rawlings) and Bourkina Faso the tales of bureaucratic corruption when goods are rationed are legion. In Guinea (under Sekou Toure) and Ethiopia, state outlets dried early and the consumer learnt the workings of the parallel market and survived through them, even as they continued to be officially castigated.

The social upshot of all this is an exodus of skills and of the business class. The economy grinds to a halt and social suffering intensifies especially among the very "ordinary" folk whom leftist populists say they cater for. When as a measure of last resort, borders are closed (as in Ghana 1982, and Tanzania 1983) to deal with smugglers and domestic racketeers, the economic situation deteriorates as the consumer products smuggled in from outside disappear. Then the state realizes it has created an economic "Gulag Archipelago" and driven into a blind alley. Hasty changes are then made to *reverse* the economic damage incurred. The left-wing rhetoric dies down and the regimes eat humble pie in the form of IMF stabilization programmes. This is the story of Ghana between 1984 and 1986, and of Tanzania in 1986.

At this point the regime turns to its critics on the left — who are invariably university intellectuals — with a vengeance. Witness the events in Liberia in 1981-82 and in Ghana in 1983-84. Terror is visited on "economic saboteurs" as was the case during the 1983 Tanzanian campaign, or as in the case of the perennial Ghanaian firing squads. In situations like this it makes no sense to speak of democracy. State apparatuses are extended for surveillance in the country, under the guise of "peoples" defence committees. As this chaos comes in, democracy leaves by the window.

Right-wing populist regimes are just as arbitrary and capricious and just as poor managers of the economy. The archetypical right-wing regime derives its philosophy and ideas from the national leader. The philosophy and ideas, often distilled from African traditions, are deemed so complete that anyone advocating contrary views or thinking in a critical vein can only be a heretic or a depraved foreign agent. A good deal of rhetoric is directed against secular ideas and intellectuals in particular. Marxism is seen as moral corruption and foreign-aided sabotage. High standards, required of life in the 20th century, exist only to be denigrated.

In fact, right-wing populists are as much against the workings of the market and capital accumulation as their leftist critics, who are also invariably their major opponents. Economic rationality is avoided by vacuous programmes of moral regeneration and moral rectitude. It is cleansing the peoples' minds which counts, not so much rational policies for increased productivity.

Thus, in the Sudan, the Numeiry regime sought to avoid difficult economic decisions by taking refuge in Islam. Yet every passing day the economy deteriorated, supplications to Allah notwithstanding. Agricultural productivity fell. A bloated government deficit fanned the fires of inflation simply because it was politically unpalatable to eliminate subsidies on basic staples. The balance of payments deficit grew to the point where it became impossible to import petroleum and the regime insisted that being responsible to Allah, it was unquestionable. Despite the *coup d'etat* of April 1985, the economic problems of the Sudan hang onto the new regime like the sword of Damocles.

In Zaire, Togo, Nigeria, Zambia and a large number of other African states, the government seeks to introduce the ethic of moral uprightness as a corrective to economic decline. It is once again an escapist ploy to avoid immediate difficult choices and the more fundamental problem of *rational,* large-scale social transformation. And because leaders think that to admit so would diminish their political stature, the issues go undebated. No public policy analysis takes place. The stage is thus set for a soldier populist from either end of the political spectrum to seize state power and engage in his own destructive escapade. Once again democracy simply is not on the agenda in these circumstances.

CONCLUSION

The economic and social crisis facing Africa today is now common headline material. It is time African intellectuals began to look at the root sources of the problem with a greater degree of sophistication than they did in the 1960s when Africa's uniqueness was purveyed as the gospel truth.

We now know better. Nobody is going to give African states a dispensation from the social and economic costs of development. Any path which points to agricultural and industrial development will require a frontal confrontation with the archaic pre-capitalist economic formations and their subjugation to either capitalist or socialist modes of moderniza-tion. To claim that external factors, "imperialism", or even "foreign ideology" are responsible for the economic retrogression of Africa is to espouse a partial and highly partisan view.

The role of democratic politics in the process is a pivotal one. Only by ventilating the issues in their full economic and political complexities will some light be shed. At the moment African regimes are content to take refuge in populist rhetoric of left or right. This simply postpones the day of reckoning. The most ignoble thing that African intellectuals could do right now is to become fellow-travellers. For by doing so they abandon their calling and imperil Africa's future.

REFERENCES

1.   U.N. Economic Commission for Africa, *Special Memorandum by the ECA Conference of Ministers on Africa's Economic and Social Crisis,* Addis Ababa, May, 1984.

2. Bequele, Assefa, "Stagnation and Inequality in Ghana" in D. Ghai and S. Radwan (eds.), *Agrarian Policies and Rural Poverty in Africa,* Geneva, ILO, 1983, p. 219.

3. Legum, Colin, (ed.), *Africa Contemporary Record,* 1981-82, p. 8422.

4. Price, Robert M. "Neo-Colonialism and Ghana's Economic Decline" *Canadian Journal of African Studies,* 18, no. 1, 1984, p. 165.

5. Recent examples range from Gromulka's Poland in 1970 to Liberia in 1979 and Guinea Bissau in 1980. Food riots in the past two years have occured in Tunisia, Egypt, Morocco and Sudan.

6. Tilly, Charles "Food Supply and Public Order in Modern Europe" in Tilly (ed.), *The Formation of National States in Western Europe,* Princeton, N.J. Princeton University Press, 1975, pp. 380-455.

7. Wangwe, S.M. "Sub-Saharan Africa: Which Economic Strategy", *Third World Quarterly,* Vol. 6, no. 4, p. 1034.

8. The World Bank, *Towards Sustained Development in Sub-Saharan Africa,* Washington 1984, p. 11.

9. The World Bank, *Accelerated Development in Sub-Saharan Africa,* Washington, 1981, pp. 45-80.

10. The World Bank, *Towards Sustained Development in Sub-Saharan Africa,* Washington, 1981, p. 13.

11. See for instance Isebill V. Gruhn, "Towards Scientific and Technological Independence", *Journal of Modern African Studies,* 22, no. 1, 1984.

12. For example: African Regional Centre for Technology (Dakar); East African Mineral Resources Development Centre (Dodoma); OAU's Scientific Technical and Research Commission (Lagos); altogether about 20. OAU and ECA are currently reviewing the status and future of these institutions under what they have called "Ad Hoc Committee" of specialized institutions of OAU and ECA.

13. Hirschmann, Albert O., *The Passions and the Interests,* Princeton University Press, 1976.

14. Berg Elliot J. "Trade Unions" in James S. Coleman and C.G. Rosberg (eds.), *Political Parties and National Integration in Tropical Africa,* Princeton N.J., Princeton University Press, 1964.

15. Moore Jr., Barrington, *The Social Origins of Dictatorship and Democracy,* Boston, The Beacon Press, 1966.

16. Warren, Bill, *Imperialism: Pioneer of Capitalism,* London, New Left Books, 1980.

17. Hyden, Goran, *No Shortcuts to Progress,* London, Heinemann, 1983.

18. Kitching, Gavin *Development and Underdevelopment in Historical Perspective,* London, Methuen, 1983.

19. Moore Jr., Barrington. *Injustice: The Social Basis of Obedience and Revolt,* London, Macmillan, 1979, deals with this concept on pp. 420-433.

CHAPTER XI

THE RELATIONSHIP BETWEEN ECONOMIC PROGRESS AND DEMOCRACY IN KENYA AND TANZANIA

N. Gatheru Wanjohi

INTRODUCTION

A study of development problems in Africa is not complete without an examination of the relationship between socio-economic progress in the continent and the existence or non-existence of democratic political systems. A close look at the history of the present-day developed countries reveals a strong relationship between their tremendous material development and their past political systems whereby the sovereign had absolute and unlimited power over the rest of the society. The power held by the sovereign, and exercised sometimes through his appointees, was no doubt necessary for the maintenance of social discipline in the process of capital accumulation and its subsequent consolidation at the time of the Industrial Revolution, a period unique from any previous one in that the accumulation of wealth had now become a matter, of course, and except in cases of war and other catastrophes, any reversion of the process had become almost inconceivable.

The interesting effect of this development was that what had become an almost fully insured process of material production was experienced in the affected societies through the increased power of the underprivileged majority *vis-a-vis* the existing ruling classes. In some cases the ruling classes recognized the necessity of accommodating the interests of the wider sections of the society by allowing them a share in the increased national wealth through social welfare facilities, as well as participation in the choice of government and the policies by which the conduct of government was determined.

The beginning of this social and political involvement of the people was not a result of voluntary action by the ruling classes, but rather of a long and bitter struggle by the under-privileged classes. What one finds as a positive relationship between democracy and economic progress[1] in industrialized societies is therefore the product of a process whereby the former emerged and grew on the basis of the latter.

One must observe from the onset, however, that even in the developed world this relationship is a very weak one, thus suggesting the direct or indirect importance of other variables such as education, improved communications and increased sense of security especially among the ruling classes. Nevertheless, the contribution of economic progress to the development of democracy cannot be underestimated considering the importance of economic factors in the development of non-economic factors. This is perhaps what Julius Nyerere of Tanzania meant when he observed that development brought freedom.[2] It is no wonder, after all, since most of society's life revolves around the economic factor.

From their policy statements, it is clear that African leaders have sought to by-pass the historical stages of social transformation whereby economic changes and progress precede the emergence and development of democracy. In particular, they seem to consider it undesirable to follow the socially costly path taken by the developed world. Indeed most leaders in Africa believe in the attainment of economic progress simultaneously with the practice of democratic ideals. Thus, for example, the post-independence government in Kenya has committed itself to establishing a society in which priority is given to rapid economic growth while at the same time ensuring that social justice and political equality prevail for all, and that the elite and the powerful economic groups do not exercise disproportionate political influence.[3]

Similar sentiments are expressed in Tanzania with Nyerere adding that "development depends upon freedom" to signify his commitment to democracy in the process of economic progress.[4] This latter position seems incompatible with Nyerere's earlier position that "freedom depends on development",[5] but all that is meant is that in Africa economic progress cannot be attained in the absence of free participation, and neither can freedom survive in conditions of economic stagnation. Kenya's position as represented in Sessional Paper No. 10/1965 is not very different from the Tanzanian one except that in the former economic growth is given greater prominence.

Having noted the large overlap in policy orientation, what remains is for us to examine the main aspects of socio-economic performance in the two countries against the background of their commitment to both economic progress and freedom and democracy.

The question we shall be asking is, "to what extent do changes in economic conditions induce changes in democratic conduct, and vice versa?" Our position is that the simultaneous realization of economic development and democracy is difficult to attain and one has of necessity to precede the other even if only by a short period of time. However, when economic progress precedes democracy, the short-term effect may be to suffocate the emergence of the latter until a well founded and secure system of economic accumulation is attained. This is the path, as we have seen, that many of the developed countries took. Where democracy precedes economic progress, the pace of economic accumulation tends to slow down.

COLONIAL HERITAGE AND THE DILEMMA OF DEMOCRACY AND DEVELOPMENT

Throughout the colonial era, the socio-economic development of the African population in both Kenya and Tanzania was generally either ignored or totally suppressed. In Kenya, for instance, some of the land areas unoccupied by the colonial settler community were set aside as African reserves, where social, economic, physical and technological change was constantly held in check and where the African population was reduced to unprecedented levels of incapacity in respect of independent production. In nearly all cases, the colonial efforts were directed at forcing the African population into complete dependence on the colonial life-line.

At the same time, some parts of Kenya underwent drastic changes as modern social and economic facilities were set up in the upcoming urban areas that became the residential and business centres for a large section of the European and Asian population. Modern physical and social facilities were also extended to rural areas set apart for occupation by European farmers. These included railway and road infrastructures linking such areas with urban centres and the Mombasa port, postal and telephone services, medical and educational facilities, as well as research and agricultural training services. The settlers were also availed of easy agricultural credit and technological services to facilitate the development of a privileged agricultural sector in the hands of European farmers. The result was a system of well established social and economic privileges which clearly placed the European population and the immigrant groups in general well above the African population in practically every respect.

A similar situation existed in colonial Tanzania except that the extent of European occupation in the agricultural sector was considerably smaller than in Kenya. This, of course, meant that when independence came, Tanzania found herself many times less favoured in terms of physical and economic infrastructure than her neighbour Kenya which, ironically, inherited an elaborate infrastructure from the out-going colonial system. This difference, however, should not obscure the fact that by the time of independence the result of colonial neglect, oppression and discrimination had become clearly evident in the social and economic stagnation of the African population, which meant that many African groups in these countries had changed little during the seventy years of colonization.

As independence approached, numerous problems of underdevelopment unveiled themselves both in their magnitude and complexity. Poverty, disease, ignorance and exploitation were singled out as the key problems constituting the backwardness syndrome in East Africa at the beginning of the 1960s.

The notion of backwardness syndrome in this case denotes a vicious cirle of socio-economic conditions each of which is a consequence of and a major factor for the existence of the other. Some economists refer to this state of affairs as the vicious circle of poverty and stagnation. However, it represents more than just problems in raising people's incomes, although the characteristic conditions ultimately affect economic progress. The main conditions include widespread low agricultural productivity; low level of average incomes with a big section of the society having no incomes at all; recurrent famine; high unemployment rates; high incidence of illiteracy and general ignorance; low life expectancy at birth; high infant and child mortality rate; and widespread social despondency. All these underline the gravity of the problems that any independent African government had to address immediately in spite of other equally serious difficulties, especially the scarcity of resources.

Under the circumstances, there could not have been a more anxiously and eagerly awaited moment than the day of independence. This was evidently to be a moment of relief and new hope for a great many people in East Africa. Apart from expecting immediate solutions to their most pressing problems, many people also entertained new and higher expectation of what independence would bring. In addition, the new independence government assumed power on an African vote and anyone dealing with designing of solutions to any of these countries' problems had to bear in mind this crucial position of the African population as the core of the political clientele both at the national and local level. In the early years of independence the centrality of the African population made it mandatory that at least some of the most salient benefits of independence should be seen to accrue, otherwise a great credibility crisis would arise on account of the failure by the new government to demonstrate political and administrative efficacy.

The task before each of the East African governments at independence was therefore enormous, and the situation presented more contradictions than opportunities. This was especially so in view of the danger that most people would seize the moment to relax rather than redouble their efforts in production. The problem of matching democracy with the drive for economic progress became evident right from the start. This led Nyerere of Tanzania to warn his people that *uhuru ni kazi* (freedom is work). On the day of independence Kenyatta of Kenya had the same message when he said: "From today onwards, I want our *uhuru* to mean: *uhuru na kazi* freedom and work."[6] The strategies adopted to implement the policy of rapid economic progress within a democratic socio-political setting therefore are interesting to analyze.

RELATIVE DEVELOPMENT DIFFERENTIAL BETWEEN KENYA AND TANZANIA IN THE EARLY 1960s

At the time of independence in 1961 and 1963, Tanzania and Kenya found themselves at relatively different levels of development. Kenya happened to have benefited from the colonial Government's desire to improve basic infrastructures for the benefit of European farming and commercial activities. Indeed, the country had not only a well developed agricultural and commercial sector, but the post-World War II era had witnessed an upsurge in the development of industrial activity with Uganda and Tanzania rapidly falling behind.[7] As such, the development policy Kenya was to adopt after independence had to be not only one that would maintain her leading economic position in East Africa, but also that would reduce European (and Asian) domination of the economy in favour of increased African participation.

By the end of the 1950s Kenya had practically become the peripheral centre of the East African region, exporting more manufactured products to her neighbours while importing substantial quantities of raw materials from them.[8] The resultant terms of trade were overwhelmingly in favour of Kenya and most disadvantageous to Tanzania which lost heavily as a consequence.

The relative development differential in Kenya and Tanzania was also identifiable through various social and economic indicators. Of these the most important was the wide gap in GNP per capita, with Tanzania resting at US$200 against Kenya's US$250 in 1963. Most of the benefits of Kenya's advantageous economic position were, however, concentrated in the European and Asian communities, thus leaving the conditions of the African Kenyans not very different from those of Tanzanians. Nevertheless, Kenya manifested a more favourable position in practically every respect (Table I) and she was therefore clearly advantaged in terms of a superior development base right from the beginning. This position was probably the most important factor in Kenya's subsequent better performance, except in the area of adult literacy which Tanzania seems to have conducted with spectacular success. The economic advantage has apparently enabled post-independence Kenya to perform better in areas requiring heavy investments, including the construction of such facilities as health centres, schools, training institutions and urban improvements, all of which have a bearing on the results reflected in Table I.

In the circumstances, it was inevitable that the two countries should start their independence era on a competitive note. Both sought to establish societies based on what they conceived as the cornerstones of a democratic social system. These included political equality, social justice, human dignity, equal opportunities and freedom from exploitation, poverty, ignorance and disease. Right from the start each country also committed itself to rapid economic growth while simultaneously upholding the tenets of a democratic society. The question was how poor and backward countries such as Kenya and Tanzania could attain rapid economic development simultaneously with the establishment of freedom, equality, justice and a

Table I: Economic and social development: Kenya and Tanzania

Country	Kenya			Tanzania		
Year	1960	1977	1984	1960	1977	1984
Socio-Economic Indicators						
GNP per capita in US$	250	330	310	200	230	210
Percentage of labour force in agriculture	86	79	81b	89	84	86b
Urban population as % of total population	7	12	18	5	9	14
Primary school enrolment as % of age group	47	105a	100	28	70a	87
Adult literacy rate	20	40a		10	66a	
Population per physician	10,000	8,840a	7,540c	21,000	18,490a	..
Population per Nursing person	2,320	3,300a	990c	8,300	1,070a	..
Child death rate (age 1-4)	25	14	16	32	20	22
Life expectancy at birth	47	53	54	42	51	52

a = 1976;   b = 1980;   c = 1981
Source: IBRD *World Development Report,* 1978, 1979, 1980, 1986.

whole range of public and social welfare facilities. Rather than put the economic horse before the democratic cart,[9] the two were expected to run parallel, none pushing or pulling the other, but each complementing the other.

While theoretically expressing more or less similar national goals, the two countries differed in approach, Kenya placing greater weight on economic progress and Tanzania on political and social goals. In the initial stages of their independence there was more similarity than difference in the way the two countries designed their development paths as expressed in their first Development Plans, 1961-64 for Tanzania and 1964-70 for Kenya.

FOREIGN INDUSTRIAL INVESTMENT AND THE DEMAND OF NATIONALISM

In keeping with the development and intellectual current of the time, leaders in both Kenya and Tanzania considered industrial development as the panacea for the problems they inherited from the colonial era.[10] Such problems as unemployment, poverty, low productivity in agriculture, poor physical and economic infrastructure, as well as poor capacity to improve technological performance, educational, health and other social facilities, were all primarily associated with the low level of industrialization in the region:

As already observed earlier the situation was viewed with greater concern in Tanzania where the size of the industrial set-up was many times smaller than that of Kenya. No wonder that one of the priority policy items in Tanzania's 1961-64 Development Plan was industrialization. Even then, however, one central bottleneck had still to be tackled. This was the acute capital shortage which seemed to threaten the country with permanent poverty and backwardness unless some form of international co-operation could be secured. Fortunately this plan was drawn largely by foreign technical experts who were already familiar with the increasing role of foreign capital in bridging a country's resource gap. The plan therefore called for foreign investments especially in the industrial sector, and, to back up this call, the newly independent government undertook to encourage foreign investments, publicizing investment opportunities available in the country, designing tax and tariff incentives, as well as giving legal guarantees to foreign investors against the nationalization of their assets or businesses.[11] The guarantees also provided for the remission of profits and repatriation of capital. These constituted very attractive terms indeed.

Luckily for Tanzania, various investors were already keen to set up industrial activities in the country for a variety of reasons. The most important of these included the fear of losing markets in the face of changes which were bound to take place in the region after independence, the desire to ward off the entry of competitors in the existing market, the need to gain a foothold in the newly independent country as well as to protect raw material supplies against possible competitors.[12]

The combined interests of the government, on the one hand, and of the international firms on the other, favoured a rapid establishment of industries in Tanzania, particularly where the market was assured as in the case of the textile industry. By 1966, the efforts had already borne fruits in that the contribution of the manufacturing sector to total exports had increased sharply, while the proportion of manufactures as part of total imports from Kenya also fell sharply.[13]

Unfortunately, the 1961-64 Plan and the First Five-Year Development

Plan, 1964-69, both of which gave a high premium on industrial growth were drawn without the consultation of Tanganyika African National Union (TANU), the ruling party, and this meant that party policy and the Development Plan were at variance.[14] This deprived the plans of the party's support and long-term continuity even on matters of such great national importance as the role of foreign capital in industrial growth. When the issue of development was presented to the party leadership in 1966 against a background dominated by the issue of independence, national pride, control and allocation of investment benefits, the outcome was the nationalization of the principal means of production, including land and industries, thus dealing a serious blow to the efforts of the period 1961 to 1966. More than anything else, the motivating factor behind the decision to nationalize seemed to be the need for national assertiveness in the face of foreign domination of the economy, a step which seemed to be taken within the spirit of democracy whereby the key policies must be in accordance with the wishes "of the people", "by the people" and "for the people", without caring about the consequences.

Although some national firms were included in the nationalization bid, the exercise was interpreted as an act of bad faith on the part of the government of Tanzania. The affected firms and indeed the Western world responded by withholding their cooperation in the implementation of the new policy. The parent companies withheld their supplies of parts, raw materials and technical know-how, while intending investors postponed their decisions in the hope of policy revisions. In their turn Western countries and international donor agencies intervened on behalf of the investors, demanding either "prompt and fair compensation", or the rescinding of the nationalization decisions. The debate that took place behind the scenes on the issue, among other things, delayed the completion and implementation of the Second Development Plan, particularly in the face of the precipitous fall in foreign capital inflows and the uncertainties regarding availability of domestic capital resources.

To all this Nyerere responded in patriotic terms, appealing to Tanzanians to discard money, which they did not have anyway, as a basis for their development. He appealed for self-reliance in the exploitation of the abundant national resources — land and labour — for development. This was the only sure way of preserving national independence and integrity.[15] The most important element of the new approach involved what came to be known as *Ujamaa* or socialism through collectivized agriculture in the hands of peasant producers organized in communal village co-operatives.

In the meantime Nyerere was aware of the consequences of his policies and particularly of the possibility of a new drift of investments to Kenya and Uganda, especially the former where yet another wave of industrial concentration would further increase its economic superiority in the region. This was indeed a dilemma of no small magnitude, and one for which no solution was to be found until the last years of Nyerere's rule when, after his resignation in 1983, yet another change of policy was adopted and denationalization began.

Meanwhile, Kenya which got independence two years after Tanzania was keen to outdo her East African neighbours in economic performance in the same way her colonial predecessors had done. Witnessing the enthusiasm with which Tanzania sought to shift the industrial set up in her favour, Kenyan leaders quickly sought to institute measures to prevent the flight of capital as well as to reassure investors. The initial years of Kenya's independence were therefore characterized by the issues of political stability and the security of foreign investments. In particular foreign investors were availed of generous depreciation allowances, tariff incentives, firm investments guarantees against nationalization on top of existing constitutional guarantees under the bill of rights, and freedom to remit profits as well as repatriate capital. These incentives were not significantly different from those offered by Tanzania. Nevertheless Kenya was predisposed to win more foreign investors in industrial and commercial sectors on account of the more developed infrastructural base as well as other economic advantages. This was particularly evident after the wave of nationalizations in Tanzania and in view of the communication facilities linking the country with her neighbours.

It must be reiterated, however, that most of the industrial concerns in post-independence Kenya were established in the period 1945-63, and that the post-1963 era was mainly characterized by expansion or takeover of existing firms,[16] as well as by entry of new firms which sought to gain a foothold in the Kenyan and East African market. A combination of various motivating factors has therefore been instrumental in the rapid expansion of Kenya's industrial sector whose most important contribution to the country's development perhaps has been the uninterrupted supply of consumer products to the Kenyan society. Thus there have been few shortages of consumer goods in Kenya as compared to the situation in the other countries in the region, a fact that may go a long way to explain the relative tolerance and peacefulness of a wide section of the Kenyan public even when it is at odds with the government of the day.

The three countries of East Africa have for a long time been regarded as three units of the same society in that events taking place in one of them have a tremendous impact on the social and political behaviour of the other two. Thus, for instance, the industrial policies of Tanzania in the early part of 1960's had an influence on the policies adopted by Kenya in 1964/65 onwards. Similarly, nationalization in Tanzania in 1966 aroused a new wave of nationalism in Kenya as both radical and moderate leaders began to question the wisdom of supporting uncontrolled foreign domination of the economy especially in the commercial and industrial sectors. The government's response to this new challenge differed from the

Tanzanian.

It differed more particularly in form, approach and the speed of implementation. Thus, the Kenya government adopted a persuasive approach, exhorting foreign investors to enter into mixed and joint ventures with Kenyans. In addition, foreign investors were requested to go public and sell some of their shares to Kenyans. In many cases international firms responded by appointing leading politicians, top civil servants or their close kins to top positions as directors or senior executives in what was later seen as window dressing. In many of these cases the central objective was to assuage the new wave of nationalism which mainly emanated frtom the up-and-coming African merchant capitalists searching for an avenue through which they could join the world of industrial capitalism.

In the meantime, although they insisted on getting priority consideration, many foreign investors and their home governments were quick to recognize the precarious situation in which the new states found themselves. The problem was how the contradictory expectations of the foreign investors on the one hand and of the East Africans on the other could be catered for without shattering the host political system. A kind of compromise emerged whereby cooperation was accepted by the investors and the governments. Thus, the investors in Tanzania and some of them in Kenya accepted the principle of shared ownership. This was primarily in a bid especially by the multinational corporations (MNCs), to save the market for their manufacturing inputs in the face of the increasingly stronger barriers that the two countries were imposing against imports. Many feared the entry into the market by new competitors, while others were keen to maintain the raw material supplies by accepting the terms of the partial localization of ownership.

The host governments were also as eager to win the cooperation of the international firms primarily in order to keep the public supplied with the consumer goods it was already used to. In Kenya, where outright nationalization has been avoided throughout the post-independence era, not much has been witnessed by way of interrupted supplies of consumer goods. In Tanzania, however, the 1966 blanket nationalization seriously interrupted production, particularly in the industrial sector. This largely meant interruption of consummer supplies which, of course, became a source of discontent especially among the urban and elite members of the population. The subsequent tension was worsened by the effects of reprisals of the multinationals who cut their supplies of inputs, spare parts and technical know-how with a hope of forcing a change of policy. For about three years there was a kind of "war of nerves" before both the government and the investors recognized the need for cooperation in spite of continued differences. By 1970 therefore the Tanzanian government had relaxed its policy regarding the actual control of the nationalized industries, and more personnel from parent companies came in to oversee the normalization of production after a spell of uncertainties.

Policy relaxation alone was not sufficient, however, to bring in the amount of capital required to have the economy running once again. So the government once more went on the offensive, wooing foreign firms into the country and assuring them of free remission of profits and repatriation of capital. They therefore went into mixed ventures with the state in an arrangement which seemed to serve as a channel through which a more unrestricted marketing of foreign products and services in Tanzania was facilitated. To the MNCs, marketing of their products and services rather than production became the main concern in the context of nationalization.

GIVE AND TAKE IN POLITICS

The benefits deriving directly from nationalization and "window dressing" localization were hardly realized by the wider population. They were restricted to a few individuals who occupied top management positions in various companies, although the workers found some salaried jobs in the foreign firms. As such, new methods of making the people feel the difference between the colonial and the independence era had to be found and it had to take a more material form. However, although the two countries had made tremendous efforts towards dealing with the more pressing social problems such as illiteracy, ignorance, disease and the worst manifestations of poverty (through the provision of community and welfare facilities like education, hospitals, water, housing, improved transport and communications), the resultant improved social justice and equality were inadequate in the absence of significant changes in the material well-being of the people.

Probably nowhere in Africa have attempts to deal with this problem been more systematic than in Kenya and Tanzania, where a unique situation of political recriprocity developed between the government on the one hand and the various sections of the public on the other. This refers to measures taken by the government to meet at least the most pressing demands of the public in general and of the economically and socially powerful groups in particular. In return the government wins support and tolerance from the public, even in times of difficulties. On the other hand, however, the government accommodates participation from interested parties in policy-making provided such participation does not seek to significantly change or replace the existing political system.

Consequently, many of the post-independence policy decisions in Kenya and Tanzania have been a product of give-and-take deals involving the state on the one hand, and various formal and informal interest or pressure groups on the other. Such groups include foreign investors and foreign government agents acting individually or collectively, the local business communities (African and Indian), professional organizations, trade unions, workers, farmers and peasant organizations, ethnic and religious groups, voluntary agencies and several other social organizations. They also include informal groups within the political parties, parliament and local authorities. Sometimes, as in the case of employment, the deals involve more than two parties such as the government, employers and trade unions, resulting in what are known as tripartite agreements. Whatever the number of specific or non-specific groups concerned, the important fact has been the development of a phenomenal chain of political reciprocity!

REDISTRIBUTIVE ADJUSTMENT AND DEMOCRACY

To begin with, the efforts of the two governments to promote fast economic development through expanded industrial activities with the participation of the foreign investors and, later on, of local individuals and state corporations, went a long way to winning the support of the public and of other interested parties. In other words, accommodation was reached through policy adjustments to take into account the demands from the public and to cater for the greater need for political stability. However, although the flow of profits may have been interrupted due to some policy adjustments, this proved to be more of a temporary or transitory experience than one which resulted in the permanent destruction of private, individual or company interests.

Subsequently and perhaps more significantly, the governments of the two countries adopted other policies which served both nationalistic and redistributive objectives. Of these, the most wide ranging involved the agricultural sector, the main sector in both countries. In Kenya, there were instituted Land Settlement Programmes (LSP), under which a big section of the former European farms was transferred to Africans who either assumed ownership of intact large-scale farms, or had the farms subdivided among several families that became settled as peasants. In addition, efforts were made to promote peasant agriculture, especially in the production of cash crops and livestock for the market. The main instruments in this exercise were public agricultural credit and price policies that offered attractive producer prices for staple foods. The latter nevertheless kept consumer prices within the reach of the urban workers in a way that seemed to subsidize the consumer (though in reality, it amounted to subsidizing the employers who sought to earn profits, not through efficiency in production, but through their low wage policies).

In spite of such problems as fluctuations in world commodity prices, the low level of innovation among many peasant producers, poor management of agricultural credit and marketing cooperatives, scarcity of capital and recurrence of bad weather conditions, agricultural production in Kenya has increased tremendously since independence and so has resulted in rising and more equitably distributed incomes. In particular, the growth of small-scale peasant production is noteworthy, though its share of the total marketed produce has tended to settle at 52% for grain (Table II), and 56% for sugarcane (Table III). For such cash crops as tea and coffee small-scale farms account for about 50% and 40% of the total marketed crop respectively,[15] while small-scale pineapple production is estimated at less than 10%.

Thus, although distributive efforts have met with spectacular success, it is clear that a big chunk of agricultural incomes in Kenya still accrues to the large-scale farmers a good number of whom are still foreign. In addition such efforts have been further affected by the fact that incomes are very poorly distributed geographically given that most of the cash-earning marketed produce involve such cash crops as coffee, tea and horticultural products, most of which are concentrated in districts most ecologically favoured for their production. Nevertheless, corrective measures have been undertaken through the introduction of drought-resistant crops and improved livestock varieties, and through the improvement of physical and economic infrastructures likely to boost production and, hence the incomes of the less ecologically favoured areas.

Table II: *Sales to Marketing Boards from Large and Small Farms 1977-1983*

Year	Large Farms K£m.	Small Farms K£m.	Total K£m.	Percentage Share of Small Farms
1977	206.0	121.9	407.1	49.4
1978	147.2	178.6	325.8	54.8
1979	148.2	165.2	313.4	52.7
1980	168.8	184.5	363.3	52.2
1981	178.6	208.3	386.9	53.8
1982	116.7	232.2	448.9	51.7
1983	271.3	284.1	555.4	51.2

Souce: *Kenya Economic Survey,* 1984, Table 8.5, p. 111, and *Kenya Statistical Abstract* 1983, Table 74 (C), p. 99.

Table III: *Sugarcane Production by Type of Growers, 1983*

Types of Growers	'000 Tonnes	Percentage
Factory Estate	789.3	25
Large Farms	617.8	19
Smallholders	1,448.3	43
Cooperative Societies	179.6	6
Settlement Schemes	232.6	7

Source: *Kenya Economic Survey,* 1984, Table 8.13, p. 118.

In Tanzania the new nationalistic and redistributive policy came to be known as *Ujamaa*, the main feature of which was improved peasant production collectively organized. This was to be the basis of Tanzanian socialism which had to derive its material support largely from small-scale agriculture. The new policy, however, encountered several difficulties, perhaps the most important being the intransigence of the peasantry whose diverse traditional land tenure systems were generally disregarded by the policy designers.[17] In addition the new system (whereby the ownership of land rested with the state while the usufructory rights rested with the tiller) itself became a bottleneck in improved production, particularly in view of the lack of security of tenure which would encourage long-term and sound investment in agriculture. There was also the problem of coercion, particularly involving urban migrants who saw their future in urban employment and who resisted being pushed to *Ujamaa* villages where agriculture remained backward and was unable to significantly raise people's incomes in the same manner as the urban areas seemed to promise.

One also cannot forget the problem encountered by peasant production by way of competition from large-scale state farms which took the lion's share of state resources towards the agricultural sector. These have been operated rather inefficiently and have been riddled with recurrent losses each year. They have nevertheless accounted for the largest part of marketed agricultural produce and have, therefore, drawn the bulk of the total income accruing to the sector. This competition notwithstanding, the other problems responsible for poor small-scale farm production at peasant or *Ujamaa* farm-holding include inadequate and poorly organized support from the state through meagre and inefficiently run small-scale agricultural credit. Transport and marketing facilities have been inadequate and the low producer prices have been a major disincentive particularly at the collective farm unit.[18] Finally, there has been little bureaucratic enthusiasm in support of *Ujamaa*, a factor which no doubt has seriously affected programme implementation and success.

While therefore noting that Tanzanian leaders were aware of the capital constraints that were likely to affect *Ujamaa* in rural development, it is also clear that the socio-cultural and even class content of top-bottom change, which Nyerere and his followers tried to introduce in Tanzania, were not clearly understood by the leadership. In particular, the context of the peasant way of life and conservatism became difficult to manage. Consequently, the post-Arusha-Declaration period experienced a sharp decline in agricultural production, a situation that ultimately contributed heavily to the economic crisis that has faced that country since 1970.[19]

In spite of implementation problems, the objectives of peasant-directed redistributive programmes in Kenya and Tanzania should not be dismissed as simply unsound. In fact, many of them were as good as any well intended objectives. They included the desire to raise and spread the incomes of the majority of the people who still lived in the rural areas. Sometimes the programmes only gave hope of rising incomes, but still they encouraged a sense of security and belonging among the rural people. Whatever one might say of the programmes, they at least conceptually constituted a clear effort on the part of the two states to cater for the material improvement of the people.

On the other hand, however, such efforts cannot always be evaluated purely economically in terms of raising people's material well-being, but also in terms of building a different quality of life for them. This is because the purpose of development is man, not things, and his dignity, his freedom, his democratic right and duty to participate in production and consumption decisions are basic, and cannot be "traded off" against a little extra income here, or a few extra jobs there.[20] In other words, some shortfalls in economic growth can be tolerated in favour of some of the more urgently needed social welfare benefits which enhance the dignity of man and his democratic status.

Distributive trends particularly in agriculture have other rather negative implications on growth. In the first place, they tend to spread the incomes too thin such that individual capacity to save as a basis for subsequent accumulation becomes inhibited. Secondly, they seem to concentrate on the peasantry with the effect that the economy of affection that Goran Hyden[21] talks about becomes more complex and reduces society's capability to leap over socio-cultural and technological hurdles that hinder growth and development.

EXTERNAL ENVIRONMENT AND DEMOCRACY

Since independence both Kenya and Tanzania have sought huge amounts of foreign aid, mainly in support of their development plans, which have relied heavily on this resource for implementation. They have used mainly external loans and credits to establish various physical and economic facilities deemed necessary for social and economic progress. In Kenya, the bulk of foreign aid has gone into agricultural development in an attempt to assist settlement programmes as well as maintain high production levels of export commodities upon which the importation of manufactured goods and services from the rich countries so much relies. In both Kenya and Tanzania, aid has been directed to trade promotion between the recipient and the developed countries.

Sometimes external loans have been used in direct investment by the state in conjunction with foreign investments under the joint mixed ventures referred to earlier. This has been in an effort to respond to the problem of capital shortage as a major bottleneck in development.

The problem of the shortage of technical manpower has also made it necessary for Kenya and Tanzania to use foreign technical personnel as advisers, teachers, engineers, doctors and planners in running some of the governmental sectors requiring technical expertise. This form of aid has accounted for nearly 15% of total aid received by the two countries since independence, while another 5% has been used towards the importation of various technical inputs and equipment in support of technical assistance.

Table IV: *External Public Debt by country and year*

Country	In million US$			As Percentage of GNP		
	1970	1977	1984	1970	1977	1984
Kenya	406	821	3062	26	20	53
Tanzania	263	1005	2654	21	32	770
Ethiopia	169	471	1384	10	14	30
Malawi	122	292	731	43	36	64
Burundi	7	37	334	3	7	36
Uganda	138	215	675	7	6	21
Somalia	77	401	1233	24	93	90
Rwanda	2	78	244	1	13	15
Sudan	307	1732	5659	15	35	77

Source: IBRD: *World Development Report,* 1979 and 1986, pp. 154 and 212.

In all Kenya received aid amounting to more than US$1336 million between 1961 and 1981 while Tanzania obtained about US$1300 million between 1961 and 1978. Since 1978, Tanzania has received a lot more aid, thus making her one of the leading aid recipients in the Eastern African region after Sudan and Kenya in that order as may be deduced from Table IV.

Of greater importance in monetary terms is the rising level of indebtedness that seems to threaten future growth in these two countries and several others in the region. As Table IV illustrates, debt has become a very serious problem for nearly all African countries with the result that a big proportion of GNP can safely be said to be accounted for by foreign aid. About half of Kenya's external debt is accounted for by multilateral aid while bilateral aid accounts for the other half. Meanwhile nearly 70% of aid to Tanzania is bilateral, while the other 30% is derived from multilateral sources. In each case, debt servicing has already become a serious problem as both countries have now to spend more than 20% of their export earnings on servicing past loans and credits. Quite often this means either doing without a wide range of imports or borrowing yet more in support of imported producer supplies. A vicious circle of debt seems to have set in and, perhaps, to have become a permanent feature of the East African way of life.

When one examines the great role played by aid especially in support of development revenue, one is bound also to consider the undue influence that his exercises on the socio-economic and even political policies of the recipient countries. This is one of the most serious unintended aspects of foreign aid as it leads not only to distortions of declared national goals, but also threatens the freedom and sovereignty of the recipient. Yet this consideration is often set aside with a view to obtaining more aid as a means of resolving the dilemma of whether to live in poverty and social depression or to borrow in order to invest in combating poverty.

The choice is nearly always in favour of the latter alternative even when national pride and planning are at stake. In this respect, the more central the position of the donor in terms of the size of aid contribution and of the influence it may have on other donors, the greater will be its power of leverage upon the recipient. Of greatest importance in these terms for Kenya and Tanzania, and no doubt for most Third World countries, has been the World Bank, which has been emphatic on the promotion of the capitalist system of economic organization whatever the social and political costs. The Bank's universal prescriptions for practically all problems of developing countries have occasionally been handed down upon Kenya and Tanzania. These are normally in the form of a package aimed at "good house-cleaning and good house-keeping". They include a series of structural adjustments such as devaluation, wage freeze, decontrolling of consumer prices, extra support for private enterprise and foreign investment, cuts on public expenditure as regards social welfare programmes and expanded production of export commodities.

If and when such recommendations, or rather, demands, are adopted, they have the short-term effect of forcing a sudden fall in the living standards of the majority of the people whose purchasing power is seriously eroded. Thus, the withdrawal of state resources from social and welfare facilities such as education and health, together with a fall in the value of money, upward movement of consumer prices and falling real wages and farm producer prices, all contribute to the dampening of incomes, with the effect that industrial expansion is hampered by the resultant contraction of the market.

In particular, devaluation in East Africa has led to greater dependence on one or two primary commodity exports whose prices fluctuate widely on a world market that lies beyond the control of weak producer nations. Some relief has been experienced in times of high commodity prices in the world market involving mainly coffee and tea, but this has been only temporary. When prices become depressed the producer nations are faced with virtual catastrophe, especially when production declines on account of difficulties in supporting imports already rendered more expensive by currency devaluation. Whenever adopted in East Africa, IMF demands for structural adjustments and good house-keeping have occasioned anxiety and latent political instability, putting the victim governments on the defensive. Many times, however, the expected social and political disruptions have led Kenya and Tanzania to politely turn down demands from the World Bank and the IMF, and when accepted the adjustments are spread over a long period of time with a view to reducing their disruptive effect on the society. Even then, however, their acceptance has more often than not been accompanied by a corresponding measure to curtail dissent from the affected groups, especially the urban workers whose livelihood depends so much on the level of real wages and prices of consumer goods.

The position of the World Bank becomes all the more crucial as the other bilateral and multilateral donors of the West tend to hinge their aid on the Bank's opinion in respect of economic performance and required changes. In both Kenya and Tanzania, efforts to resist the IMF and World Bank's recommendations have led the other donors to suspend their aid flows, insisting that differences with these institutions be settled first. The two countries have thus been pushed into accepting the recommendations even when their value to their people is very doubtful. Coupled with the debt problems cited earlier, both multilateral and bilateral donor demands upon recipient nations have grave implications on the sustenance of democratic principles in conditions of poverty.

ECONOMIC LIMITATIONS ON DEMOCRACY AND FREEDOM

The kind of efforts taken to promote economic growth and increased participation of the nationals in the economies of the two countries have created several opportunities as well as difficulties for further stabilization of democracy. The establishment of settlement schemes, promotion of peasant cash crops, and greater involvement of local people in the public bureaucracy, in industry and in commerce, have greatly enhanced the legitimacy of the government in the eyes of the public. Furthermore, the presence of foreign investors and their official and unofficial interaction with local members of the bureaucracy, local businessmen and executives, have all contributed to consensus on the overall need for political stability, and one way of preserving it has been the hope-raising regular general elections. Both Kenya and Tanzania have closely adhered to regular elections so far. Sometimes, when conditions such as corruption, smuggling and ineffective provision of public facilities threaten stability, there has been direct intervention by the head of state whose remedial decisions are widely applauded.

Sometimes, however, the cooperation between foreign investors and local upcoming bourgeoisie has led to an abrupt change of attitudes on the part of the latter who turn to viewing the less-privileged members of the society with contempt. This development in Kenya took place during the 1974-78 coffee boom when smuggling and corruption were rampant and when a good section of senior politicians, bureaucrats and security personnel became wealthy on account of state support. This was the time when state repression held sway as the senior political, bureaucratic and security individuals identified themselves with the government or state, seeking to protect it by any means, including violence. Their enthusiasm was motivated by the enormous support they received from the state and which they would not easily forego.

Such brief or, sometimes, prolonged moments of totalitarian behaviour by those in positions of power have been experienced in several African countries. Their effect on overall economic development has been negative, with less state resources being availed to the public for expanded production. Modernization is hampered as most technical, financial and input resources are concentrated in the hands of the powerful and wealthy individuals. Governmental policies become difficult to communicate to the micro-levels as apathy and cynicism set in. This latent state of anarchy threatens the entire political edifice in many African nations.

In spite of occasional drawbacks, various empiricist adjustments in economic structure have gone a long way to answering peasant, worker and national bourgeois demands, thus enabling both Kenya and Tanzania governments to win some reciprocal support from the public on many issues. When that support is not readily granted, especially when the public strongly feels the actions of the government leave a lot to be desired, difficulties arise and the government has to either back down in order to avoid stalemate and uncertainty or to use repressive measures.

It is for the sake of avoiding a stalemate that both governments have allowed limited criticism and debate on various aspects about how society is being run, provided such are not aimed at the overthrow of the government or at the replacement of the system. Thus, Tanzania still encourages individual accountability as well as collective responsibility which requires the leadership to heed public criticism and adjust accordingly. It is in this spirit that debate and criticism are not only entertained at party conferences, but that their deliberations are also broadcast live over the national radio in the interest of the national audience. Similarly, criticism of the government and the party is entertained in Kenya's National Assembly whose deliberations are also broadcast over the national radio. Such debates are also given wide coverage in the press. Occasionally the press initiates debate on particular issues of national importance such as detention, official corruption, economic policy and so on, while the Church and the Kenya Law Society have expressed their opinions and even their opposition to various issues including family planning programmes, political detention and proposals for "turncoat" constitutional amendments deemed harmful to the public interest and democracy.

In response, the two governments have resorted to such tools as persuasion, warning or threat, propaganda and patronage in a bid to rally public support over controversial issues such as the recent KANU decision to have the constitution amended so as to provide for queueing behind the candidates in the preliminary elections. This decision was vehemently opposed by the leading Churches, the Kenya Law Society and various veteran national politicians in Kenya with the effect that a lot more caution had to be taken regarding the move.

It was largely in order to reduce the amount of debate that both Kenya and Tanzania moved away from the principle of the multi-party to the single-party system. The pretext was the need to expedite decision-making which if delayed due to prolonged debate, could do harm to development programmes as a result of under-utilization and wastage of resources. In Kenya, the move has also been justified on the basis that the multi-party system would encourage tribal and sectional rivalry which would seriously weaken national development efforts due to difficulties arising out of competition for resources.

All the same, single-party systems have led to degenerate systems whereby outmoded and primodial traditions are invoked in giving credence to personal rule which gradually replaces modern forms of collective leadership, thus threatening these societies with resultant authoritarianism. In the circumstances, the sanctity of constitutionalism suffers as the personal interests of the leadership are accorded preference over public interest. It is here that the greatest threat to democracy in Africa lies as efforts are made to institute security agents to safeguard the personal interests of the leadership, and as harassment is meted out on dissenting politicians, intellectuals and others who are either imprisoned, detained, killed or forced into exile.

In nearly the whole of Africa post-independence governments have made efforts to control interest and pressure groups with a view to rendering them ineffective as sources of opposition. In this direction, the state has sought to sponsor these groups or to regulate them through the system of registration or through planting government agents in their leadership. In this respect, perhaps the most affected group involves the trade union movement which in Kenya and Tanzania has been reconstituted under a single, centralized body which is rigidly controlled by the state in a bid to forestall strikes considered antithetical to the high growth rates that these countries seek to attain. Although the right to withhold labour is still presumed, practically all strikes in Kenya, for instance, have been declared illegal. However, some form of principle of equity has been created whereby controversies between labour and employers are adjudicated by the Industrial Court, while under various tripartite agreements involving trade unions, employers and the government, some form of reciprocity is once again achieved, at least temporarily.

In many African countries, however, numerous economic problems and the dire need to maintain high production levels have been responsible for extreme harassment suffered by trade unions at the hand of the state. Their plight has been summarized by Wogu Ananaba whom we quote in full:

> "Laws and policies which violate international labour standards abound in most African states. *Bona fide* trade union organizations have ceased to exist in many countries, and have been replaced by outfits created or sponsored by governments, politicians or military leaders. Trade unionists have been arrested and detained without trial, some have been detained for months or for years, and some have been shot in cold blood. There are probably more African unionists in jail or detention, killed or driven into exile by independent African countries than was the case during the whole period of colonial rule. In certain countries, so-called union leaders have been imposed on trade unions without any reference to them or the workers they are supposed to represent, while in others elected officials have been removed from office by persons or organizations which did not elect them."[22]

In accordance with the experience of developed countries in the days of initial development efforts, a shift towards totalitarian regimes in developing countries has been rationalized on the premise that the "imperatives of capital accumulation require the establishment of an authoritarian political regime, capable of dealing with the tensions and frustrations engendered by the economic growth process."[23] When applied to Africa, however, the implied discipline fails to take place, a state of corruption, smuggling and economic anarchy sets in, while production and general rate of growth decline substantially. Totalitarianism in Africa, as exemplified by Uganda in East Africa, therefore, seems to have the effect of increasing social, political and economic indiscipline. Rather than promote expanded production and augment wealth, it leads to greater poverty and misery of the affected societies. Nevertheless, various aspects of freedom and democracy have been suspended, controlled or completely removed in the name of political stability which has strongly been associated with economic progress in East Africa.

CONCLUSION

It appears that what we have called political reciprocity has more impact than anything else in promoting economic progress on the continent. A large measure of governmental responsibility, based on acceptance to be accountable to the public on many policies, could no doubt lead to the development of a motivated society as a crucial resource in social and economic progress. In its turn, such progress would give any responsible government a feeling of security, and, rather than become totalitarian, it is likely to prefer increased freedom and to accept more public scrutiny and questioning in respect of how public policy is being handled.

In both Kenya and Tanzania much has depended on redistributive efforts that widened the range of the nationals benefiting directly from involvement in agricultural and small-scale industrial activities. It has also depended on the two governments' efforts in promoting industrial expansion to cater for the ever-growing urban population. In Tanzania, the readiness of the state to force change on the rural way of life without giving due consideration to peasant traditional land tenure systems, or to individual incentives, has rendered much of *Ujamaa* efforts useless. The willingness of the state to accommodate some elements of individual enterprise preferred by a wide section of the society was yet another example of reciprocity that made the government tolerable even when its record of performance in the area of economic and bureaucratic management left a lot to be desired.

The two countries have undergone various periods of economic success and failure. In Kenya, however, an exceptionally good economic record in some years was also responsible for the emergence of a small clique of wealthy local businessmen who in conjunction with some senior politicians, bureaucrats and security personnel became contemptuous of the less privileged members of the society and nearly threatened to flout all rules of restrained governance. Though open totalitarianism proper did not establish itself, at least there was an indication of how easily such a state could set in once the national wealth was over-concentrated in a few hands. The effect is the exact opposite of what Sessional Paper No. 10/1965 sought to prevent, that is, the exercise of disproportionate political power by powerful economic groups.

In spite of efforts to accommodate criticism and debate both the Kenya and Tanzania governments have been more sensitive to dissent and critical debate. As long as criticism is not aimed at pulling down the government, it is tolerated and somehow answered by the state through warning and propaganda meant to weaken the effect of such criticism on the general public. This approach, together with the system of reciprocity coupled with some respect for rule of law, seems to reinforce the importance of maintaining a balance between democracy and economic progress. At least examples from some African countries are a clear demonstration that in Africa totalitarianism does not lead to development-oriented discipline, but rather to chaos and poverty.

REFERENCE

1. Lipset, S.M., *Political Man,* London, Heinemann, 1959.
2. Nyerere, Julius K., *Man and Development,* Dar es Salaam, Oxford University Press, 1974, p. 27.

3. Republic of Kenya, Sessional Paper No. 10/1965, *African Socialism and its Application to Planning in Kenya,* Nairobi, Government Printer, 1965, pp. 1-4.

4. Nyerere, *op. cit.,* p. 29.

5. *Ibid.,* p. 25.

6. Kenyatta, J., *Suffering Without Bitterness,* Nairobi, East African Publishing House, 1961, reprinted 1978, p. 216.

7. Rweyemamu, J.F., "The Historical and Institutional Setting of Tanzania Industry", in Kwan S. Kim, Robert B. Mabele and Michael J. Schultheis, *Papers on the Political Economy of Tanzania,* Nairobi, Heinemann Educational Books Ltd., 1979, pp. 69-70 and Nicola Swainson, *The Development of Corporate Capitalism in Kenya, 1918-1977,* London, Heinemann, 1980, Chapter 3.

8. Rweyemamu, in Kim *et al., op. cit.,* p. 79

9. Hyden, Goran, *No Shortcuts to Progress,* London, Heinemann, 1983, reprinted 1985, p. 2. The author argues that by putting welfare above growth, both the African leaders and foreign donors alike placed the cart before the horse which soon proved unable to push the cart from behind while there was nobody to pull the cart.

10. Earlier on, India had led the way in this trend of thought by placing industrialization at the top of her development priorities after independence, particularly in her Second Five-Year Plan 1956-1961.

    A.N. Agrawal, *Indian Economy,* New Delhi, Vikas Publishing House PVT Ltd. *Economics of Development and Planning,* New Delhi, Vikas Publishing House PVT Ltd., 14th Revised Edition, pp. 507-508.

11. Rweyemamu, *op. cit.,* p. 71.

12. *Ibid.,* pp. 71-72.

13. *Ibid.,* p. 71.

14. Rweyemamu, J., "Development Planning in Tanzania", *U.N. Economic Bulletin for Africa,* Vol. XII, No. 1, 1976, pp. 46-48.

15. See Arusha Declaration in Julius K. Nyerere, *Ujamaa: Essays on Socialism,* Dar es Salaam, Oxford University Press, 1968, (reprinted 1971), pp. 24-33.

16. Swainson, *op. cit.,* p. 214.

17. For the centrality of traditional land systems in designing agricultural programmes, see Raymond Noronha and Francis J. Lethem, *Traditional Land Tenure and Land Use Systems in the Design of Agricultural Projects,* Washington D.C., World Bank Staff Working Papers, No. 561, 1983, and Peter Dorner, "Land Tenure Institutions" in Melvin G. Blouse, *Institutions in Agricultural Development,* Iowa, The Iowa State University Press, 1971.

18. Also see Livingstone, I., "Some Requirements for Agricultural Planning in Tanzania", in Kim *et al., op. cit.,* pp. 34-37.

19. Miti, Katabaro, "Crisis after Crisis: Tanzania's Post Independence

Development", Economic Research Bureau, Dar es Salaam University, 1982.

20. Temu, Peter, "The Ujamaa Experiment", in Kim *et al., op. cit.,* p. 200.
21. Hyden, *op. cit.,* pp. 8-22.
22. Ananaba,Wogu, *The Trade Union Movement in Africa: Promise and Performance,* London, C. Hurst & Company, 1979, p. 6.
23. Roxborough, Ian, *Theories of Underdevelopment,* London, Macmillan, 1979, p. 115.

INDEX